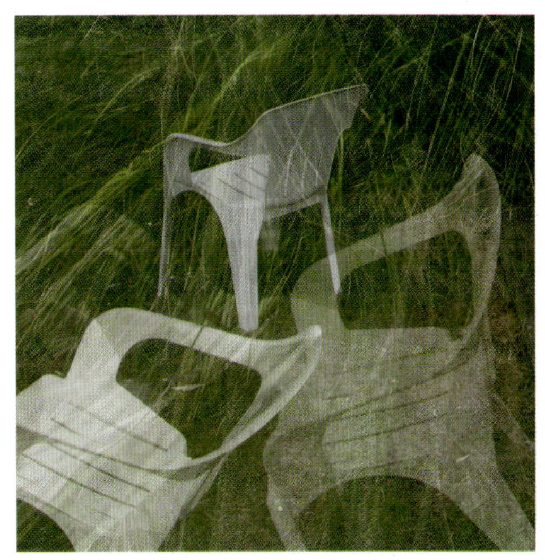

Digital Photo Artist

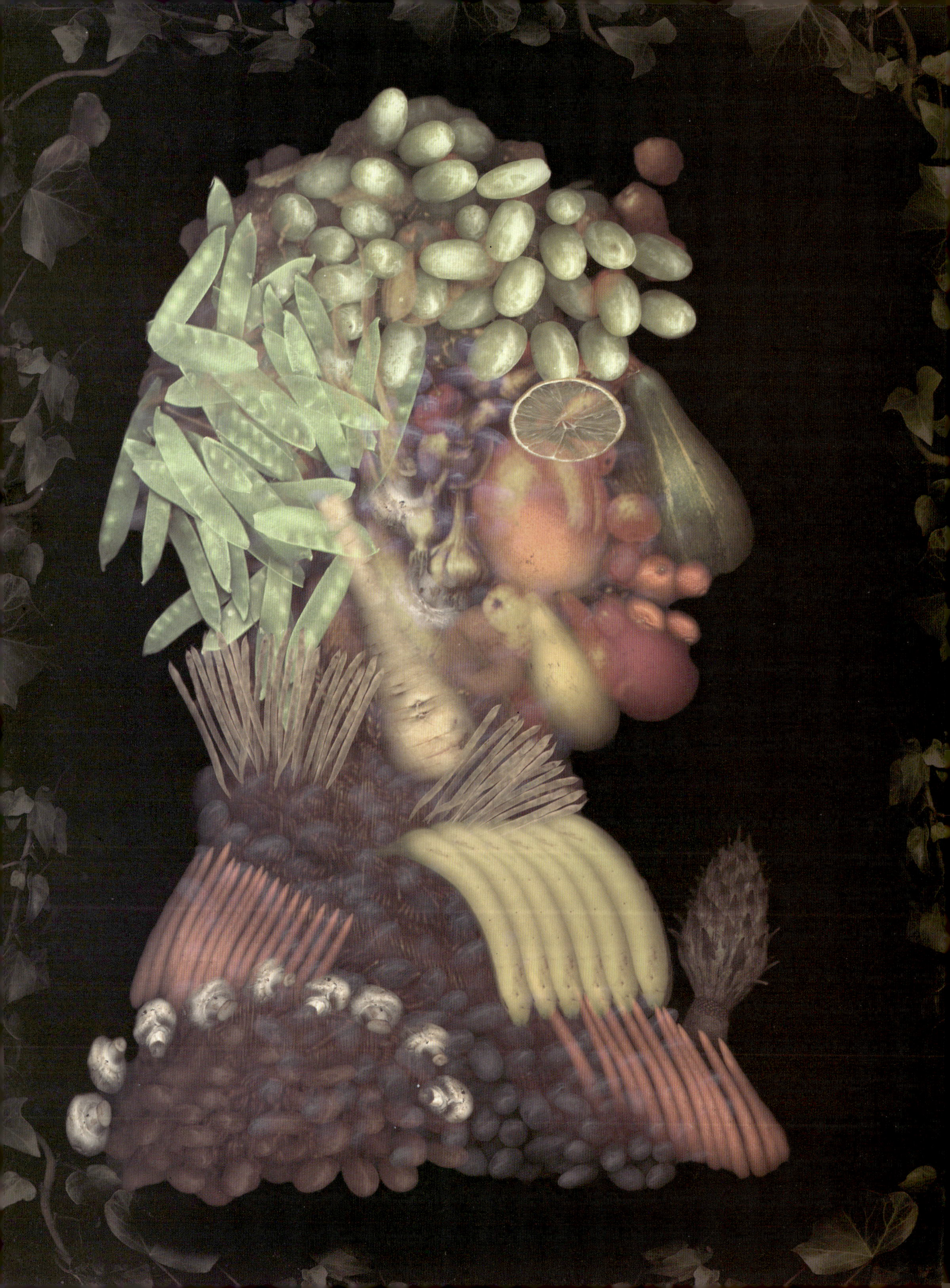

DIGITAL PHOTO ARTIST

Tony Worobiec
and Ray Spence

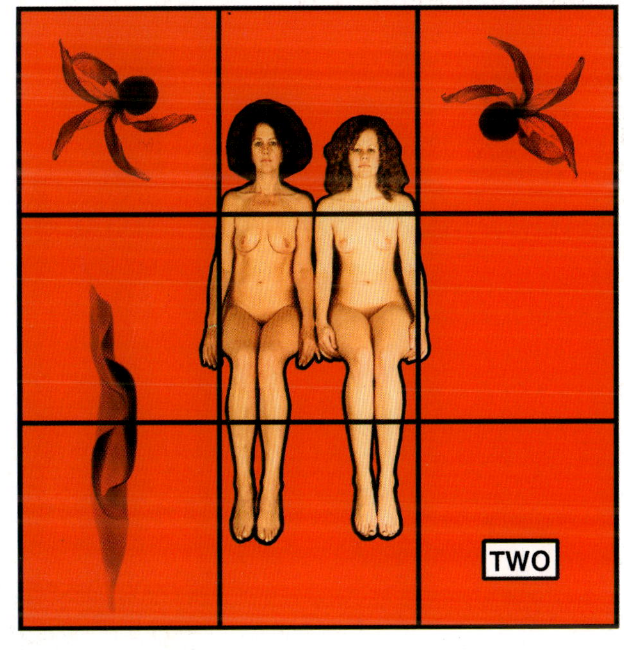

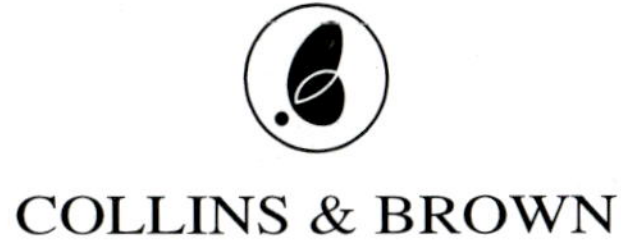

COLLINS & BROWN

Collins & Brown
The Chrysalis Building
Bramley Road
London
W10 6SP

An imprint of **Chrysalis** Books Group plc

Distributed in the United States and Canada by
Sterling Publishing Co.
387 Park Avenue South, New York, NY
10016, USA

British Library Cataloguing-in-Publication Data:
A catalogue record for this book is available from
the British Library.

ISBN: 1-84340-148-7

Designed by Roger Hammond@Blue Gum
Edited by Ian Kearey
Indexed by Isobel Mclean
Proofread by Fiona Corbridge

Reproduction by Classic Scan, Singapore
Printed and bound by Times Printing Co, Malaysia

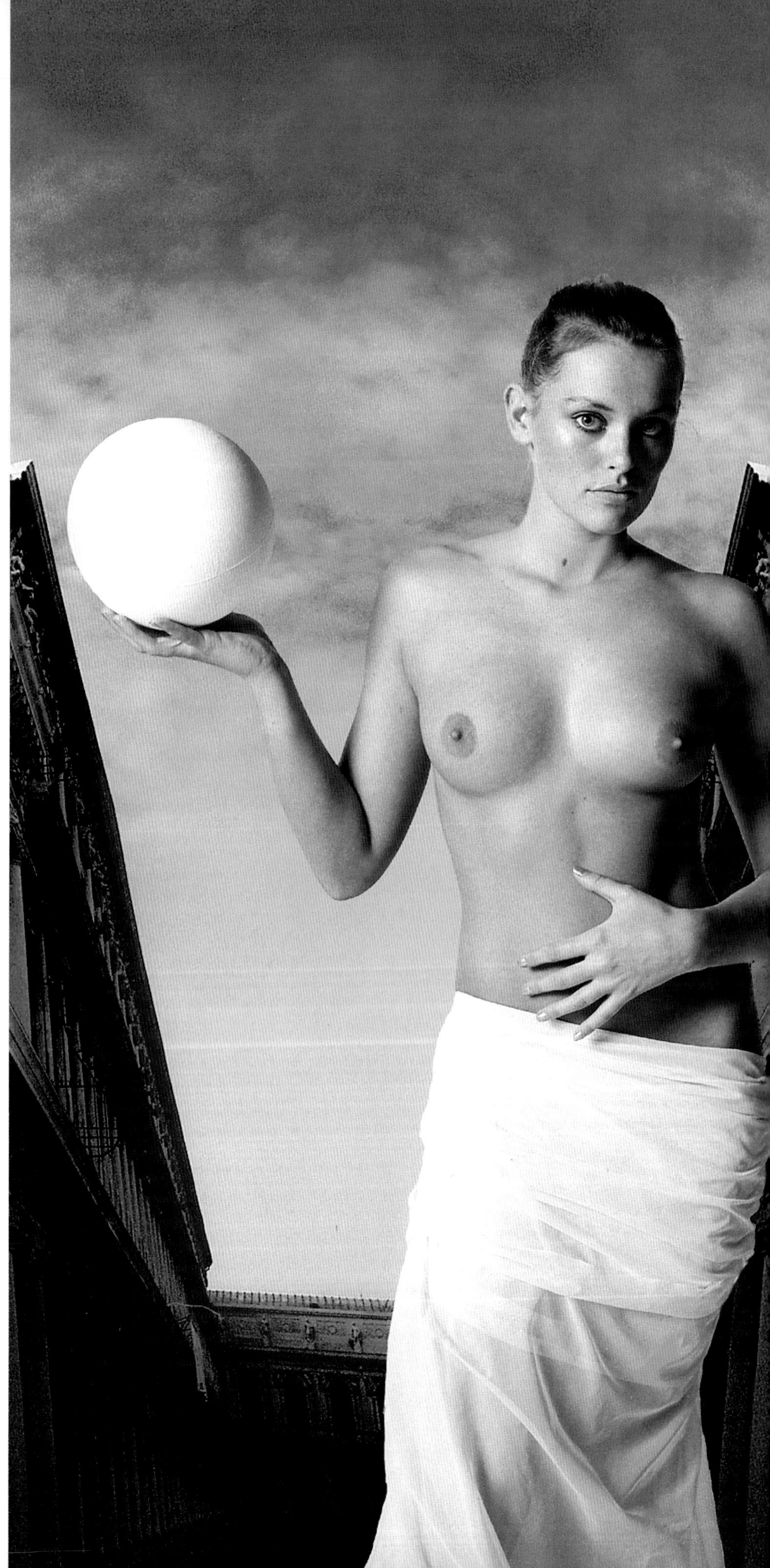

Contents

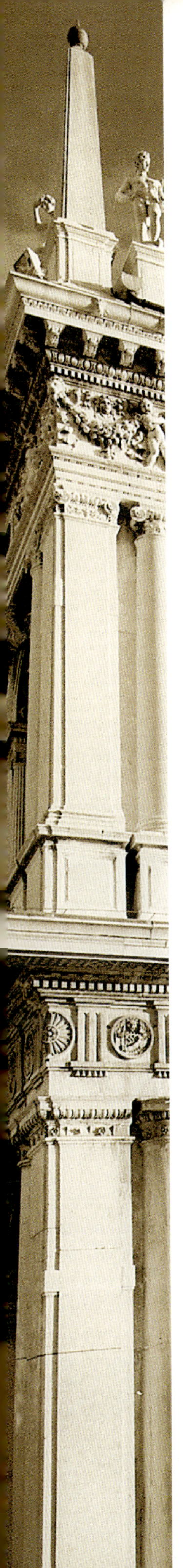

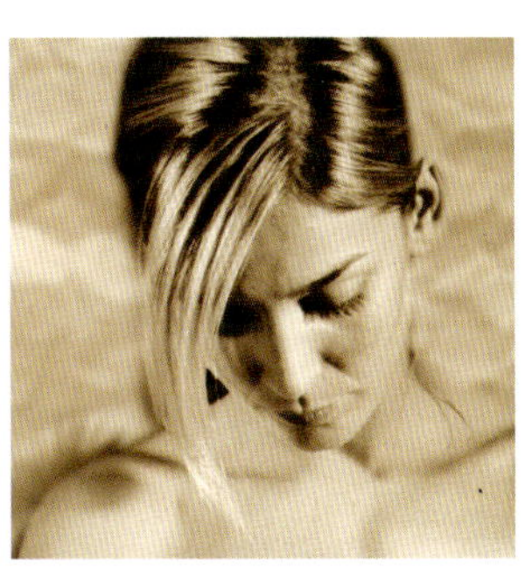

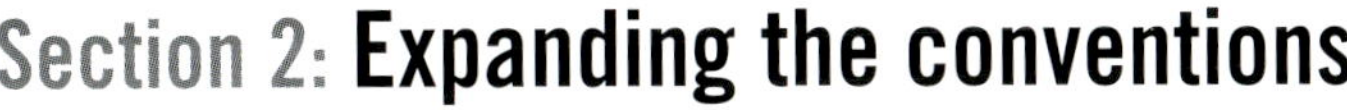

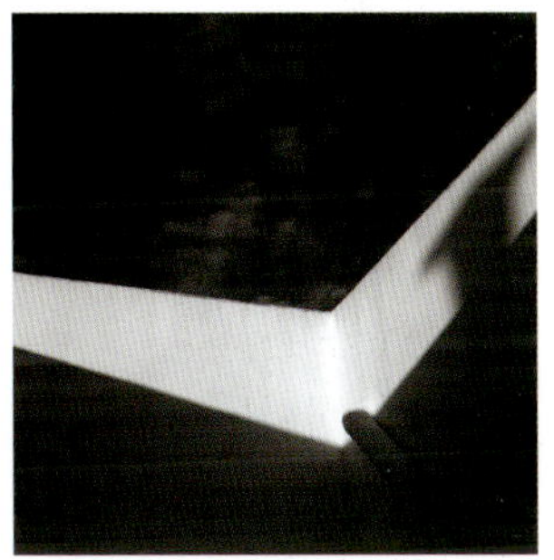

Introduction

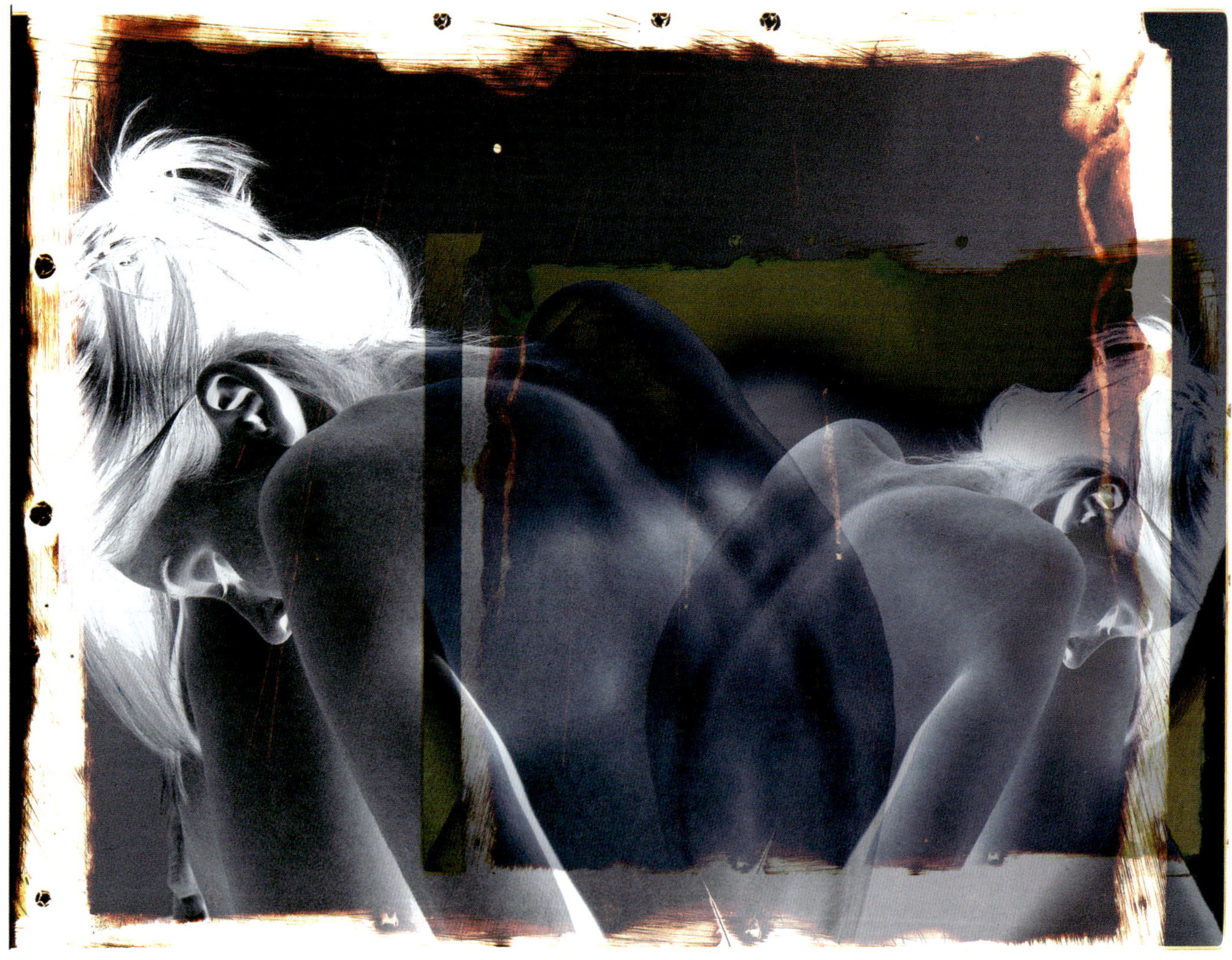

BEARING IN MIND the closeness of art and photography, there has been a symbiotic relationship between the two activities ever since the latter emerged as an independent art form in the middle of the 19th century. The earliest photographers inevitably looked to art for guidance regarding composition, while the very nature of painting changed with the advent of the camera, as artists were able to explore motion in depth, which they had been unable to do previously. This interdependence continued throughout the 20th century, with artists and photographers exploring the same issues, and each deriving sustenance from the other.

In many ways, photography did art a great favour – painters were no longer required to slavishly represent reality, as photography was far more able to assume this role; artists suddenly found themselves liberated and willing to investigate alternative avenues of thought. New and vibrant schools developed as artists explored styles and techniques that had hitherto been unimaginable: Dada, Cubism, Surrealism and Abstract Art were all fashioned in a period of great liberalization, when artists felt that they were entirely in control of the images they produced.

The problem for photographers is that they can only photograph what is there, which greatly contrasts with the artist's blank canvas. But the emergence of digital photography has dramatically changed all that, and suddenly photographers find themselves enjoying the same freedom as their artistic counterparts. While photographers still rely on captured images, sophisticated programs now allow them to explore interesting visual ideas in a totally new way. The scope of what a photographer can achieve has broadened, and the finished print can match the individuality and style of a painting. One of the aims of this book is to explore how this can be done.

We have not set out to methodically explore each and every digital technique or process: a much larger book would be required to do that. Instead, we have sought to illustrate how flexible digital imaging has become, and to explore ideas within the context of contemporary

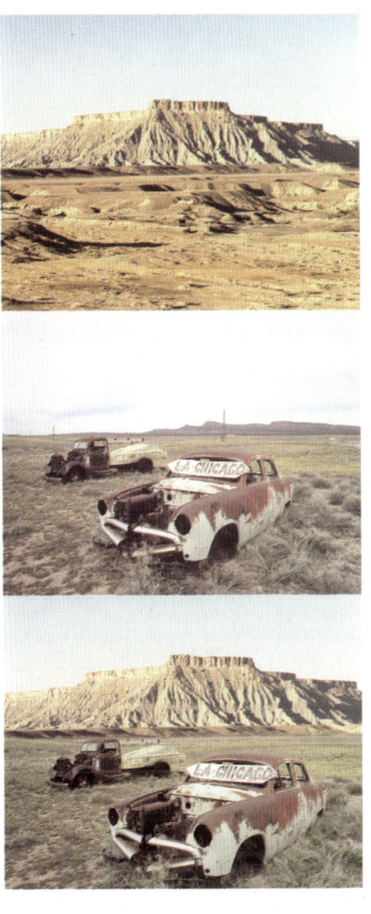

practice. By examining what current photographers and artists are doing, we have produced examples that can easily be done by the reader. Moreover, we are very aware of beautiful traditional photographic processes that could easily be forgotten, and have explored ways of mimicking

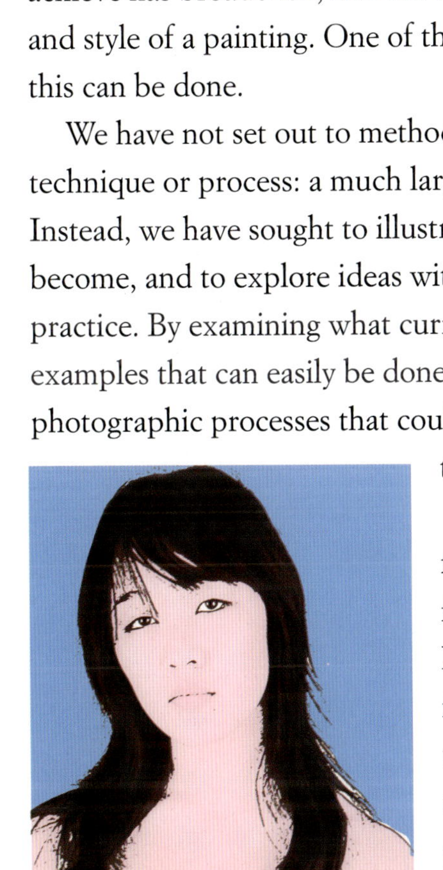

them digitally.

Finally, while we recognize that Photoshop is the industry standard for digital imaging, we have used a variety of its programs, ranging from Elements to CS. This book is not intended to be used as a Photoshop manual, but we have instead tried to identify its generic features, so that it is as inclusive as possible. We are confident that any user of Photoshop should be able to use this book to develop their skills and expertise. In addition, we have tried to identify noteworthy practitioners in both camps who explore this interesting interface between art and photography, and our hope is that the issues and techniques covered prove instructive, inspiring photographers and artists alike.

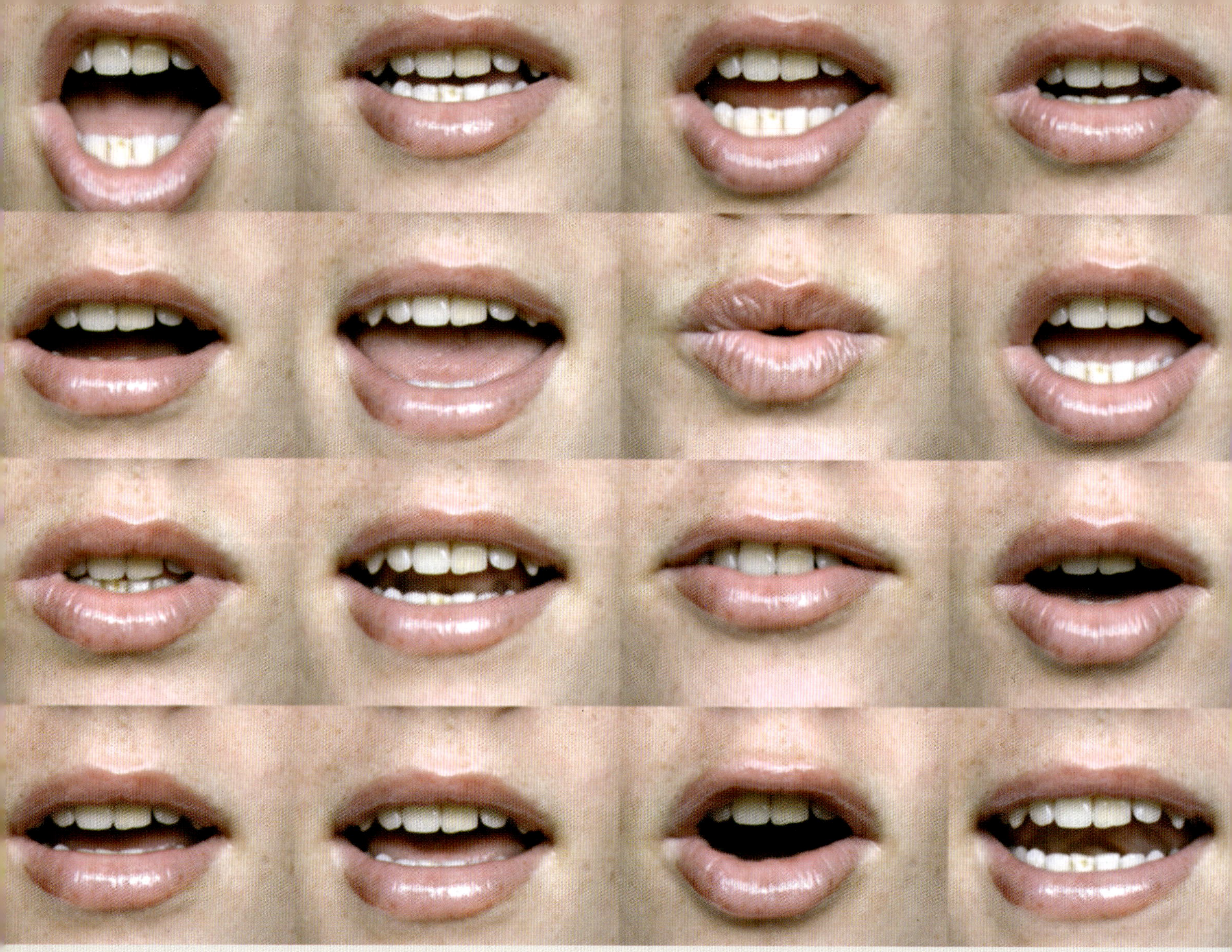

Section 1

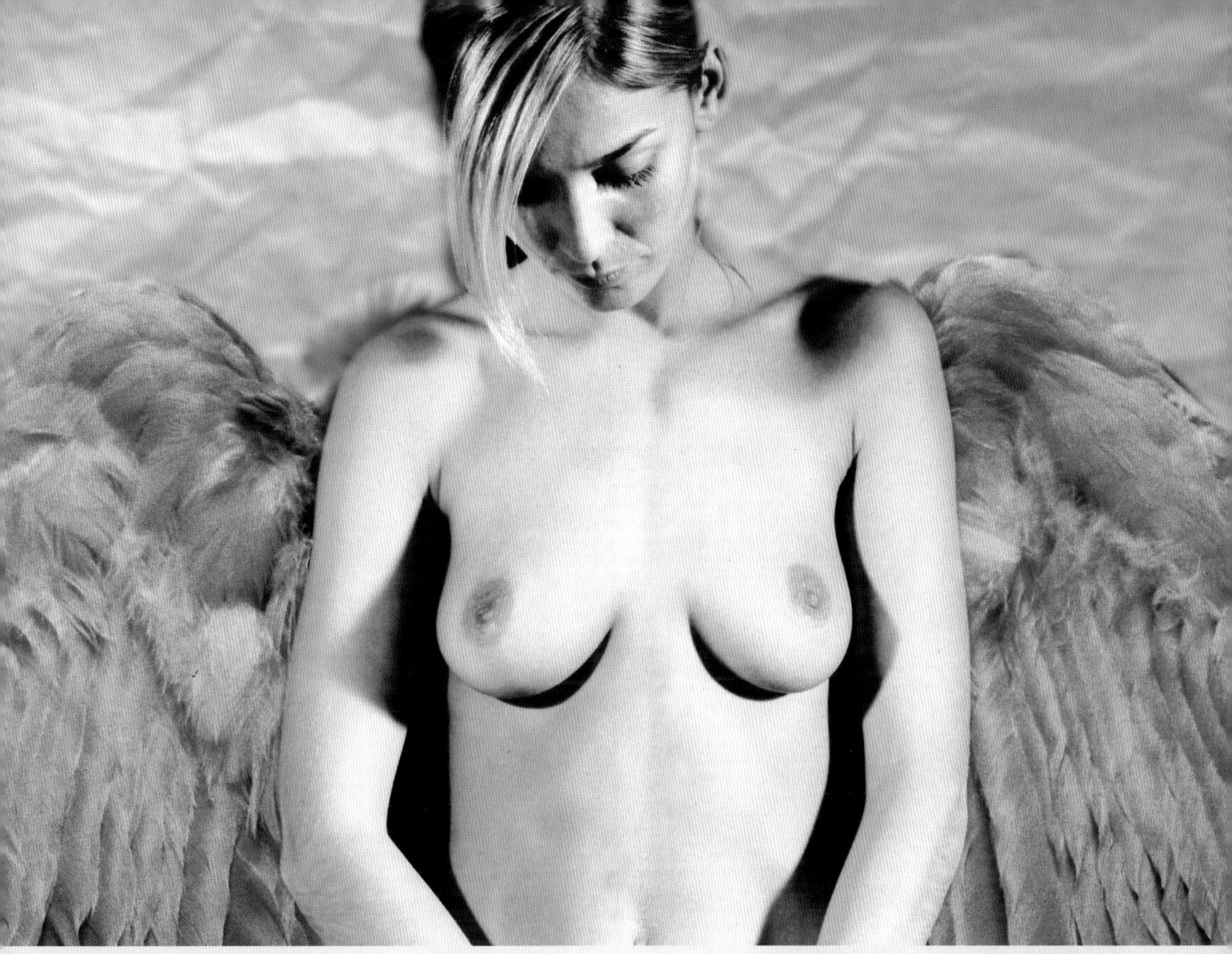

Fundamental skills

Exploring technology

There is much debate about the "digital revolution", and no doubt the arguments between those who use film exclusively and those who are converts to digital photography will continue for some time. We have never really understood this polarity of views and have always argued for taking the best from whatever technology is available, and view digital imaging as an evolution of the photographic process, which offers many new possibilities.

IN ADDITION TO incredible control over the content of an image, and how it can be manipulated and printed, the capture of images digitally also offers new opportunities – one often overlooked area is the use of scanners as cameras in the creative field, which is dealt with later in the book.

The features on modern digital cameras are now astounding, and as prices continue to tumble there is an enormous amount of choice; almost any feature for any type of photography is now available. Inevitably there will be gimmicks that come and go, but there have been true innovations that should only improve our creativity. There has certainly never been a better time to invest in the new technology.

Instant playback

This is probably the most obvious feature, and is of enormous use. It is especially useful when trying out new techniques, such as slow shutter speed and movement, new lighting techniques and so on. The possibility of using it to constantly monitor progress can interrupt the flow of a photographic session, especially when photographing people – use it at the beginning of a session to determine the camera settings and lighting, then forget about it and concentrate on taking images. It can also be enormously useful when photographing strangers on location, as you can reassure them of your intent by showing them the images on the LCD screen. Once you've done this, they are usually more than willing to humour your demands.

Playback levels

The exposure of digital images is crucial to the final quality. Using digital capture is analogous to using colour transparency film – overexposure is definitely to be avoided. One of the major features of digital cameras is the ability to play back images almost

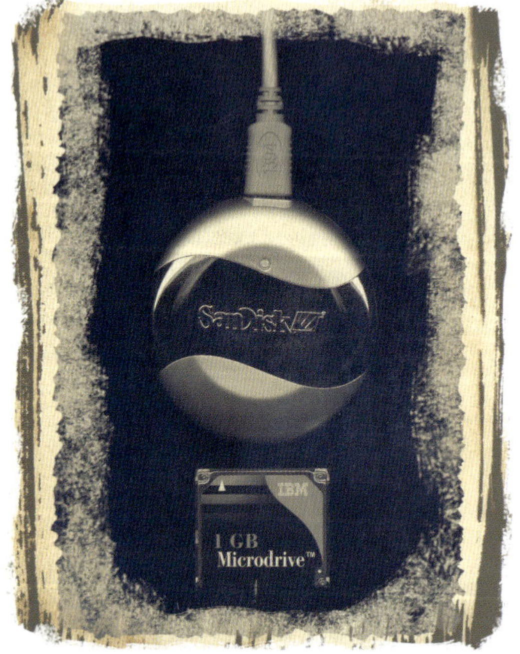

Card and Reader

Digital storage media – Compact Flash Card and Card Reader

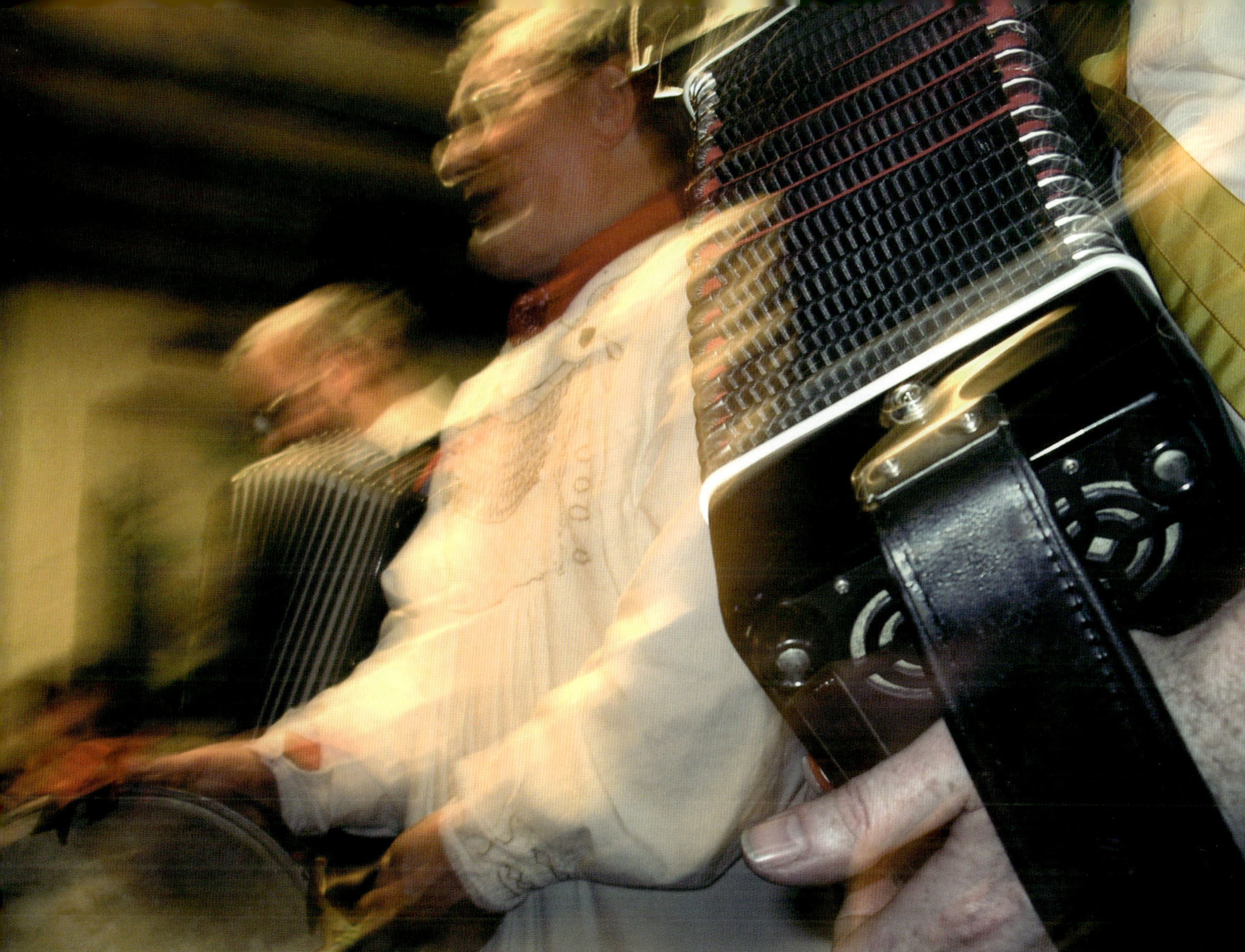

immediately; although you might think that this is a failsafe method of achieving the correct exposure, LCD monitors are not particularly accurate – they are small, and reflected light can affect their appearance.

One almost indispensable feature on most digital cameras is the ability to play back not just an image which has been taken, but a record of the pixel make-up of the image as a histogram. This shows the recorded pixels from shadow to highlight and is an accurate method for determining over- or underexposure (otherwise known as accurate zone system control. This is particularly valuable in studio situations, where light or dark backgrounds can fool the camera meter.

Morris men

Traditional English morris men tend to have a good time with plenty of ale and song. Fortunately I happened to have my Pentax digital camera in my pocket when they visited my local hostelry. I wanted to capture the atmosphere of this occasion and gain permission to photograph literally within inches of the revellers. By using the instant playback on the LCD screen I was able to show the accordion player my intentions, and by experimenting with slow shutter speed and flash I could determine the optimum settings. Once these had been established I could shoot with confidence and enjoy the occasion. I was also able to hold the camera at arm's length and still observe the LCD. In this way I could put the camera much closer to the musicians without becoming too intrusive.

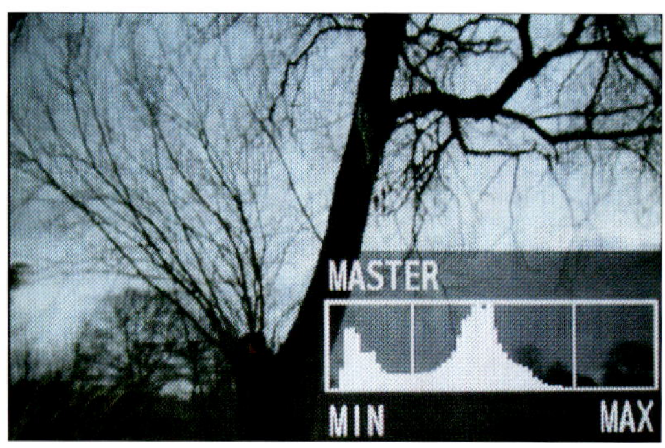

Underexposure

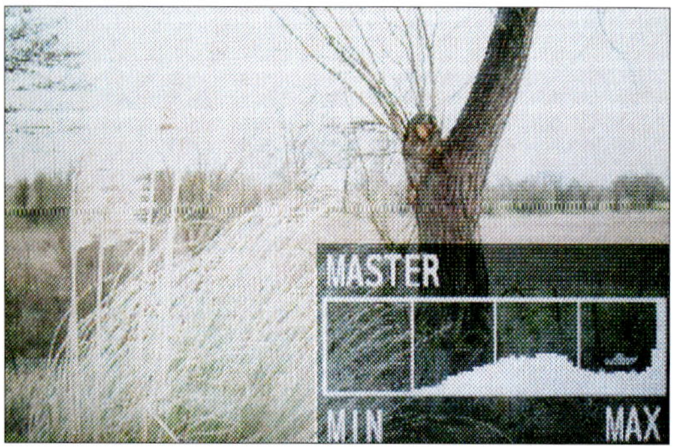

Overexposure

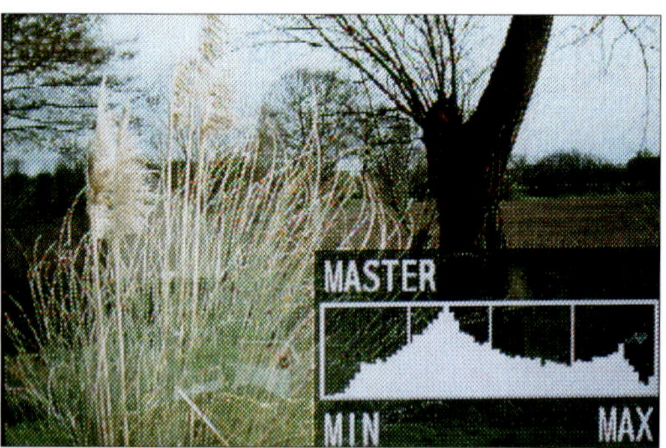

Correct exposure

The histogram is identical to the Levels dialog box in Photoshop: one that is weighted to the left represents underexposure, and one weighted to the right shows overexposure (see Fig 1).

White balance

Photographers have always had a problem working in artificial light if they are trying to reproduce true colour, as tungsten and fluorescent lighting usually lead to unwanted colour casts. Not any more – auto white balance and, in more advanced cameras, manual white balance and preset fluorescent and tungsten settings, have ensured that colour-corrected images are produced.

Colour or black and white

No longer do you need to stock different films or use several cameras to take both colour and black-and-white images. A digital camera produces a colour image, but many models have the facility to produce black and white or even sepia tone at the flick of a switch. With the power of Photoshop, however, it is much more controllable to produce monochrome effects from an original colour file, so it is a good idea to always take images in colour and work on them later.

ISO

Claims that certain films can be exposed at a range of ISO sensitivities have led to many people believing that the ISO can be changed between exposures. Of course this is not true; it depends purely on the latitude of the film. Digital sensors, however, can be changed between each exposure – it is now possible to take one image at ISO 100 and follow this with one taken at ISO 1600. As with film, the quality of the image usually deteriorates with increased sensitivity, so with digital images, the higher the ISO setting, the more the likelihood that certain digital artefacts, such as "stuck pixels", can creep in. Fortunately, many of these can easily be repaired or masked in Photoshop.

Multi-image

One of the most exciting pre-digital cameras was the Lomo camera, which was capable of taking a series of images on a single frame of 35mm film; the most basic model had a single fixed shutter speed and aperture, and was great for producing sequences of images, each separated by about $^1/_4$sec. In the digital field, the Nikon Coolpix has a similar but more versatile feature.

Panoramas

A variety of specialist panoramic film cameras exist; they are great fun to use, but you have to be pretty dedicated to fork out the cash required. Alternatively, digital technology allows you to "stitch" images into panoramas, either manually or with a certain amount of automation. Many digital cameras now have features that make this process easier by playing back images and showing where the next image should be taken to provide the correct overlap, and an increasing number of cameras also include software for stitching the images together for printing.

Multi-exposure

Multi-exposure with film is both exciting and frustrating – welcome accidents and unexpected juxtapositions can occur, but it's more likely that overexposed or poorly framed images will result. Imaging software such as Photoshop can combine images in a vast variety of ways and allow infinite experimentation, but the ability to produce multiple images in camera is highly developed with digital cameras.

Many cameras allow the image to be viewed and accepted at each separate exposure so that decisions can be made at that stage to see what is really working. The image can be seen developing in the playback mode, and such instant feedback can really get the creative juices flowing. By starting with a base image that is replayed in the viewing screen, the effect of the next image is superimposed before the shutter button is pressed. Each

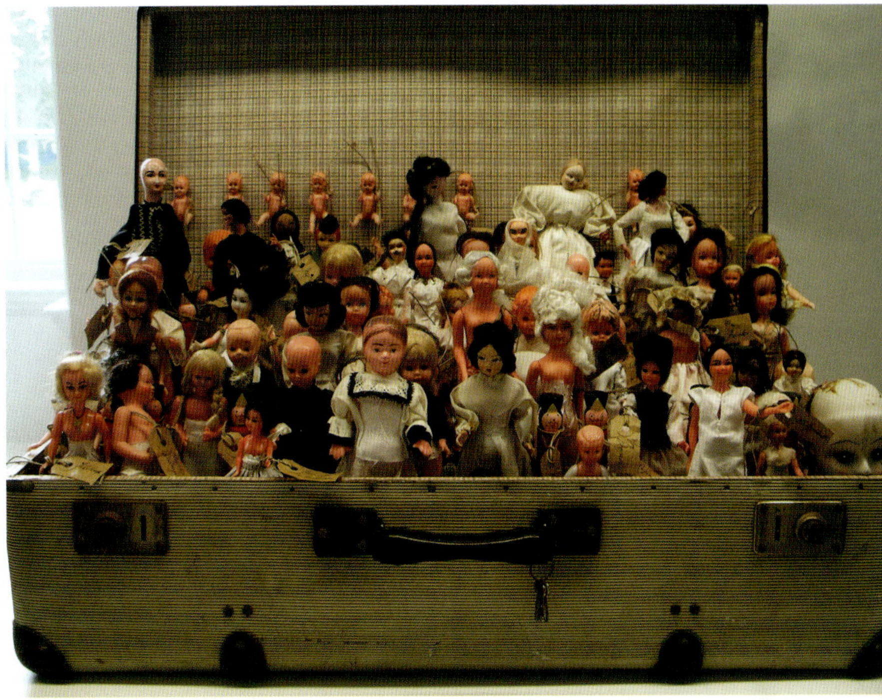

stage can then be added until the final image is complete.

Moving images

This feature is not a substitute for a dedicated film or digital video camera, but useful for short videos, for Web or Internet use, for example. The length of the sequence will depend on the memory card installed, but a 256MB card can easily store up to 12 minutes of moving images with sound, which could be ideal for recording the latest exhibition of your work.

Timed sequences

Self-timers on film cameras allow the photographer to take an image 2–10sec after pressing the shutter, but many digital cameras now have the ability to take a preset number of images separated by discrete time intervals – for instance, 20 images at 90sec intervals. This facility is marvellous for making series and sequences.

Suitcase

This image, taken on a Pentax Optio 555 digital camera at an exhibition by Peter Greenaway, clearly shows how the auto white balance has coped with the tungsten light. If you look carefully, the view through the left-hand window to daylight in the background is blue – the camera has effectively used a blue filter to correct the warm tungsten light.

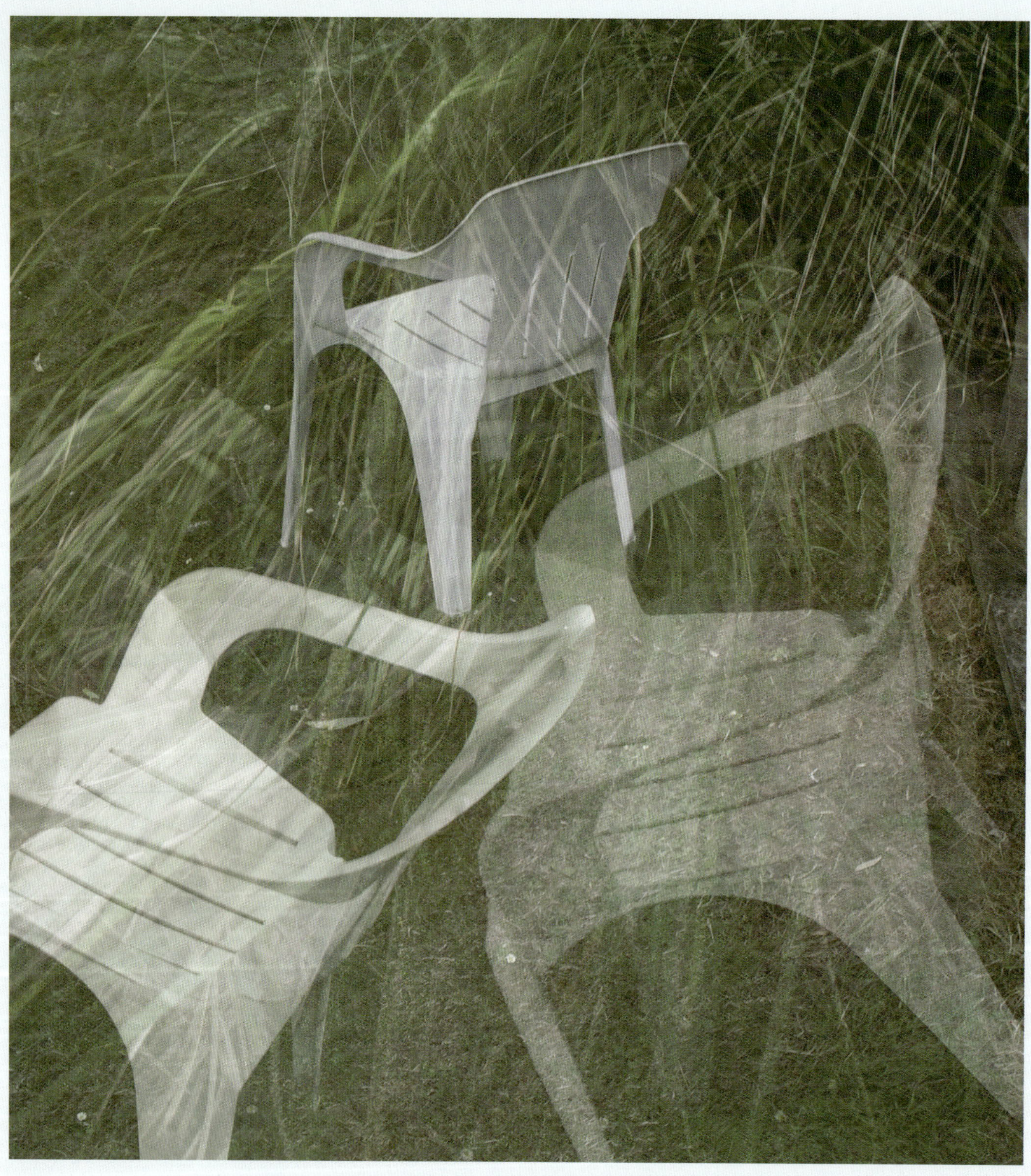

Chairs

By using the multi-exposure facility on my Pentax Optio digital camera, I was able to observe each exposure and see the effect it was having on previous exposures. I could then decide if I wanted to add each exposure or delete it and try another one.

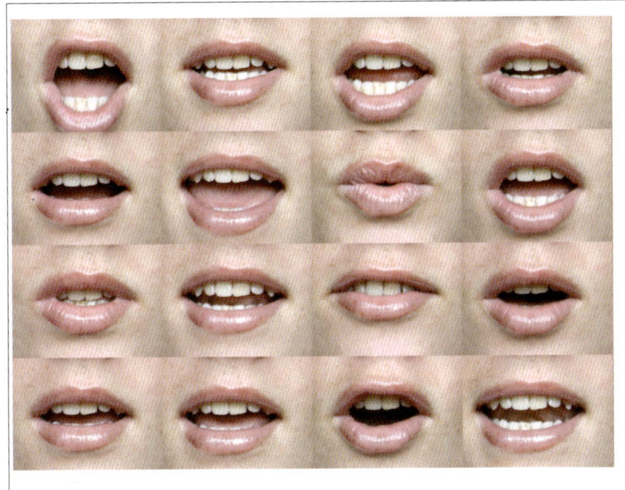

Speech

This sequence was taken with a Nikon Coolpix digital camera, which can take 16 images with a slight time delay between each shot and combine them into a single image in camera. This was part of a project on communication.

Maypole dancing, Welford, 2004

Some children's activities are best captured with moving images and sound. Obviously a dedicated digital video camera is best for this, but even a pocket Pentax can take low-resolution moving images and sound. In some ways the low quality is rather charming and is reminiscent of very early home movies.

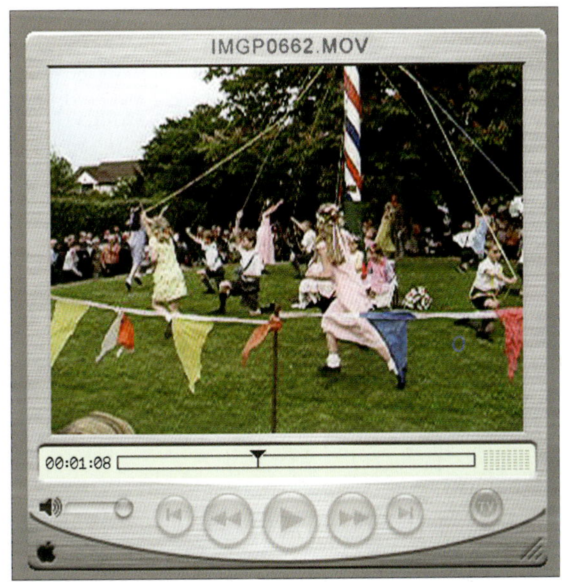

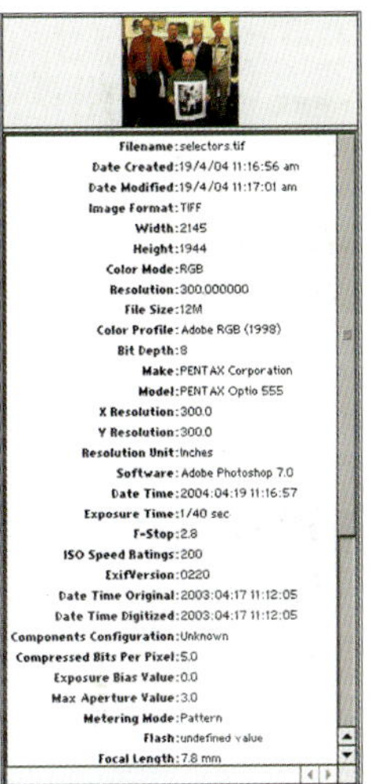

Fig 2

EXIF data is information that is automatically stored with every digital image you take. It includes the date and time the image was taken, the f-stop, shutter speed, ISO, make of camera, file size and much more. This can be immensely important when evaluating your work and trying to improve your results.

Sound

At first sight this is not necessarily a feature that appears to be of much use to a photographer, but it can be an invaluable tool when important information needs to be kept with an image. A biologist would find it useful to be able to record the exact Latin names of the plants and animals he or she photographs, especially if they would be difficult to identify accurately at a later date; and documentary, social, news and even landscape photographers would find this feature useful for keeping accurate information in the field. The pre-digital technique was to record information on paper or via a tape recorder, which meant extra effort and the chance that the image and the data might become separated or difficult to match. Sound files recorded by the camera are linked with the image, and so are never separated or lost.

Working with layers and masks

If there is one single feature about working digitally that is particularly valuable, it is the capacity to work in layers. This allows the user to select elements from one source and to fuse them with those from another in an extraordinarily controlled way.

IMAGINE VARIOUS INDEPENDENT images stacked one over the other, rather like a pile of acetate sheets – it is possible to fuse together whole images, or just parts; the order of the images within the stack can be changed and alterations can be made to single layers, without those changes impacting on the other layers. In essence, this is a particularly sophisticated aspect of Photoshop and lies at the heart of successful digital imaging.

Multiple printing in the darkroom is a demanding skill that is fraught with dangers; the big problem is that it is impossible to see what has been achieved until the very end. If there have been any miscalculations, it only shows at the printing stage, but of course that is too late. Working digitally, we are able to see the changes as they take place and make the required alterations before printing. Most darkroom workers limit the number of images they are prepared to merge together to just two or three, but when working digitally it is possible to use considerably more.

Multiple printing can be achieved in two ways:

1 Two or more negatives can be stitched together to produce a plausible new image. For example, it is perfectly possible to print the foreground from one image and combine it with the background from another, merely by removing the unwanted areas. If the overlap within the images shares common characteristics, then a very realistic result can be created. In many respects, this is a continuation of the darkroom tradition of multiple printing.

2 Overlapping one image over another so that the characteristics of one blend with the other. With the numerous editing facilities available in Photoshop, very subtle controls can be

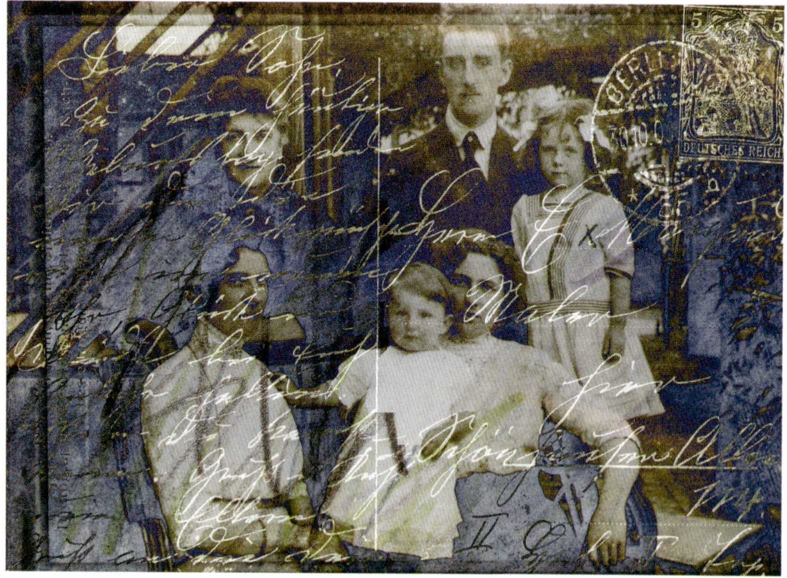

Family album

Increasingly photographers envy the freedom many contemporary painters enjoy, whose slavish commitment to "reality" was jettisoned 150 years ago. They have pioneered a new way of presenting the visual world, and encourage the viewer to interpret images at a much more personal level. With the emergence of digital imaging, photographers are increasingly recognizing that they can also abandon reality.

In this example I started with a very old family photograph dating back to the early 1920s. I never knew the people featured, or much about their backgrounds. But by creating overlapping layers, a new and personal meaning is introduced. In some respects this contains some of the complexity and beauty of a banknote.

made. Traditionally this has been very hard to achieve without muddying the printing paper, because of the risk of overexposure; and as the image only appeared at the printing stage, meaningful editing was difficult to do.

Selecting your elements

Multiple printing using layers is quite a different task from montaging using masks (which is examined later), and more thought is required concerning how various negatives will match. Obviously this is partly governed by the intended visual statement, and whether a realistic or surrealistic outcome is required. But generally speaking, it is important to ensure that the elements being used have some shared characteristics, and simply cobbling together random negatives rarely works.

First, think about the lighting. If one of the negatives is clearly backlit, then ensure that the others are as well, otherwise the final result could look rather strange. If one of the negatives is strongly illuminated from one side, but the others are illuminated from the other, be prepared to rotate that negative to ensure that the lighting remains consistent throughout.

Then consider the areas that need to be blended. For example, it will be difficult to convincingly combine a dark, rocky outcrop with a delicate sandy beach. The most successful blends occur when both the texture and tones match. The problems are increased when working in colour, as not only do the colours need to match, but the relative warmth of the colours also needs to – a sandy yellow desert can look quite different at dawn from how it does in the middle of the day, and this needs to be considered when matching colour images.

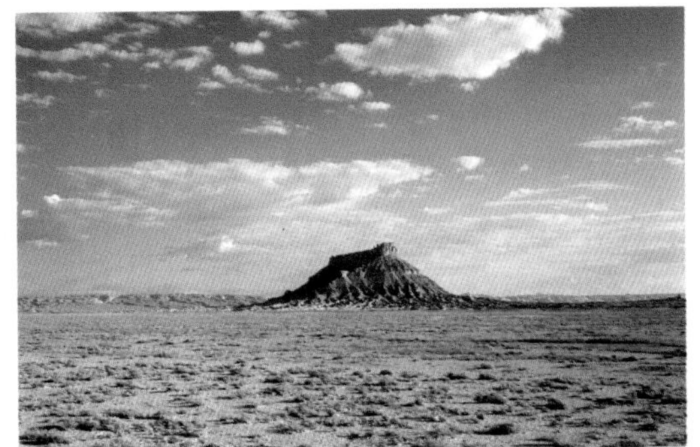

Original image 1 (layer 1)
While this image has certain endearing qualities, the foreground and the sky lack sufficient character to make the picture truly interesting. My aim is to replace both elements.

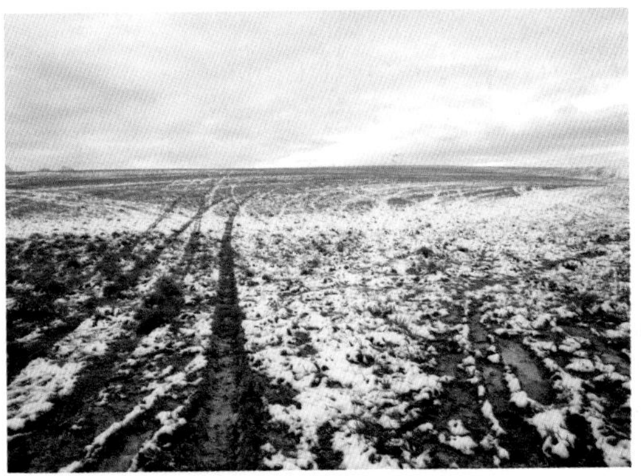

Element 1 (layer 2)
The foreground in this image is far more interesting, and the tracks leading towards the horizon offer greater visual impact.

Fusing elements together

Both these black-and-white negatives were scanned in RGB mode and resized to ensure that they matched. I saved them as files just in case I needed to redo the join. With both images on screen, the Move tool was used to drag layer 2 over layer 1, ensuring that both horizons matched (see Fig 1). By doing this, layer 2 completely obscured layer 1, but by carefully removing the top portion of layer 2 using the Eraser tool, the upper portion of layer 1 began to emerge. (It is important to appreciate that the Eraser tool offers various options that can prove to be particularly useful; double-click the Eraser tool to reveal the Eraser tool palette (see Fig 2) or use the tools options bar.)

1 Select the appropriate mode. While Photoshop defaults to Paintbrush, other options can be selected, including Airbrush, Pencil and Block. Each has its own characteristics, which can prove useful when removing areas.

Fusing elements together

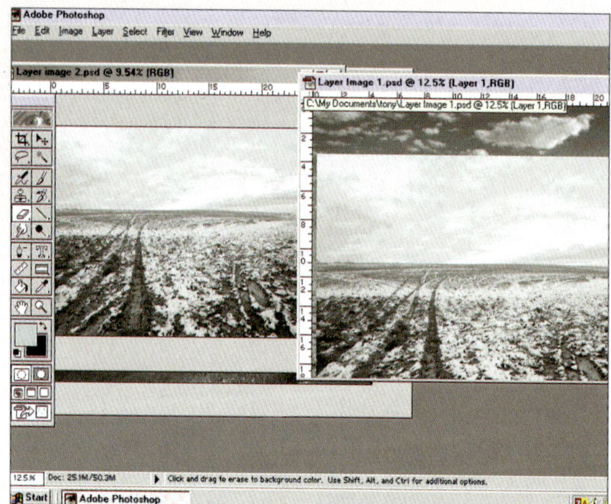
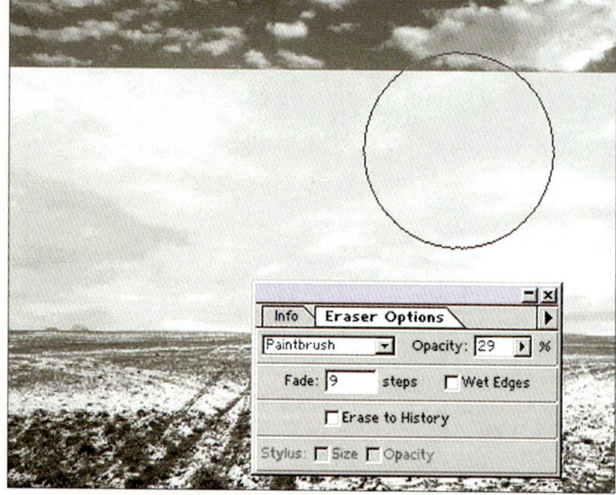

Figs 1 and 2

Element 2 (layer 3)

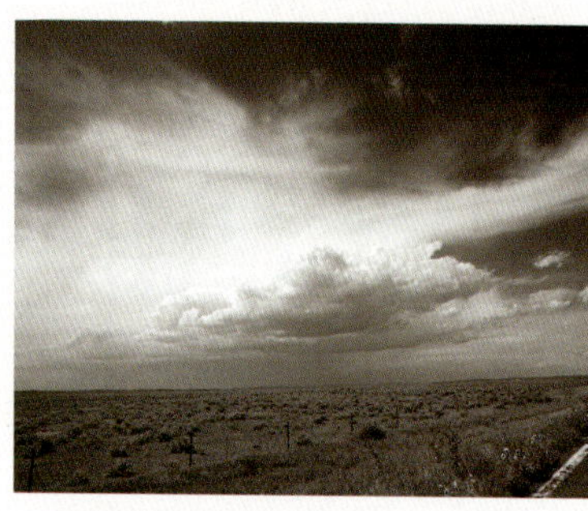

The sky in the original image lacks drama and cohesion, but introducing layer 3 creates a more powerful and exciting image. The procedure is virtually identical to the previous one, except this time the aim is to remove most of the sky from layer 1. Once again, using the Move tool, layer 3 was dragged over layer 1 (see Fig 3), ensuring that the horizons roughly matched up – this repositioning can be done more precisely later on. By using the Eraser tool, the lower portion of layer 3 was carefully removed to reveal the butte with its newly acquired snowy tracks below. Great care was then required to ensure that the skies from the two elements blended successfully.

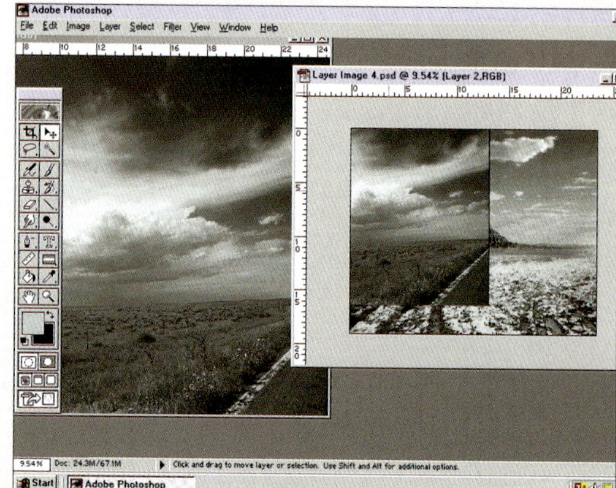

Fig 3

2 The Opacity setting allows for partially erasing pixels, which can be particularly helpful when trying to achieve a subtle blend.
3 By using the Erase to History option, it is possible to return the pixels to their former state by clicking the History Brush column within the History palette.
4 The size and softness of the Eraser used is governed by the Brush palette.

Initially I used a large Eraser, set to a soft paintbrush mode, to remove most of the overlapping sky right down to the butte. I then changed the Eraser to Airbrush mode and reduced its size in order to be able to work with greater accuracy. Using the Navigator at this stage proved to be essential. As I worked nearer to the point where I required a subtle overlap, I used an Opacity setting of 50% to ensure a gentle transition from one layer into another. It is important to set the Navigator to normal from time to time, in order to get an overview. If a mistake is made, go to Edit > Undo Eraser or Control Z on the keyboard; alternatively use the Erase To History facility. Once all the elements have been removed, review the join once again, and if necessary carefully reposition the two layers until a more satisfactory blend is achieved. Remember that they are still two independent layers at this stage and can be moved using the arrow keys on the keyboard.

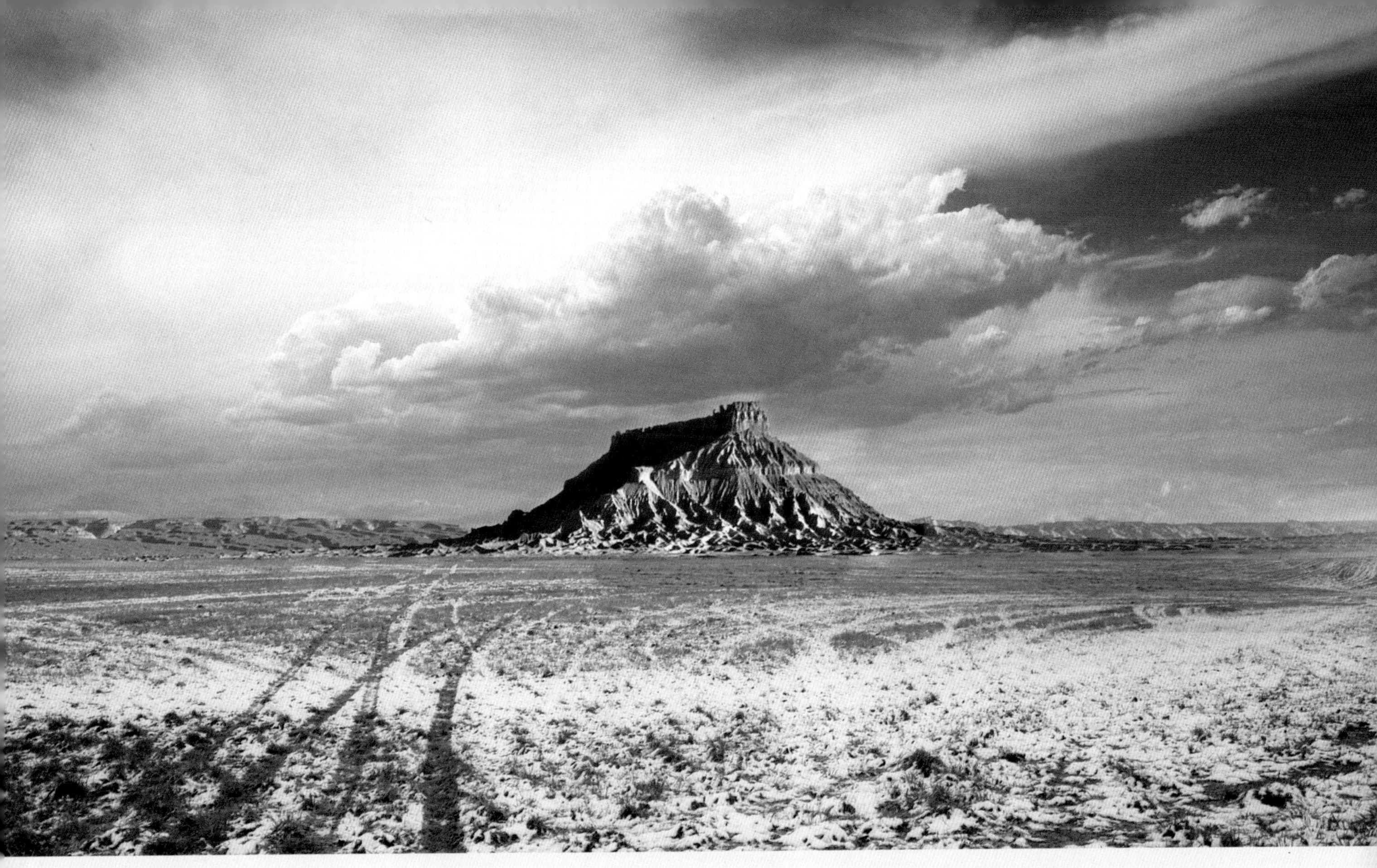

The added sky and foreground have helped to make this a far more interesting picture. Obviously, it is useful to have an idea of what the final outcome will look like, but once all the elements within the composite are in place, further small adjustments can still be made. For example, there is evidence of snow in the foreground, although none appears on the butte, but by selectively lightening the highlights using the Dodge tool, a light covering of snow is suggested there as well. Once I was satisfied with the final outcome, the three layers were merged into one by going to Layer > Flatten Image, thus reducing the file size.

Overlapping layers

While plausible composites can be created by layering and removing elements, far more challenging images can often be achieved by producing numerous layers and allowing the qualities of each to show through. This is particularly difficult to do using conventional photographic means, but it is not difficult to achieve digitally (see page 20).

1 The decaying bird's wing was photographed from above, using a piece of white card as a background in order to ensure that other layers could be introduced without creating too much confusion.

2 A visual palindrome was created. The left side of the image with the bird's wing was selected and copied: Edit > Copy, then Edit > Paste (or Control/J to copy and paste in one go). This produced two layers containing the image of the wing. Using Edit, the copy was flipped horizontally: Edit > Transform > Flip Horizontal, and then repositioned using the Move tool.

3 A distressed piece of metal was used as the background, thus creating the second layer.

4 It was important to ensure that the background layer mirrored the first layer, so a duplicate layer of the metal image was created, rotated through 180° and then merged using Multiple Blend in the Blending options (see Fig 4). The amalgamation of the two layers increased density, so it was

Decaying wings

As I was sweeping the patio one summer's day, I spotted a decaying wing which I initially mistook for a dried leaf. Whilst it was only several inches in length, I could immediately see that it had strong figurative qualities. It reminded me of some strange figure wearing a bizarre headdress. I chose to place it in a new context, using a piece of discarded metal I had also found. Creating independent layers and then joining them together in this way helped to introduce a new meaning to this otherwise uninteresting subject.

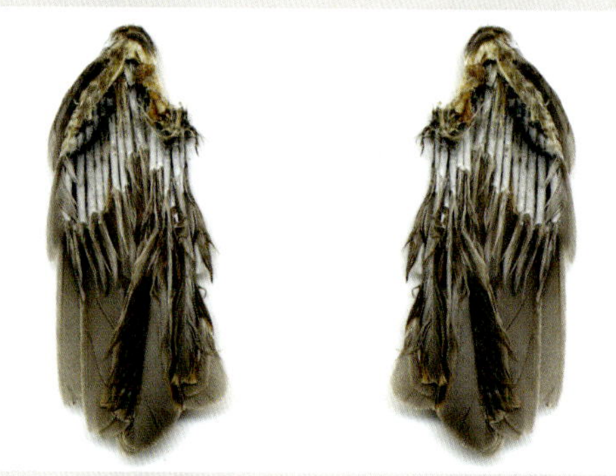

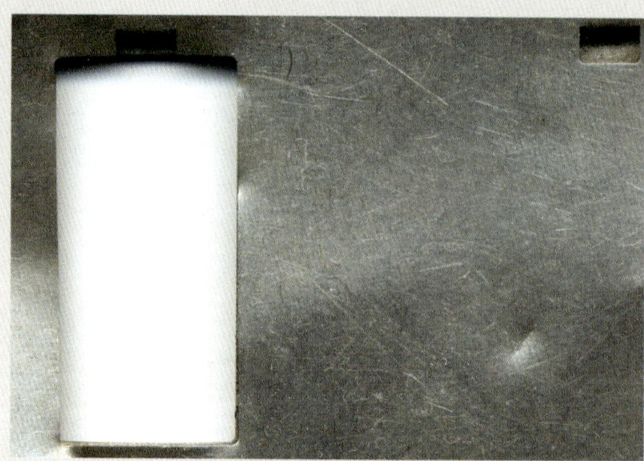

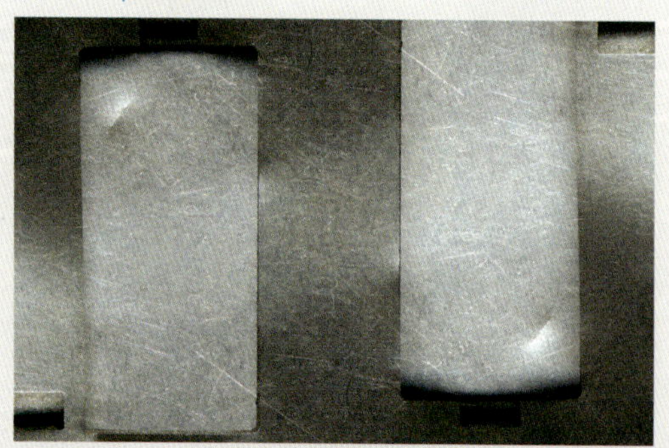

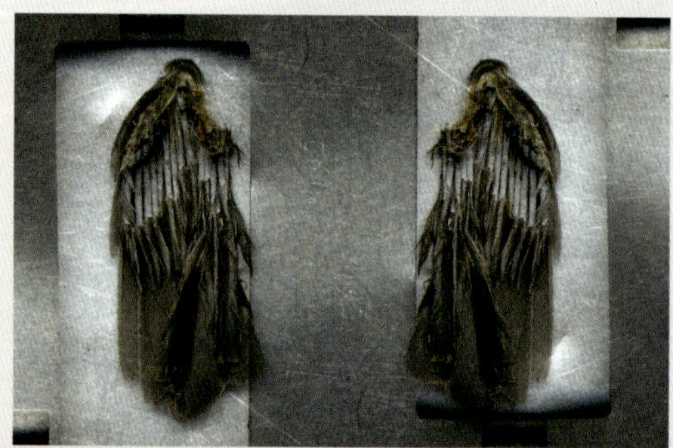

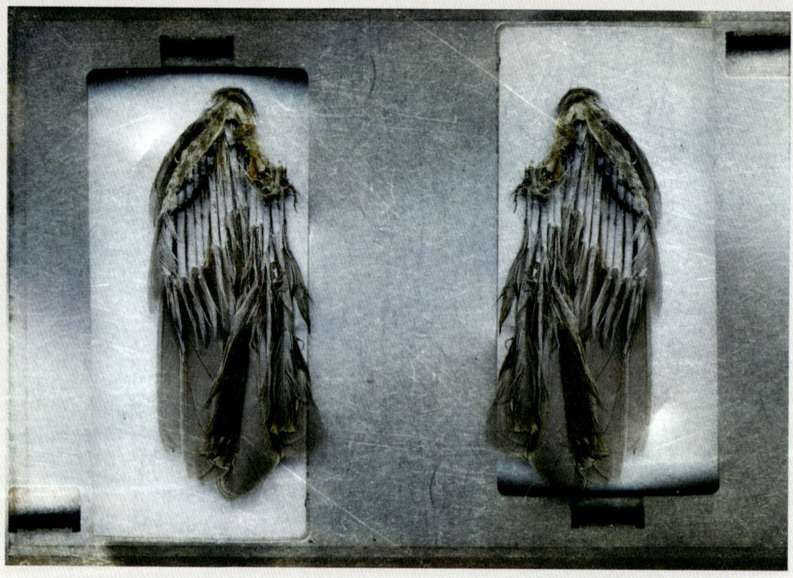

Fig 4

necessary to lighten them using Levels. Presented in this way, this new layer ceased to be just a discarded piece of metal, but could instead be interpreted as an architectural structure revealing mysterious doorways.

5 The layers with the bird's wing and the metal background were combined using the Layer options; but as all the layers were still independent, it was possible to make further slight alterations concerning position, tone, contrast and colour.

6 Finally, a layer was made by using a discarded Polaroid negative; this served not only to create a subtle border, but some of the

Fallen angel

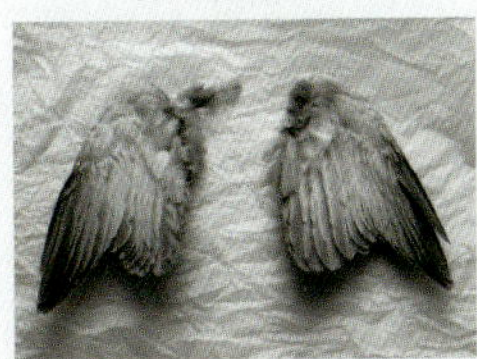

Layer 1

Having found a dead pigeon in the garden, I decided to remove its wings before burying it. They were then arranged on a crumpled piece of light tissue paper and photographed.

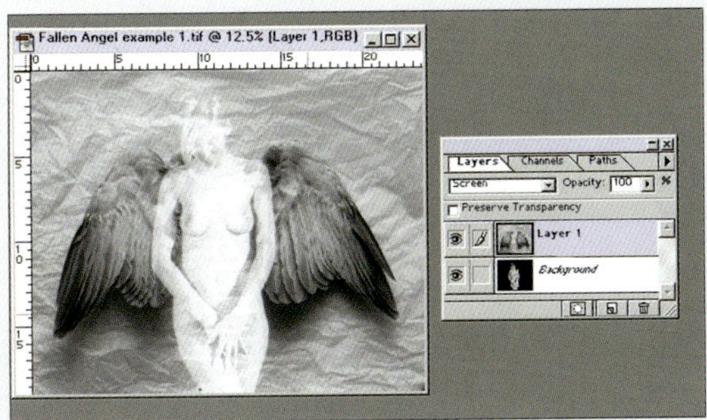

Fig 5

Both layers were carefully resized to ensure a perfect match, and by using Edit > Copy, then Edit > Paste, the two layers were stacked. By blending the two layers using the Screen mode, a lightened and slightly ghostly image of the model appeared over the wings.

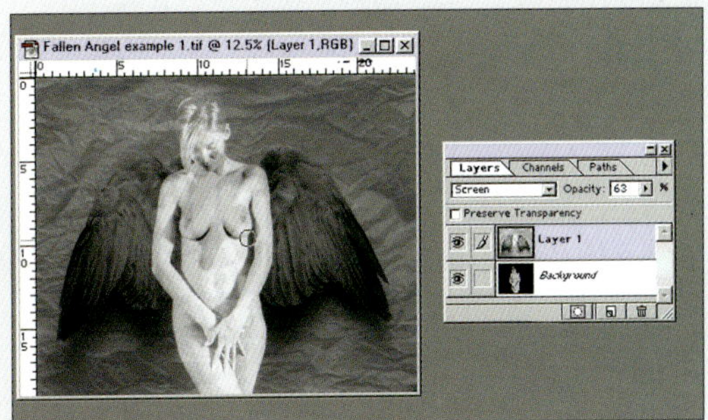

Fig 6

By reducing the opacity of layer 1, the strength of the background layer increased; parts of layer 1 that were obscuring the model were removed using the Eraser tool, which was set on a large but soft setting. It was not necessary to be too accurate at this stage, as allowing something of layer 1 to show through actually helped the image.

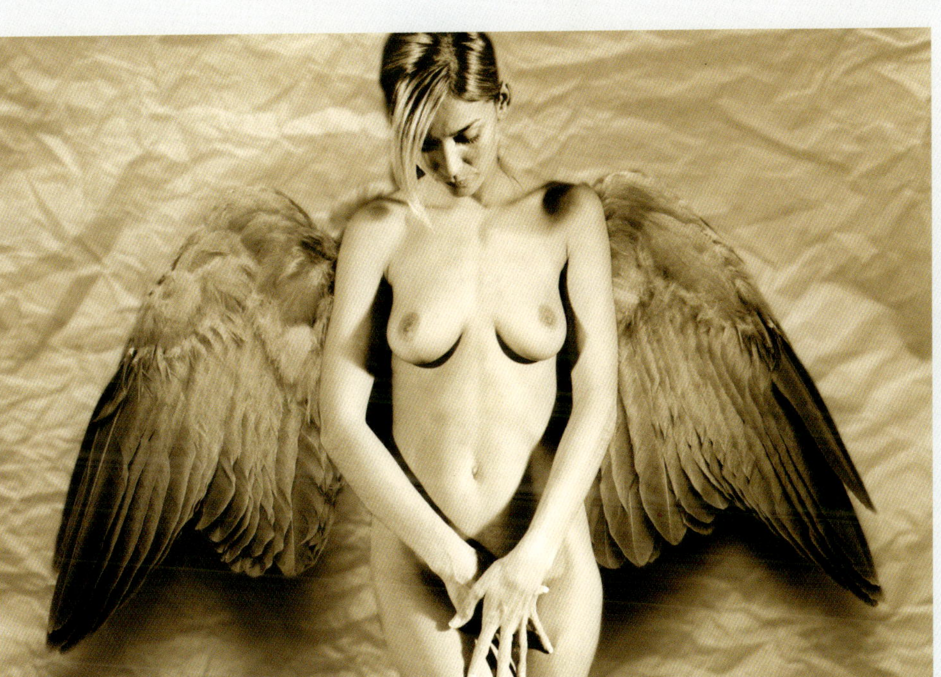

Final composite

The crumpled paper background was selected, feathered and then a Gaussian Blur filter was applied in order to create a sense of distance between the "angel" and backdrop. The two layers were merged and the entire image was coloured using Hue/Saturation.

oily colours apparent in the film were also allowed to infuse the final image. The Polaroid layer was carefully resized for an accurate fit.

Fallen angel

Some composites can be easily constructed and this is a case in point. I had a clear idea of how I wanted to use this model, and ensured that she was photographed against a dark background.

Adjustment Layers

The use of the Layers palette to combine images is probably its most obvious feature,

Antiquity

There is a well-established tradition within art photography of layering images, thus producing visual fragments, which invites the viewer to identify stimulating new realities. With the advent of digital photography, this way of producing an image has become far more accessible.

Occasionally we encounter such images in our everyday lives. This composite, for example, was inspired by old, peeling frescoes. Twenty separate layers were required to produce this, and while I had a general idea of how things might turn out, there were still one or two surprises. Despite its apparent complexity, it was easy to do, and every element within this image derives from purely photographic sources. Initially I created a new file, proportioned it to the size of the intended print, and then resized and imported each of the new files. Careful use was made of Blending modes and the Opacity slider at each stage. The Eraser tool was also extensively used.

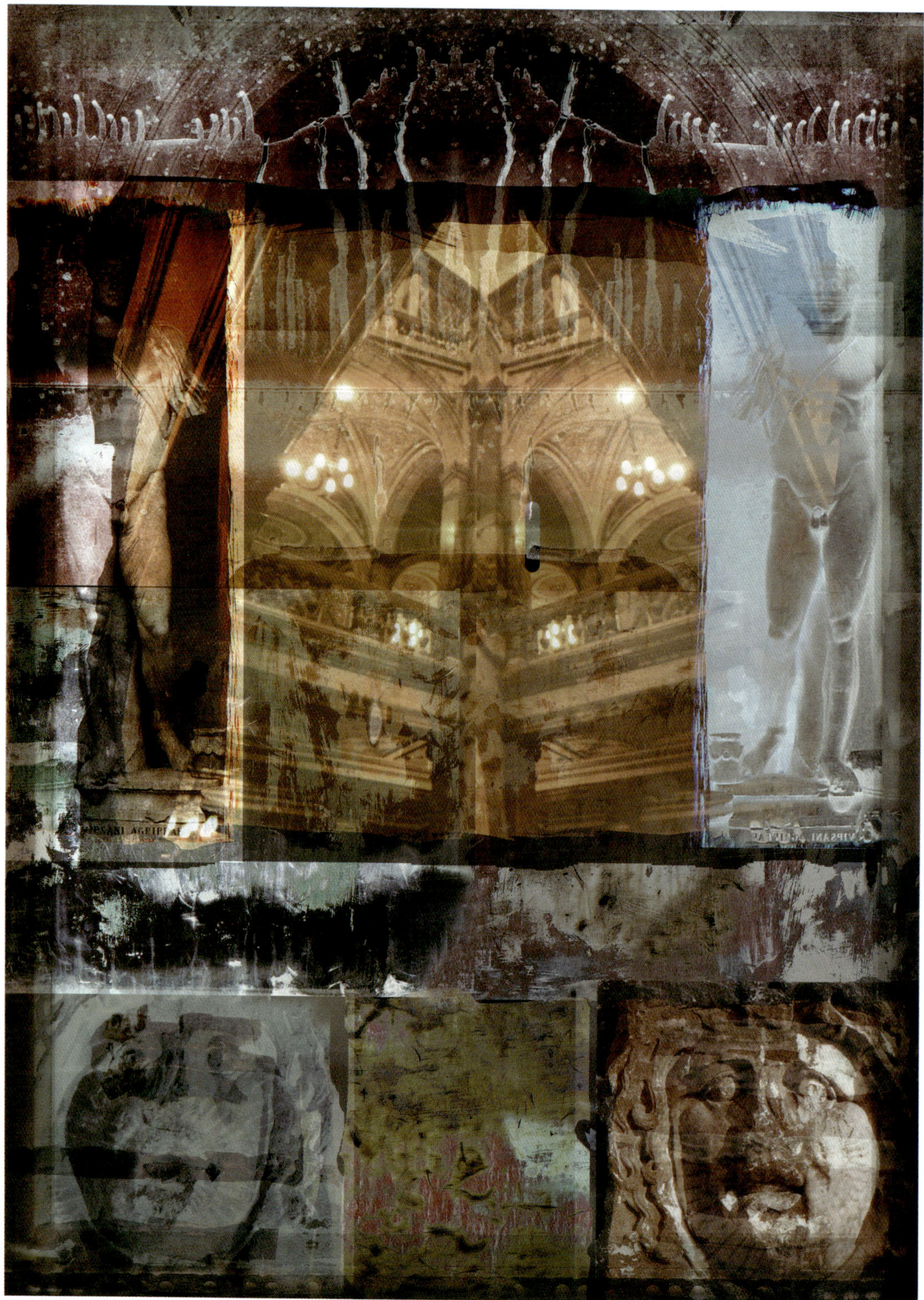

but as useful is the ability to include so-called Adjustment Layers. These are basically image adjustments that can be applied to individual or groups of layers. The important thing is that they can be revisited and changed at any time – only when an image is finally flattened are the adjustments committed to the image. For example, you may decide to sepia-tone a monochrome image using the Hue/Saturation option, but when the image is printed, it may not be quite the tone you expect. Using the normal route, you could use the History palette or start again. If the Hue/Saturation had been applied as an Adjustment Layer, it could be reopened and appropriate changes made. Not only this, but Multiple Adjustment layers can be made for different types of image adjustment, such as Curves, Levels, Color Balance and so on – each one can be switched on or off at will to show its overall effect on the image.

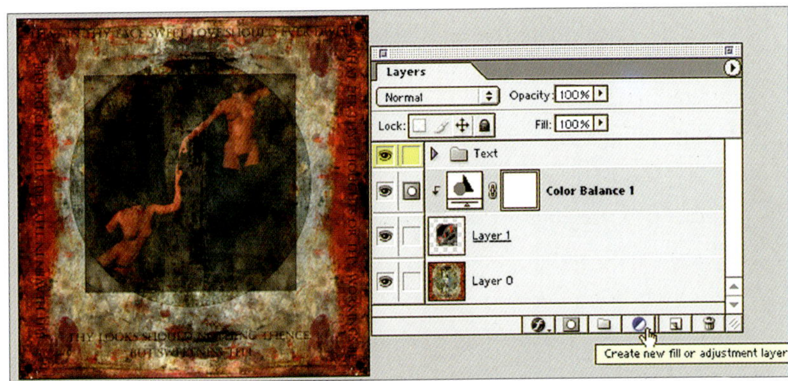

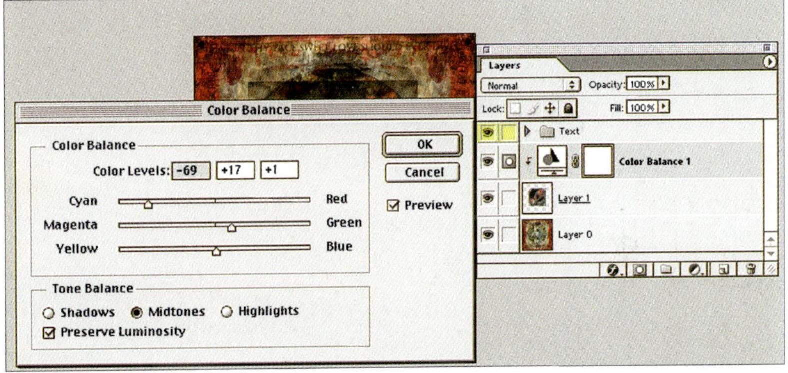

Applying an Adjustment Layer

Click on the Create New Fill or Adjustment Layer icon at the bottom of the Layers palette (see Fig 7).

A number of image adjustment options now become available from the drop-down menu. Select the appropriate option, which will appear above the highlighted layer in your layer stack. A dialog box where adjustments can be made also appears. Once an adjustment is made it can be altered at any time simply by double-clicking on the adjustment icon in the Adjustment Layer (see Fig 8). The Adjustment Layer also creates its own mask, which can be used to add or subtract adjustments, so they can be applied to selective parts of the image.

Linking Adjustment Layers

An Adjustment Layer will affect all layers below itself. If you want the adjustment to apply only to a single layer in a stack, it can be linked by moving the cursor between the two layers whilst holding down the Alt key. A double circle icon will appear. Click on the dividing line, and the Adjustment Layer will now only affect the layer it is linked to. Repeat the procedure to unlink it.

Applying Adjustment Layers to multiple images

If you have a number of images that you want to alter in identical ways, it is a simple matter to drag Adjustment Layers from one image to another. In this way, the identical adjustments, are added. This is particularly useful if complex Curves adjustments have been made – in normal circumstances it would be extremely difficult to make precisely the same curves adjustment from scratch, but dragging the Curves Adjustment Layer to another image applies the Curves directly and identically.

Fig 7 (top)

To add an Adjustment Layer, click on the Create New Fill or Adjustment Layer icon.

Fig 8 (bottom)

Select the type of adjustment required. In this case, Color Balance was used to alter the colour of the figures, which were originally scanned from a monochrome negative. The Adjustment Layer was linked to the figures so that it only affected them and not the background.

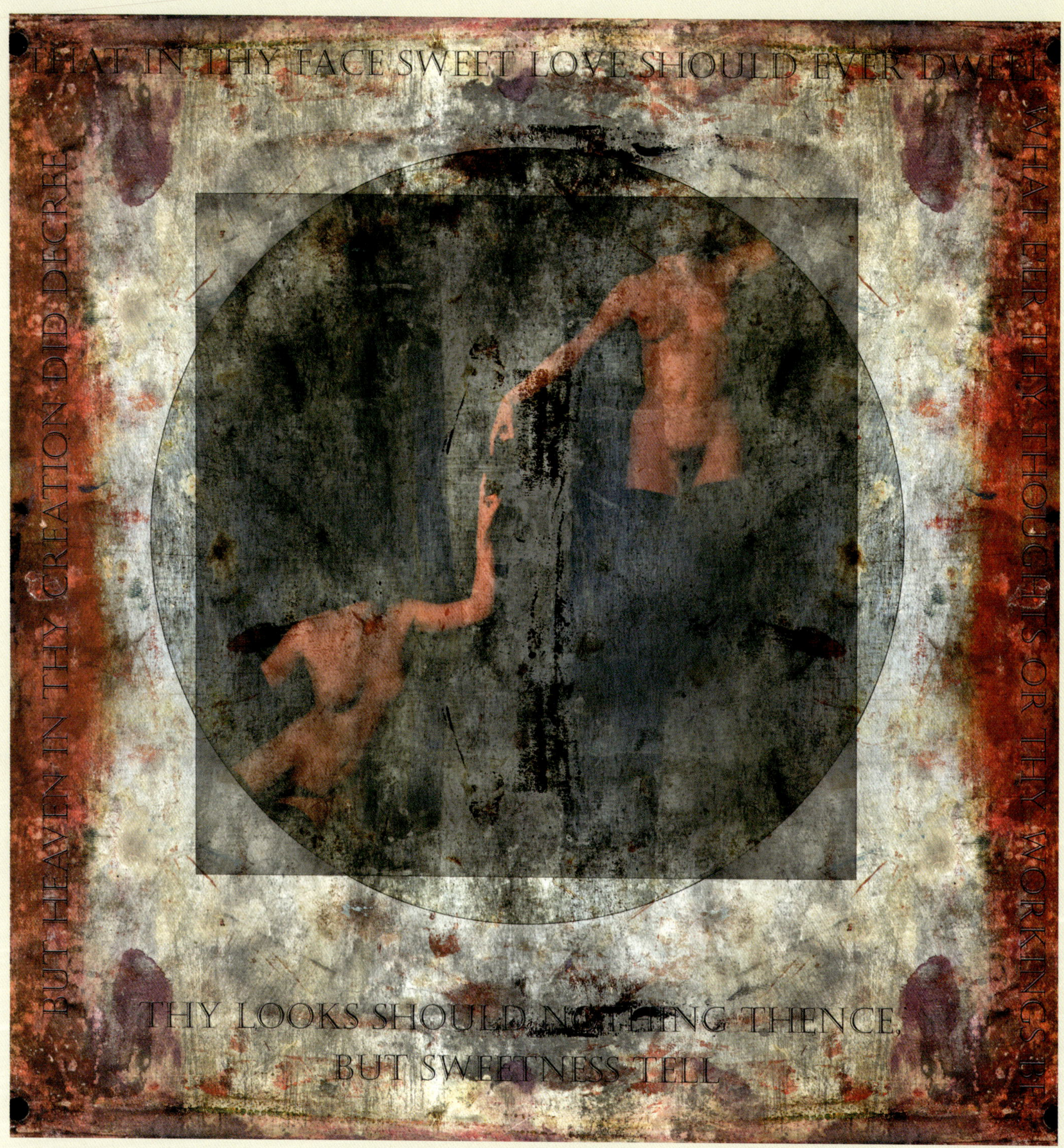

Creation

The background to this image started as a waste piece of card from a print room. I found the colours of ink interesting and scanned on a flatbed scanner, then duplicated and flipped the image twice to create a symmetrical background. The figures were imported from a scanned monochrome image as a separate layer. On yet another layer, a circular and square selection were made and then stroked with a dark colour. Finally, text was added as four separate layers around the edge of the image.

Using masks

Photoshop is a particularly sophisticated piece of software that allows us to produce images we could only dream of creating in the darkroom, and one of its most potent elements is its capacity to make masks. Masks are not a new concept, and traditionally any photographer wishing to produce a difficult composite would construct one so that various negatives could be printed onto a single piece of paper. The problem was that the masks were difficult to create, there was a limit to their accuracy, and the process relied on precisely registering the mask during the printing stage; even the slightest misalignment resulted in a ruined piece of paper.

Using masks was not a technique that photographers entered into lightly, but with the advent of Photoshop, all this has changed. It is now possible to digitally construct masks that are accurate up to 1 pixel – in fact they can be so accurate that in order to gain the best results, it is recommended that the mask is blurred ever so slightly. There are various ways of producing masks, but the most popular methods are by using the Quick Mask mode or Layer Masks.

Using the Quick Mask mode

The easiest way of using Quick Mask is to make a rough selection using the Lasso or other selection tool, and then apply a Quick Mask to produce a red, semi-transparent overlay which can then be further refined, if required. This overlay is similar to the old rubylith masks that were used by professional printers when producing composites, and has the added advantage of showing both the mask and the image at the same time, which allows some fine-tuning to be done. While Photoshop defaults to a 50% red transparent overlay, this can be changed by double-clicking the Quick Mask mode icon, which introduces the Quick Mask options box – using the Quick Mask set at 40% is easier to operate.

To apply the Quick Mask, select the Quick Mask mode icon (see Fig 1), but make sure that the default foreground and background colours are set to black and white.

This is important, because by toggling between these two, it is possible to add or delete elements from the mask, which allows for fine-tuning. Select the Brush tool and a brush size that seems appropriate for the task – often it is helpful to use a large Brush initially and then to progressively reduce its size as you work on more demanding areas. If the foreground colour is set on black, the brush will add to the mask, but if the foreground colour is set on white, the brush will remove the mask; by alternating between

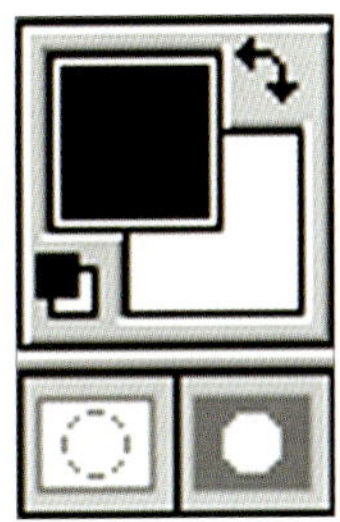

Fig 1

Genesis

Here, 27 separate layers were used. Each of the smaller outside images was carefully scanned, sized and then placed in position. Finally, the colour of the entire composite was inverted (Control/I) in order to induce a sense of unreality.

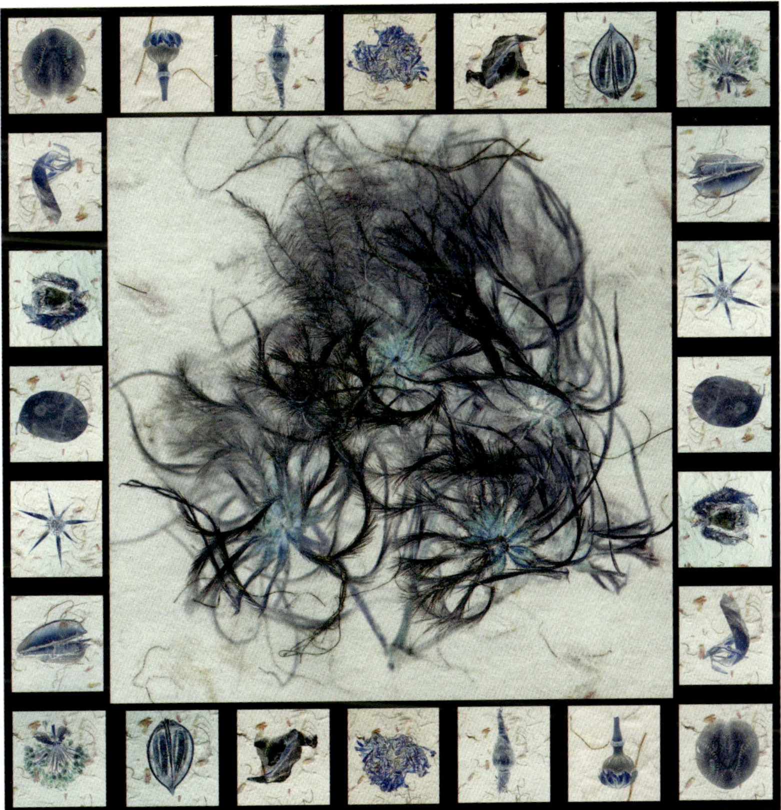

Dropping in a sky

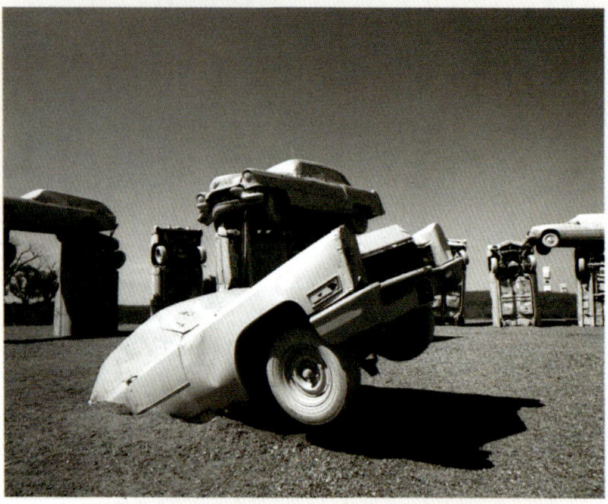

This is a classic situation where an otherwise promising photograph has been let down by a flat and uninteresting sky.

Fig 2

Making accurate selections is a particularly important part of the process, and if it is possible to use an automatic selection process, the task becomes far easier. Although logic told me that I should select the landscape and cars, I decided to select the sky first, as it revealed an even tonality, which would make the job separating the sky from the rest of the image simpler. I initially did a rough selection using the Lasso tool, but then opted for Color Range: Select > Color Range, to make a more accurate selection of the sky. I inversed the selection: Select > Inverse, and then applied Quick Mask. Finally a bit of fine-tuning was required, which I did using the Brush and Eraser tools.

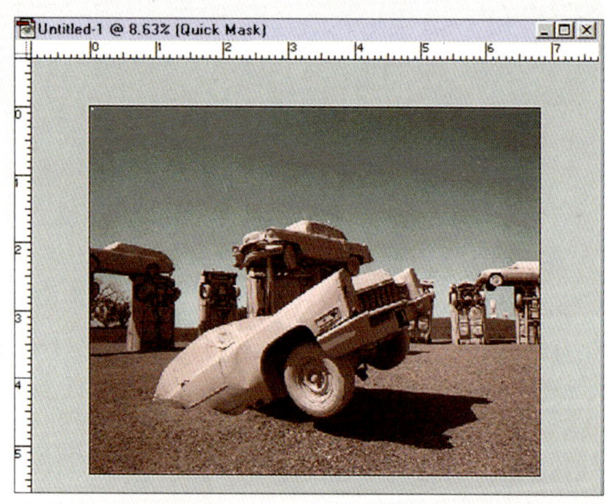

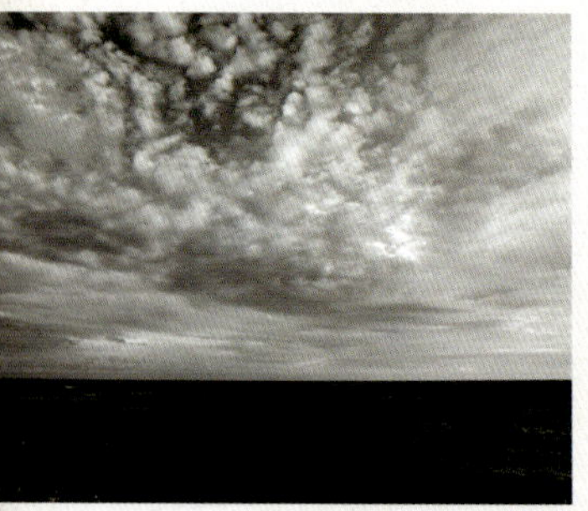

Fig 3

A suitable sky taken from another negative.

Fig 4

It is important to ensure that the size and resolution of the two windows match, and to appreciate that the destination window will determine the dimensions of the final composite, therefore the horizon of the destination window has been adjusted to match that of the source window. This was easily done using the Measure tool. Once these slight adjustments had been made, the Move tool was used to drag the source window over the destination window. (It depends on the file size, but this can take several seconds, so avoid the temptation to repeat the task. Once in position, the join between the two layers can appear too sharp, but this can easily be countered by defringing by 1 pixel: Layers > Matting > Defringe. It is useful to remember that the composite still comprises two layers at this stage, so each of the layers can be tonally adjusted independently of the other.) Once all the required adjustments had been made, the two layers were flattened to reduce the file size.

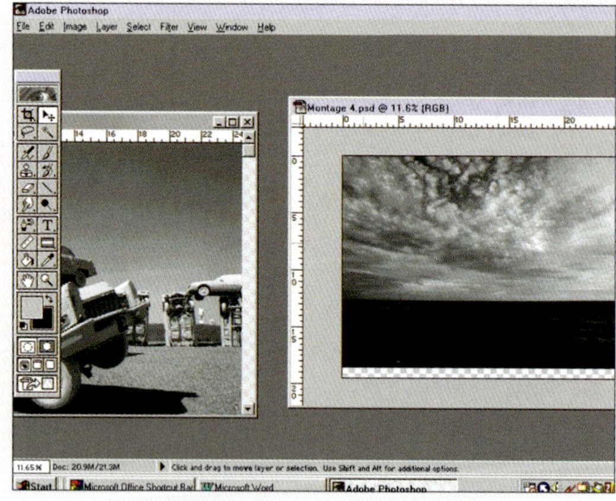

these two controls, a fairly accurate mask can be made. The Eraser tool can also be used to remove parts of the mask. Working with the Navigator at this stage is critical in order to achieve an accurate mask.

Once this has been done, click on the Standard Mode button, and the red mask will disappear to be replaced by the characteristic "marching ants", which indicate that a selection has been made. It is important to remember that it is the area that has not been covered by the red mask which becomes the selection. By selecting the Move tool, it is now possible to position the selection over another window.

Dropping in a sky

One of the most common improvements most photographers make is to "drop in a sky" when they encounter interesting landscapes

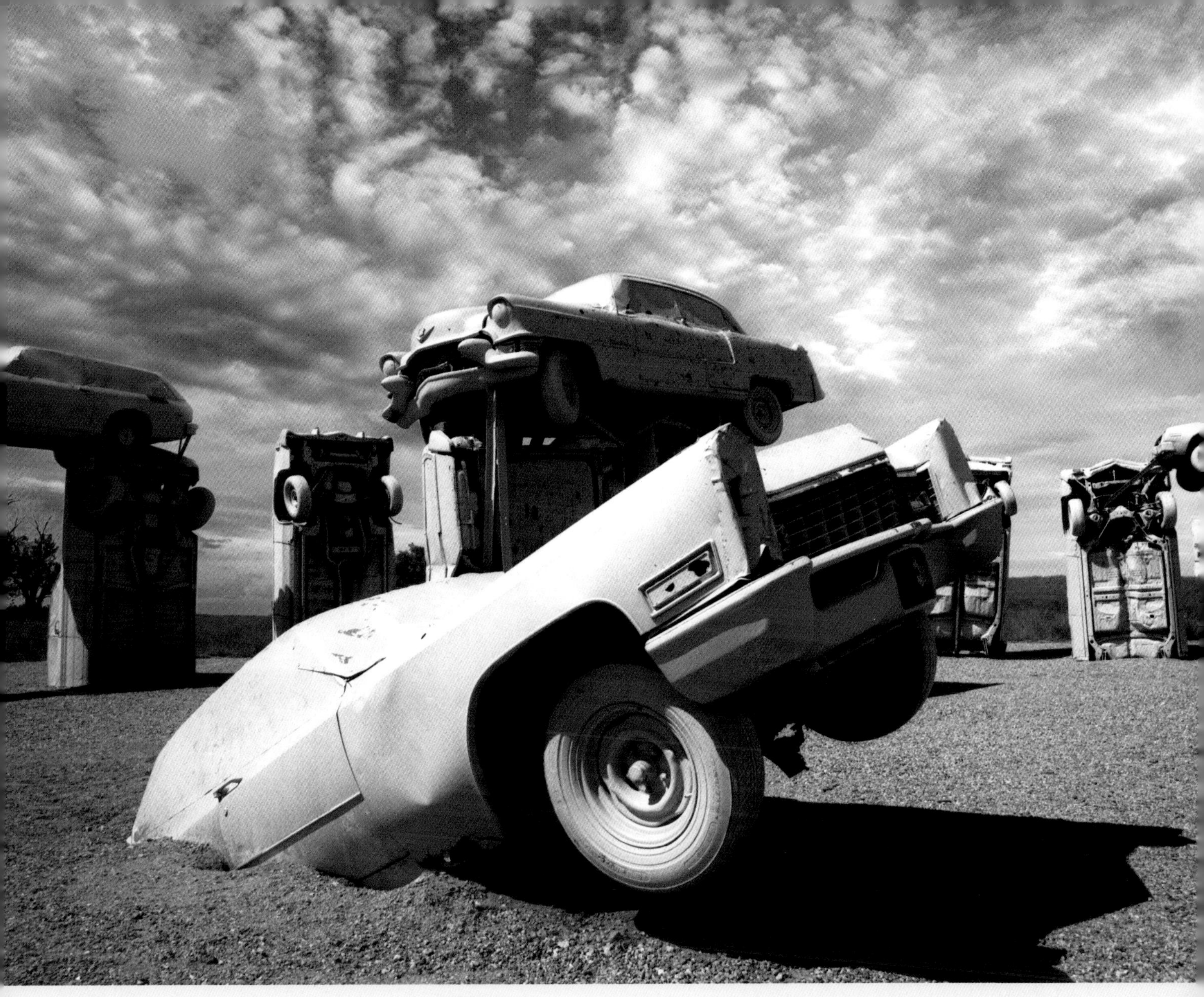

The final composite. "Carhenge" is a humorous parody on the ancient English site of Stonehenge, and this parallel is made all the more obvious when the dramatic, yet mysterious sky is introduced.

that are let down by boring skies. In the darkroom this is easily rectified, so long as there is a straight or uncluttered horizon, but as soon as other features protrude over the horizon, an accurate mask of some sort is required. This is beyond the scope of many photographers, but when working digitally, it is a relatively straightforward task.

Creating composites

Photoshop permits far more complicated montages than merely dropping in skies, and often the real challenge is to show restraint. Working with an idea in mind is often a good way to start. Trying to create a montage by simply cutting and pasting various unplanned negatives rarely works, as critical problems concerning lighting and perspective cannot be

Creating a scenario: model with globe

While images such as this are of questionable artistic value, it does not do any harm to set oneself a technical challenge, which is largely what this is. In order to succeed, it was important that the figure was carefully removed from its original context and imported into this new background.

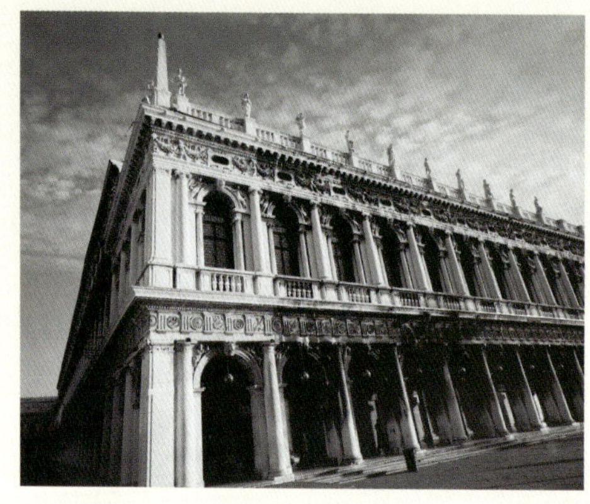

Fig 5

The best montages are often pre-planned. When I took this photograph in St Mark's Square, Venice, I already had it in mind what I intended to do, which is why the dark background building to the extreme right of the image was photographed perfectly horizontally thus making a potential join easy to achieve.

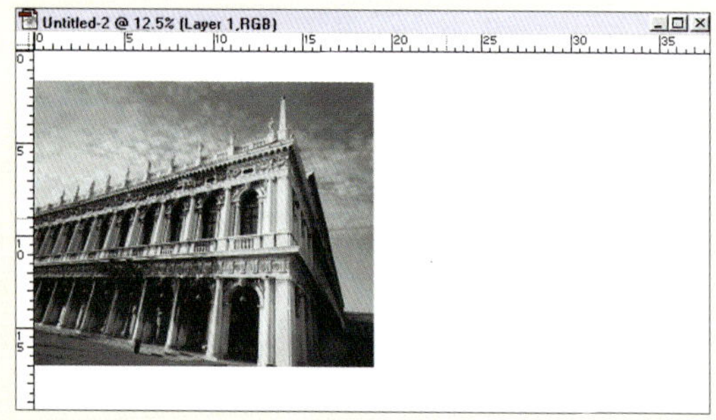

Fig 6

I created a new layer precisely double the width of the image of St Mark's Square.

Fig 7

Next I created a duplicate layer, flipped it horizontally and carefully positioned it using the Move tool. The Navigator was used in order to ensure a perfect join.

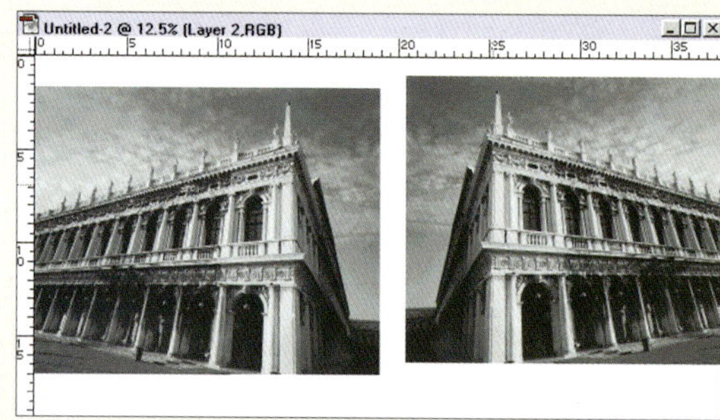

The finished montage.

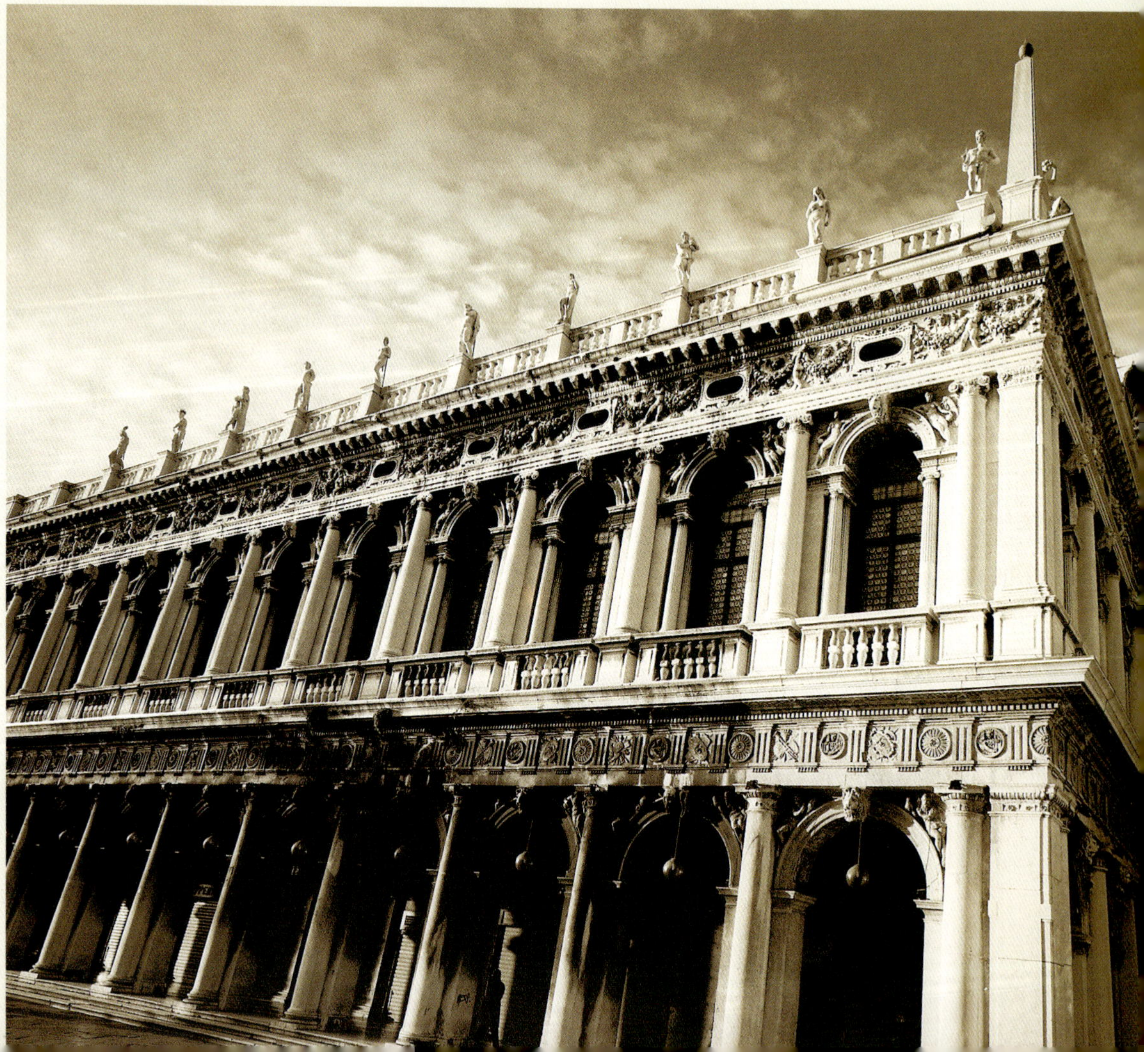

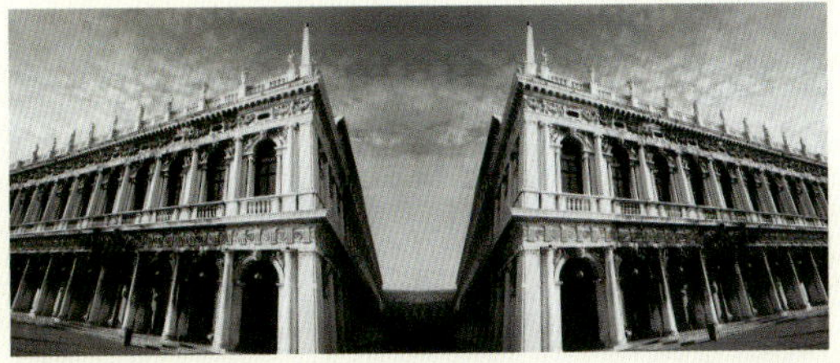

Fig 8

Once the two halves of the building had been joined, a small amount of cloning was required in the middle portion of the sky.

Fig 9

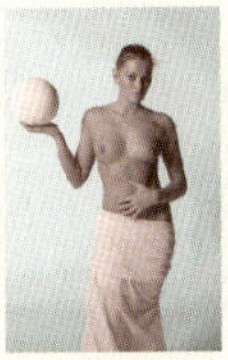

I opted to use this image because, in a quirky sort of way, her pose echoes the classical sculptures encountered around St Mark's. First, I needed to make an accurate selection. I used Color Range: Select > Color Range, and experimented to see which Fuzziness setting gave the best selection. Often this tends to be a compromise, and some of the selection needs to be done manually. At this point I applied the Quick Mask.

Fig 10

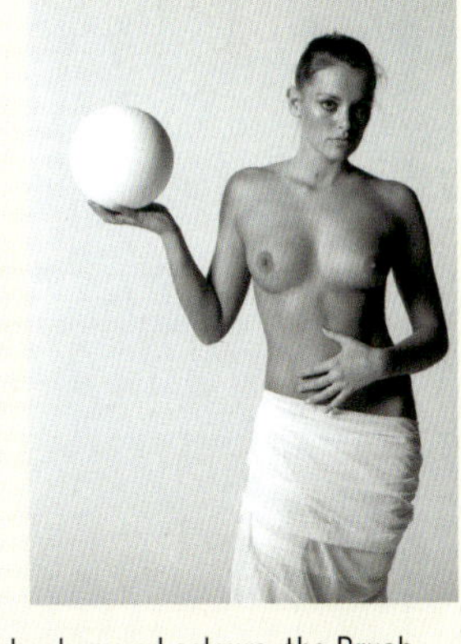

There is no escaping the issue: accurate selections take time and skill. While good results can be achieved using a mouse, if you anticipate doing a lot of this kind of work, investing in a graphics tablet can be worthwhile — they operate like a pen and pad, so drawing on screen becomes far easier. When applying the Quick Mask, it is important to set the default foreground and background colours to black and white respectively. Initially use a large Brush size to remove unwanted areas of the mask, but also to add to the mask where required. By toggling between the foreground and background colours, the Brush can be used for adding or removing the mask. As the requirements become more demanding, be prepared to reduce the Brush size, even up to 2 pixels. Once you are satisfied that the Quick Mask is as accurate as it can be, select the Standard Mode button, which makes the area not covered by the mask into a selection. In order to select the figure, I needed to inverse the selection: Select > Inverse. The "marching ants" then transferred to the model; using the Move tool, I repositioned the model over the building composite (see Fig 4). It is important to remember that the model layer is still independent from the background layer, so alterations regarding scale and tone can still be made. Once all the required changes had been made, I flattened the layers to reduce the file size and toned the entire image using Curves.

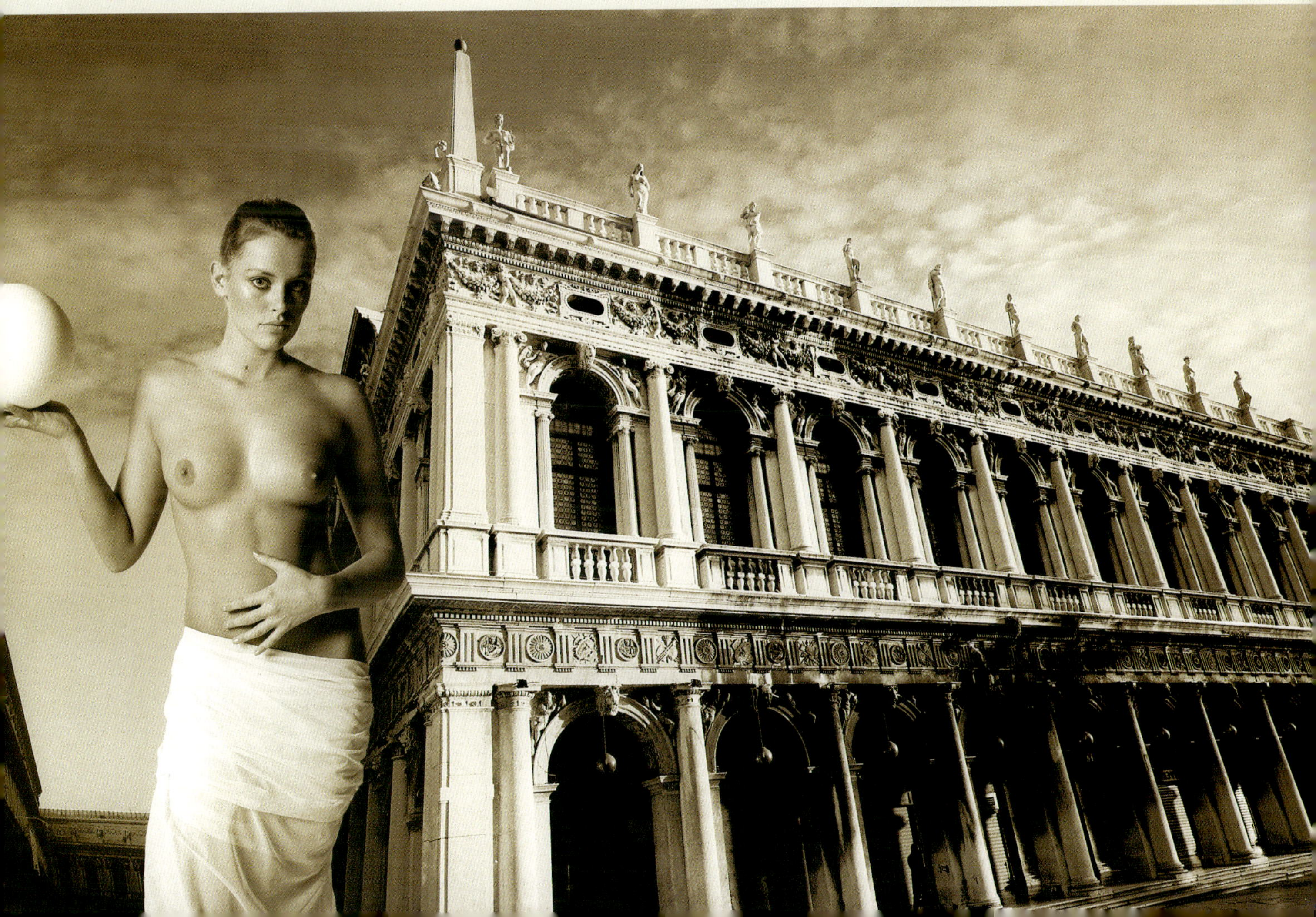

resolved digitally. The best montages are usually thought out and the negatives taken specifically for the task.

Think about the scenario

Another very important consideration when designing a composite is the scenario. The easiest montages are when elements are cut from one source and then pasted into another. The more complete the background, the less work there is to do. It is also important to choose an uncluttered background, otherwise obtrusive elements might appear and compromise the overall design – simple interiors, landscapes or seascapes can make excellent scenarios for composites.

Layer Masks

Combining elements in layers using selection techniques and cut and paste is all very well,

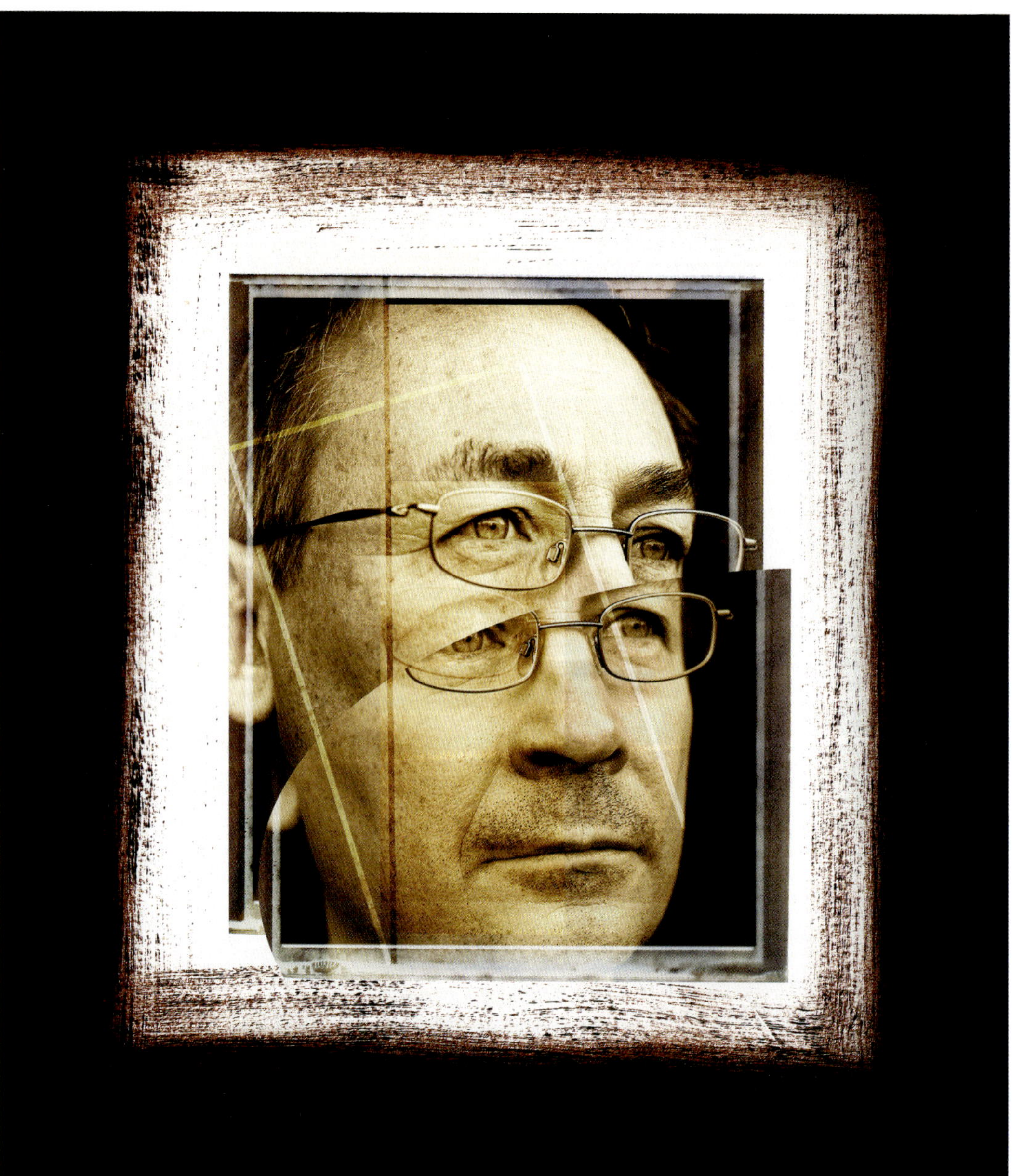

 WORKING WITH LAYERS AND MASKS

but such operations lead to irreversible changes to an image. The advantage of using Layer Masks is that such changes can be produced in a non-destructive way. Any change to an image applied through a Layer Mask can be reversed or edited at any time, or removed totally if required. The mask is formed as an alpha channel, so it can easily be copied or converted to a selection. Masks are particularly effective ways of making cutouts or combining images (see Chapter 14: Joiners and Panoramas).

Creating a Layer Mask

A Layer Mask is created by clicking on the Layer Mask icon at the bottom of the Layers palette (see Fig 11). The mask then appears next to the image icon in the Layers palette. This can only be done on a layer, not the background.

As with Quick Mask, set the default colour on the toolbox to black as foreground and white as background. Now you can paint with any paint tool – Brush, Gradient etc. – and as you do, a mask will be painted within the mask icon. Again, if black has been selected it will conceal (mask) the image. The beauty of this technique is that any part of the mask can be removed by painting with white (reverse the colours using keyboard key X, so the mask can be modified at any time, especially if you make mistakes). The mask is stored in Channels as a separate alpha layer (see Fig 12).

Layer Masks can be an intuitive and effective way of making selections, especially if a graphics tablet and pen are used. By varying the pressure on the pen, different densities of mask can be painted to gradually reveal or conceal detail. If using a mouse, this can also be done using various shades of grey as the foreground colour.

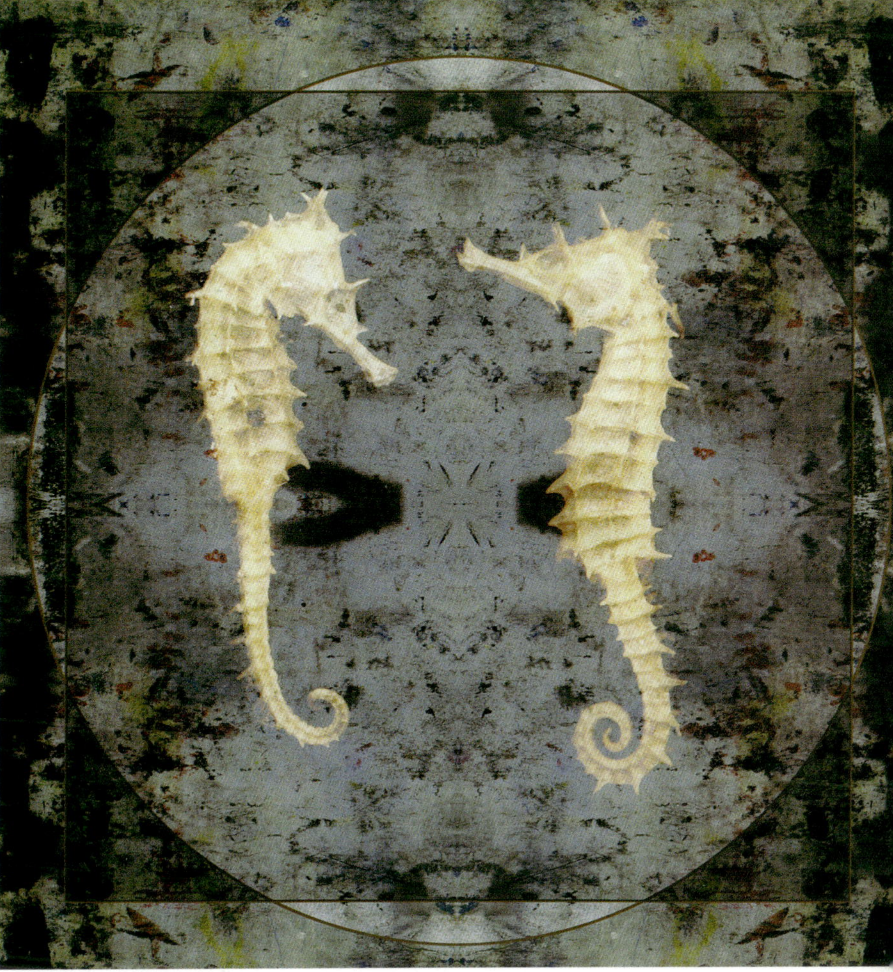

When using masks, be aware that the mask icon must be selected. Within a layer which has a mask it is easy to get confused. By clicking on the mask icon a black line will appear around its edge. If you then want to change to working directly on the image, you must click on the image icon; a black line will then appear around it, showing that it is the active layer.

In conjunction with Blending modes, Layer Masks are a good way to make selections, as any mistakes can always be altered at a later date: edges can be softened and blended, and so on.

Seahorses

This image started life as a flatbed scan of two dried seahorses against a black background. The texture of the background was the created on a new layer by scanning a piece of scrap metal which had paint marks on. This was then duplicated and flipped to create symmetry. The geometric shapes were drawn with the marquee selection tools and stroked. Whilst the selection tools were active changes were made using curves to alter the areas of the background within them.

Creating Layer Masks

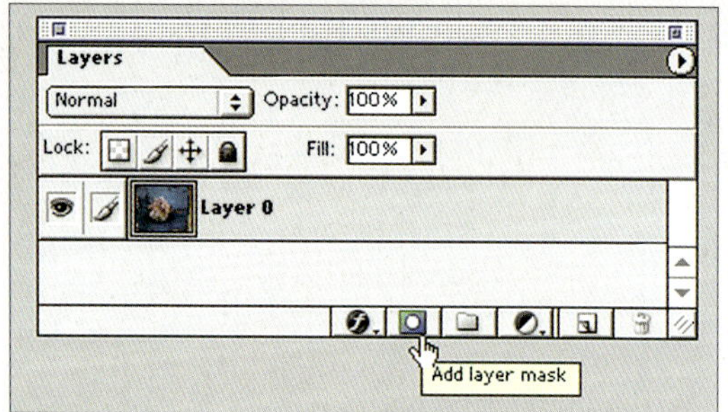

Fig 11

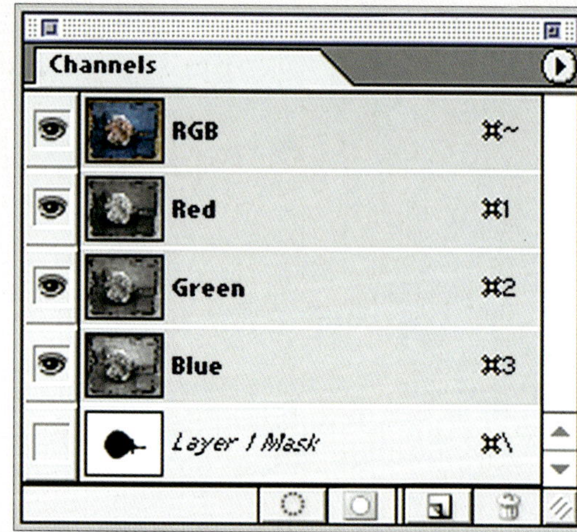

Fig 12

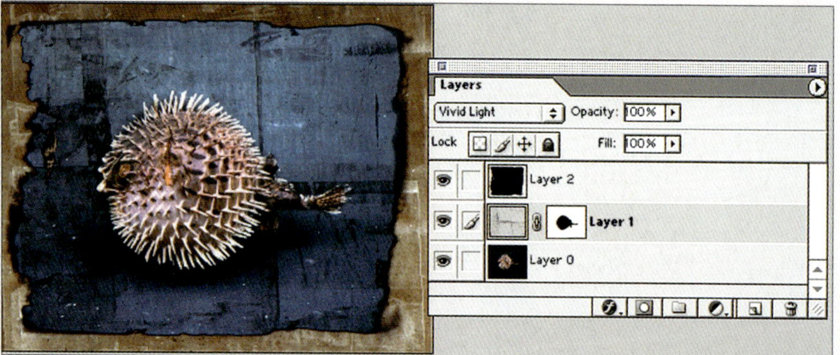

Fig 13

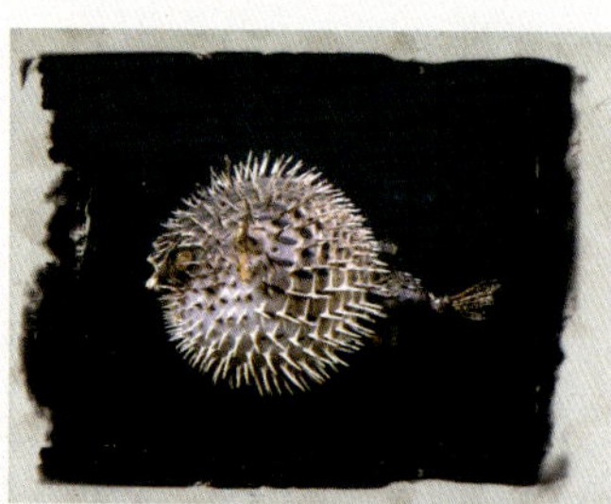

Puffer fish 1

I wanted to add texture to this image of a puffer fish, but wanted the texture to affect the background and not the fish. Therefore a mask was made on the texture layer, which was then painted with black over the area of the fish with a soft-edged Brush (see Fig 13). This prevented the texture being applied to the fish.

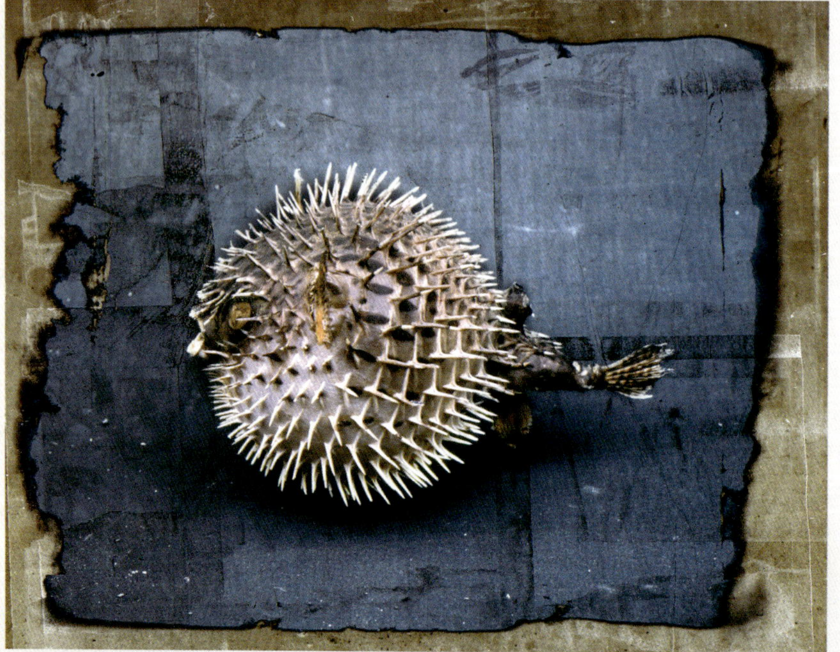

Puffer fish 2

The final image shows texture in the background with the fish "floating" above it. The colours and texture were exaggerated using Blending modes. The texture layer was Vivid Light Blending mode.

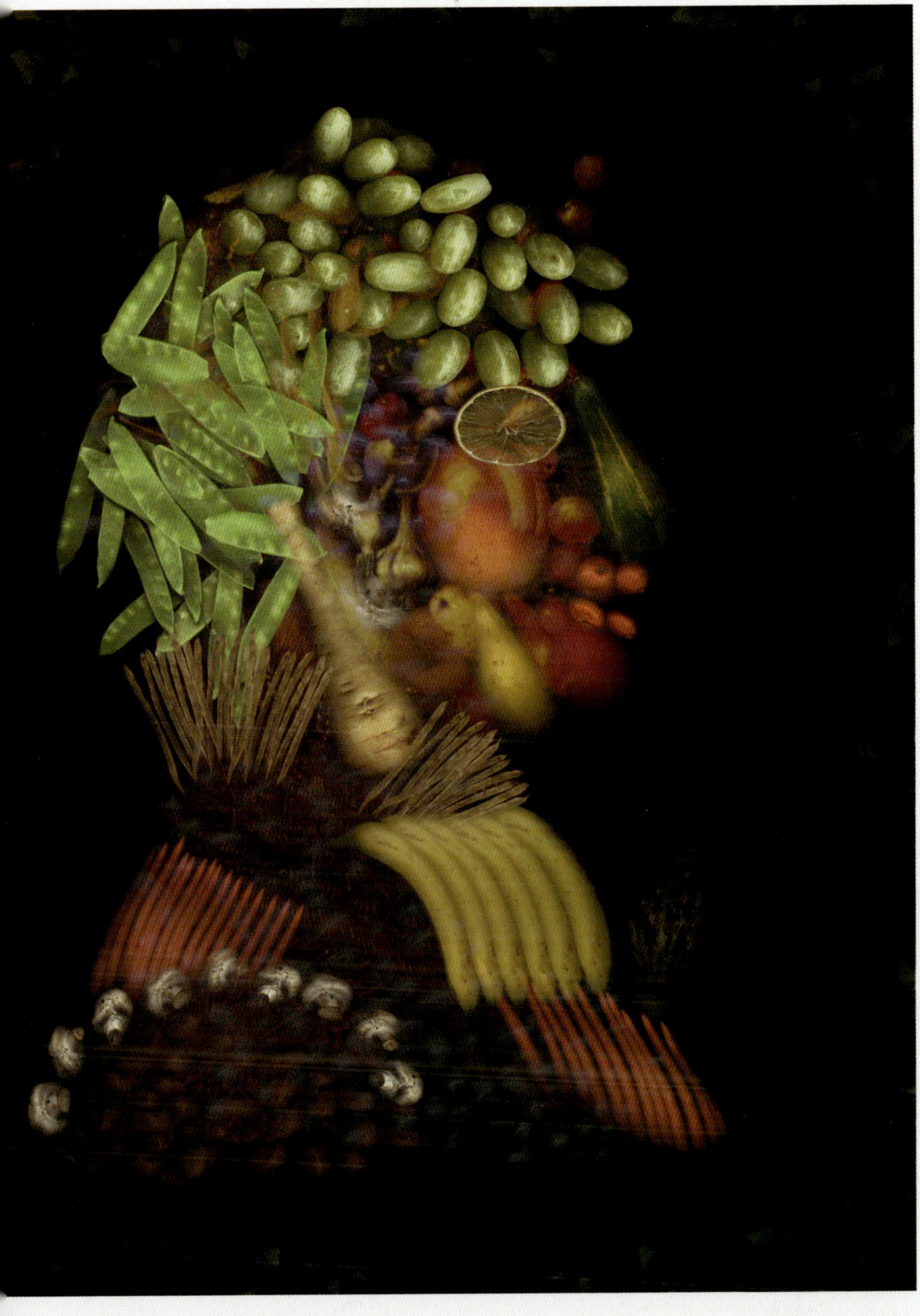

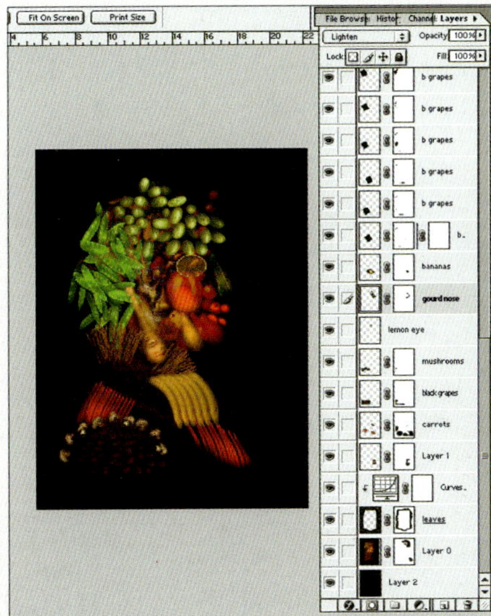

Fig 14

The Layer Masks were mainly used to merge individual vegetables with the background, which was built up gradually. By using soft-edged Brushes and painting on the Layer Masks, I was able to reveal or conceal the separate elements of the composition.

Homage to Arcimboldo

The great 16th-century Italian painter Giuseppe Arcimboldo was probably best known for his unique portraits, which he would create from compositions of fruit, flowers and even fish. Inspired by his work, I made a trip to my refrigerator and selected a variety of fruit and vegetables. These were then scanned on a flatbed scanner, and two days later I had an image composed of 36 layers with associated Layer Masks.

3   Creative use of flatbed scanners

A very large number of people own a flatbed scanner, but when you inquire about how much they use it, apart from copying the occasional document, it remains largely untouched. The flatbed is a much undervalued means of capturing images – used as a macro lens, it is easy to photograph small man-made and natural forms in abundant detail. Once captured, these scans can be merged effortlessly with other more conventional photographic sources to produce dramatic and exciting images.

IN THE 1970s and 1980s photographic artists used photocopiers for quick recording of informal images. The disadvantage was that the images were extremely ephemeral, as photocopy prints are cheaply produced and not designed to last. But the notion that a "photographic" image need not be captured using only a camera helped to define what we now mean by photography – dictionary definitions vary, but most suggest that it is a process of producing permanent and visible images by the action of light. The source can be either natural or artificial, so by most definitions, using a scanner is a legitimate means of capturing a photographic image.

When compared to a photocopier, a flatbed scanner has considerably more advantages. First, the quality of the scan is infinitely more precise. Second, the images captured can be reproduced using sophisticated printers of varying formats, which employ archival pigments and use a full range of quality art papers. Third – and potentially more interestingly – images captured using a flatbed can be amalgamated with a variety of other sources, including conventional film, drawings, text, maps and illustrations. A flatbed offers opportunities that exceed those available in the past, and so it should come as no surprise that within the contemporary artworld the use a flatbed scanner is a recognized means of recording images.

What is a flatbed scanner?

Flatbeds were designed to replace the role of the photocopier in offices, allowing the user to make copies of documents, scan pages of books and magazines, and even make copies of photos. Most flatbeds scan at A4 size (215 x 298mm or $8^{1}/_{2}$ x $11^{3}/_{4}$in) although it is now also possible to buy scanners that will scan up to A3 size (298 x 430mm or $11^{3}/_{4}$ x 17in). As with a photocopier, the document is placed

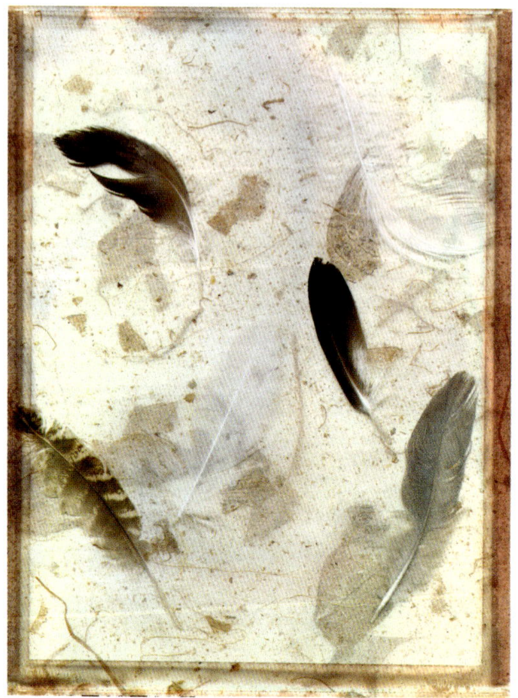

Feathers on rice paper
Very complex images can often be created using the very simplest of techniques. While this image may appear to be a composite made up of various layers, it was all done with one single scan: the feathers were randomly distributed over the platen, and then a sheet of rice paper impregnated with leaf fragments was placed over them. Once again the border was created using a discarded Polaroid negative.

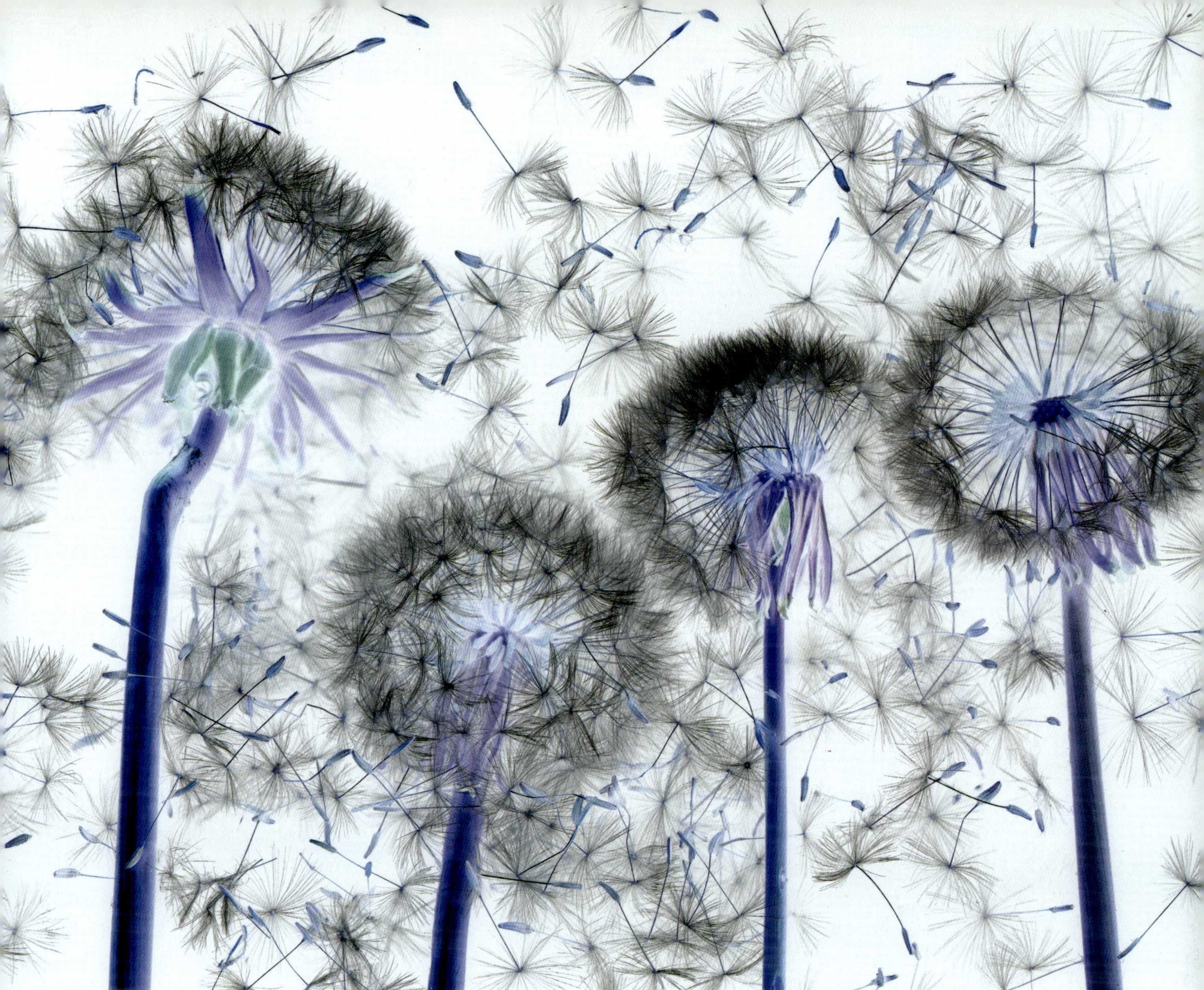

face down onto a glass platen and is then copied onto the computer to which the flatbed is linked. The big advantage of working in this way is that the document can then be imported into other documents or even e-mailed.

Flatbed scanners should not be confused with film scanners, which operate to much finer margins. Aware of the growing interest in flatbeds within photography, some manufacturers are suggesting that film – even 35mm film – can be scanned on a flatbed. It can, but the results are often disappointing, unless a scanner that can deliver a minimum

of 2400dpi is being used. Having said that, technology is moving fast and at the time of writing, flatbed scanners are being produced with a scanning resolution of 4800dpi and digital ICE technology. With inexpensive flatbeds, scanning prints is often the best solution.

Using a flatbed to scan objects

The first thing to understand is that using a flatbed allows you to capture images that vary from the very simple to the highly complex. In addition, it allows you to scan a wide variety of objects in astonishing detail. Although you

Dandelions

When scanning these dandelions, I wanted to convey the sense of the seed heads being dispersed by a gentle breeze. Because only some of them are clearly in focus, a sense of distance is suggested. As no background was used on the original scan, it appeared very dark. By inverting the entire image, a subtle sky background is implied.

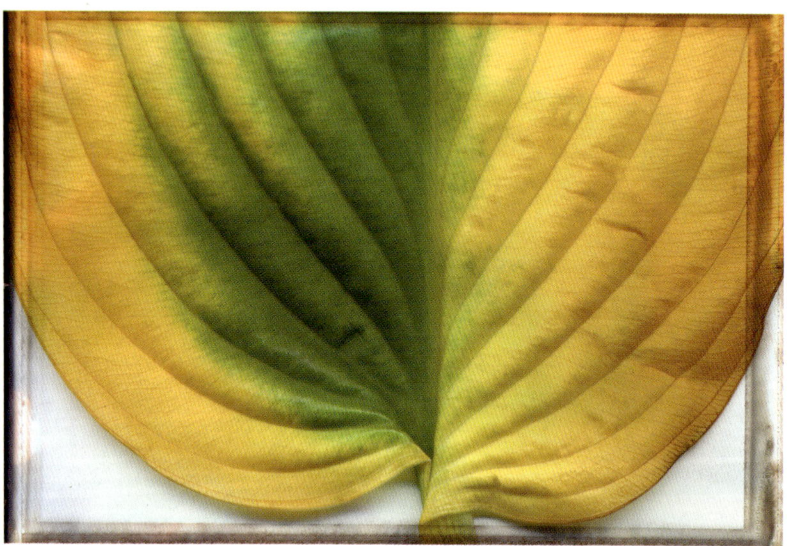

Hosta leaf

This was spotted late in the summer. When I examined it more closely, I was drawn to the delicate textures and colour. To retain all the delicate venation, a flatbed seems to have few rivals. The border was created using a rejected Polaroid negative.

Physalis

After a collection of Physalis (commonly known as Chinese Lanterns) was scanned on a flatbed, the subsequent image was abstracted using the Pattern Stamp tool, set to Non-aligned. This tool works in a similar way to the Rubber Stamp tool, except that it creates repeating patterns. In this example the largest Brush size was used.

may be restricted by the size of the scanner you use, it is possible to methodically scan parts of an object and then digitally "stitch" these elements together later on – but even if you decide to restrict yourself to only scanning objects that will comfortably fit onto the platen, the variety of things that can be successfully scanned is simply amazing, including material that proves difficult to photograph using other, more conventional techniques.

The obvious choices are small, natural objects such as shells, feathers, cones, leaves and so on, because when they are viewed close-up, they often reveal an intricate beauty that is difficult to show even when using a close-up macro lens. With such objects it is important to exercise care, particularly when scanning hard objects that might scratch the platen. A sensible precaution is to place a clear OHP transparency onto the glass surface, which then serves as a protective barrier. Occasionally, the texture of the transparency can show up, particularly in the darkest areas of the scan, but this can easily be removed by selectively using a Noise filter.

Some photographers are concerned about being unable to control the depth of field, but it has to be remembered that flatbeds are not cameras and are not designed to scan in depth; their primary function is to scan documents and flat objects. The important principle is to view this limitation as a strength. Photographers can be overly keen to maximize the depth of field, and as a consequence fail to appreciate how interesting some images can be when this is greatly reduced. It is always foolish to generalize, but it appears that professional photographers are much more willing to use a narrow depth of field than most amateurs. It should also be recognized that when using a powerful macro lens, the depth of field is probably less than when using a flatbed scanner, particularly when it is used at high magnification.

The process of scanning

When scanning using a flatbed, the image needs to be placed face down on the platen; therefore it is difficult to see what the scanner sees. There are two simple ways of resolving this problem:

1 Try to compose the elements away from the scanner, and once this is done, place them carefully on the platen.

2 Place the objects on a sheet of glass and then view it from below: in this way it is possible to see what the scanner will see.

Most flatbeds have a cover that can be removed. While it is useful to keep the cover in place when scanning shallow objects, it does need to be removed when scanning objects much deeper than 10mm ($^1/_3$in). When the cover is removed, the scanner is theoretically capable of picking up detail from the room, but in reality unless there is a light directly overhead, the illumination fall-off

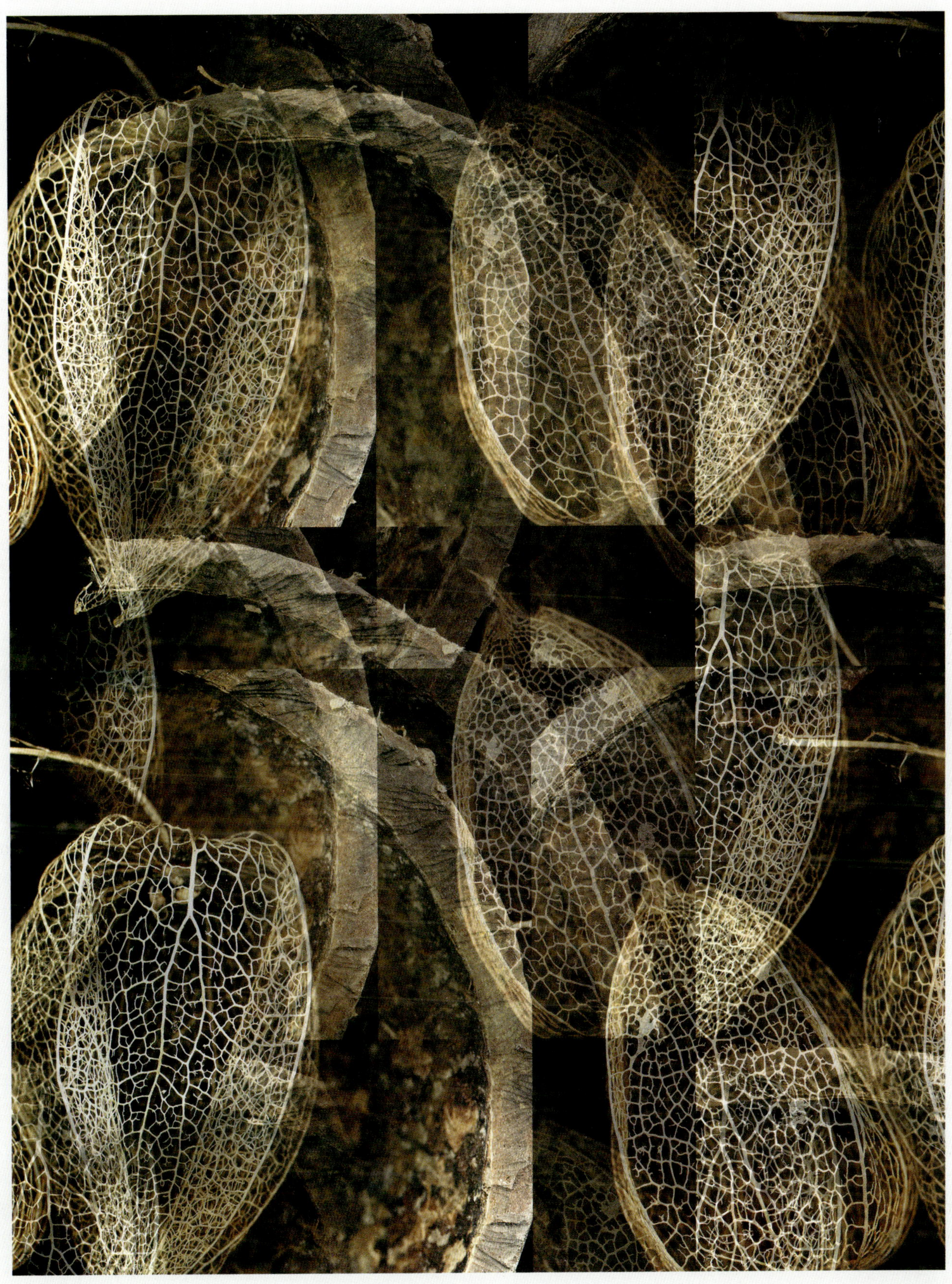

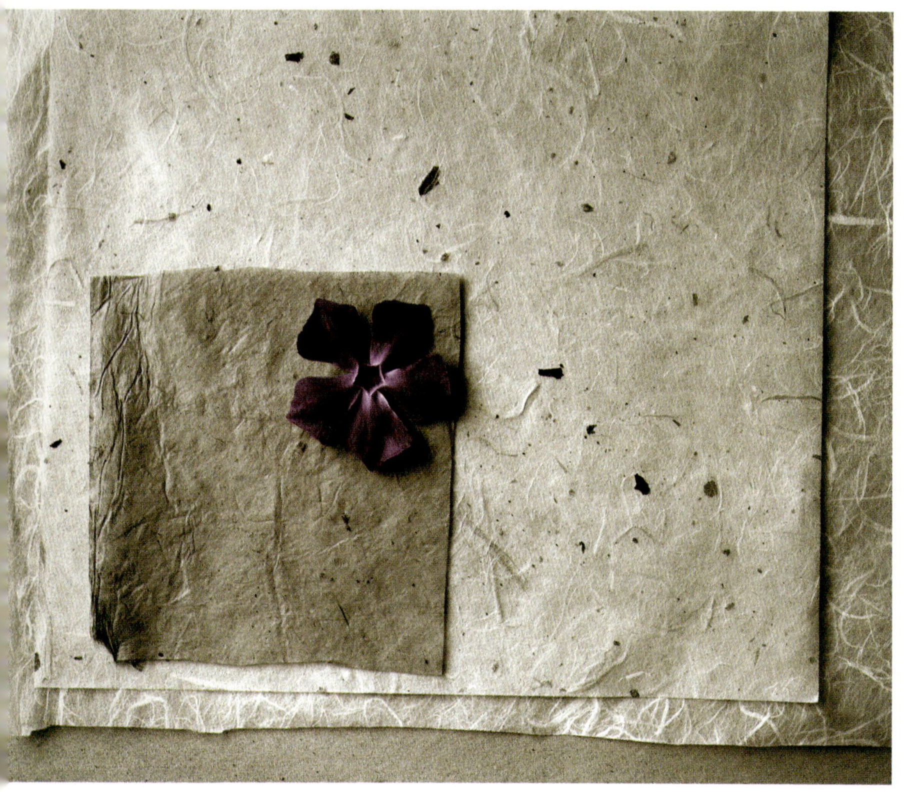

magnify the image output to a longest edge of 300mm (11³/₄in). If scanning in RGB mode, an output scan of 300 x 200mm (11³/₄ x 8in) at 300dpi will give an image file of 24MB.

Unlike a dedicated film scanner, a flatbed will scan the entire platen (unless otherwise instructed), and it is therefore capable of recording an astonishing amount of information. It is important to be aware of the computer's memory capacity before creating enormous files. When scanning objects that are close to the maximum size of the flatbed, there is no harm in starting with the lowest resolution, and then if that proves to be unsatisfactory, increasing it a little.

Constructing backgrounds

One of the simplest ways to create a background is to support a sheet of firm card directly behind the scanned objects; this can vary in terms of texture, colour and tone, although changes can also be made depending on where the card is placed in relation to the platen – the greater the distance, the darker the background colour.

Backgrounds can be quite elaborate, as all manner of materials can be used: in addition to paper or card, try using metal foil, textured wooden board, mirrors, fabric or even parts of the human body. Each has its own unique qualities. You could construct a purpose-made hood that fits directly over the scanner, to ensure a consistent black background. One photographer has constructed a box, lined with black velvet, which he fits over the scanner. Each scanning task offers its own challenges, and the problems must be thought out.

Constructing supports

Flowers are a popular subject for scanning with a flatbed, although soft objects such as these can pose problems. Flowerheads in

Purple flower

After this image had been scanned in full colour, I felt there was no reason why the colours should not be changed – I desaturated it and then introduced new colours using Hue/Saturation and Color Balance.

is so severe that the background will appear black. Often this can prove to be advantageous, as dark, uncluttered areas can easily be merged with images from other sources using Layers. But there will be occasions when a lighter background is required, and it may be necessary to construct one (see below).

Resolution

The resolution you use depends on various factors, but should be governed by the size of the object being scanned and by how large you want your final print to be.

There is little point in creating image files that make for memory problems or greatly reduce the computer's performance, particularly if you intend to add further layers. For optimum printed quality using A4 paper, select the desired scanning "input" area, and with the printed resolution fixed at 300dpi, particular can distort under their own weight, but one way of resolving this problem is to support the flower so that a much smaller surface area is in contact with the glass platen. This can be done in two ways:

1 Try supporting the flower on the edge of the flatbed using Blu-tack. If this proves impractical because of the size of the flower, attach the Blu-tack onto the platen, making sure, of course, that a protective OHP sheet is in place.

2 Construct a small wooden block that sits to the side of the flatbed and can then serve as a kind of fulcrum for the flower. By adjusting the length of the overhanging stem and counterbalancing this with Blu-tack, subtle adjustments can be made.

Overcoming the obvious source of light

Another problem when using a flatbed is that the source of light is usually very apparent; although this is something over which there can be very little control, as ever there are ways of dealing with it. Sometimes it does not appear to pose a problem, as the light appears to come from above the subject, although on other occasions the lighter areas that are in direct contact with the platen can appear burned out.

Most flatbeds allow the user to make adjustments at the pre-scanning stage by using either Curves or Levels. Reducing the highlights at this stage is an obvious way of overcoming the problem. If this is not possible, an alternative is to make the adjustments once the object has been scanned. By making an Adjustment Layer, selective changes can be made to the highlights without affecting the other tones.

Debris on the platen

No matter how careful you are, it is easy to litter the platen with small pieces of debris; this is particularly likely when scanning organic objects. It is important to be aware of this and to remove any loose material that is likely to create problems, using an old lens brush. If, despite your best efforts, debris appears after scanning, this can be dealt with digitally using a variety of tools. Debris can be particularly evident if a black background is used, although one simple solution to this problem is to select the background and then apply a Noise filter.

Working with scanned images

While it is possible to achieve wonderful images by simply doing a straight scan, these can often be greatly enhanced by introducing other elements. It is important to appreciate that just because the main source has been

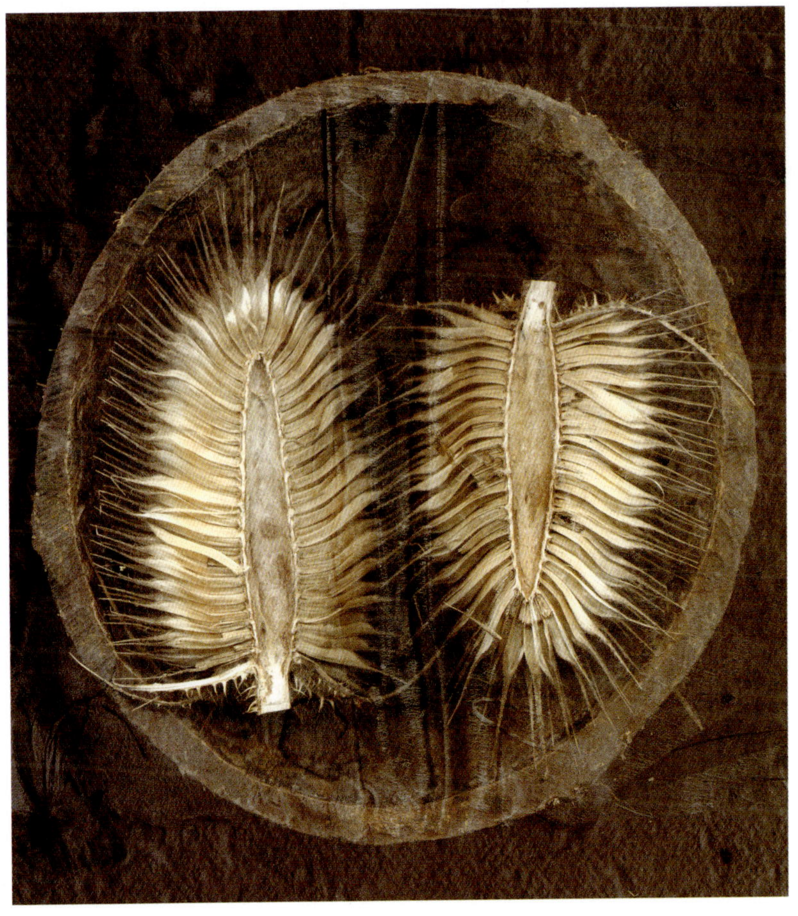

Working with scanned images

Fig 1

A small section from a bird's wing, scanned using a flatbed.

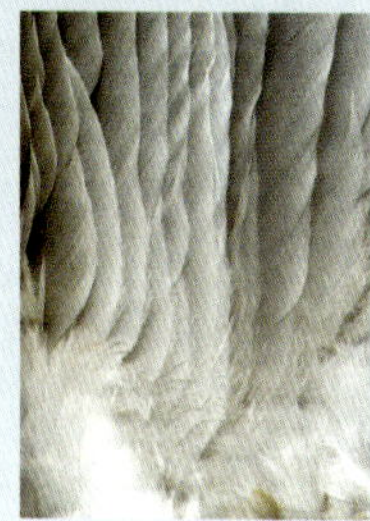

Fig 2

In order to create a mirror image of the bird's wing, open a new file large enough to accommodate both this and a duplicate image: File > New. A dialog box appears, allowing you to determine the height and width of the new file. Using the Move tool, import the image of the bird's wing into it.

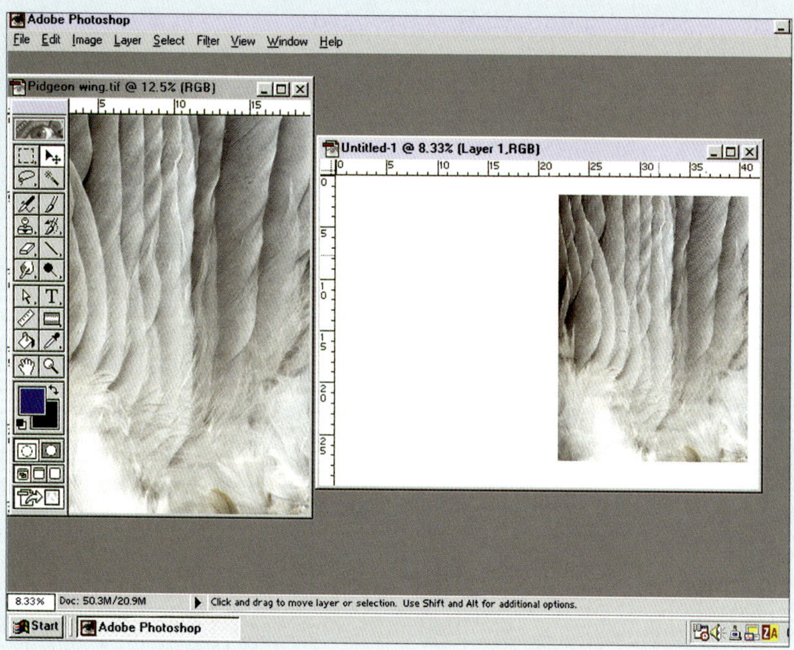

Fig 3

To create this visual palindrome, it is necessary to make a copy. Carefully select the image of the bird's wing and then make a duplicate copy: Edit > Copy, Edit > Paste. Transform the duplicate copy: Edit > Transform > Flip Horizontal. Using the Move tool, drag the duplicate copy into the empty space within the new file. It is now possible to see the two halves of the join. Once again using the Move tool, carefully reposition the duplicate copy so that a perfect match is made; it helps to use the Navigator at this stage. Finally, gently soften the edges of these two layers to ensure a seamless join.

OPPOSITE

Wings: The finished composite.

drawn from a flatbed, there is no reason why elements from other sources cannot also be used. Not only is it possible to use film (colour or black and white), but other disparate elements, such as old photographs, letters, pieces of fabric, maps, illustrations from magazines, books and drawings can also be drafted into the final image.

Collecting potential objects is part of the fun of using a flatbed. The American Pop Artist Robert Rauschenberg and the photographer Olivia Parker have both, in their own unique ways, developed an art form that attempts to amalgamate apparently disparate and unrelated elements into new and exciting creations.

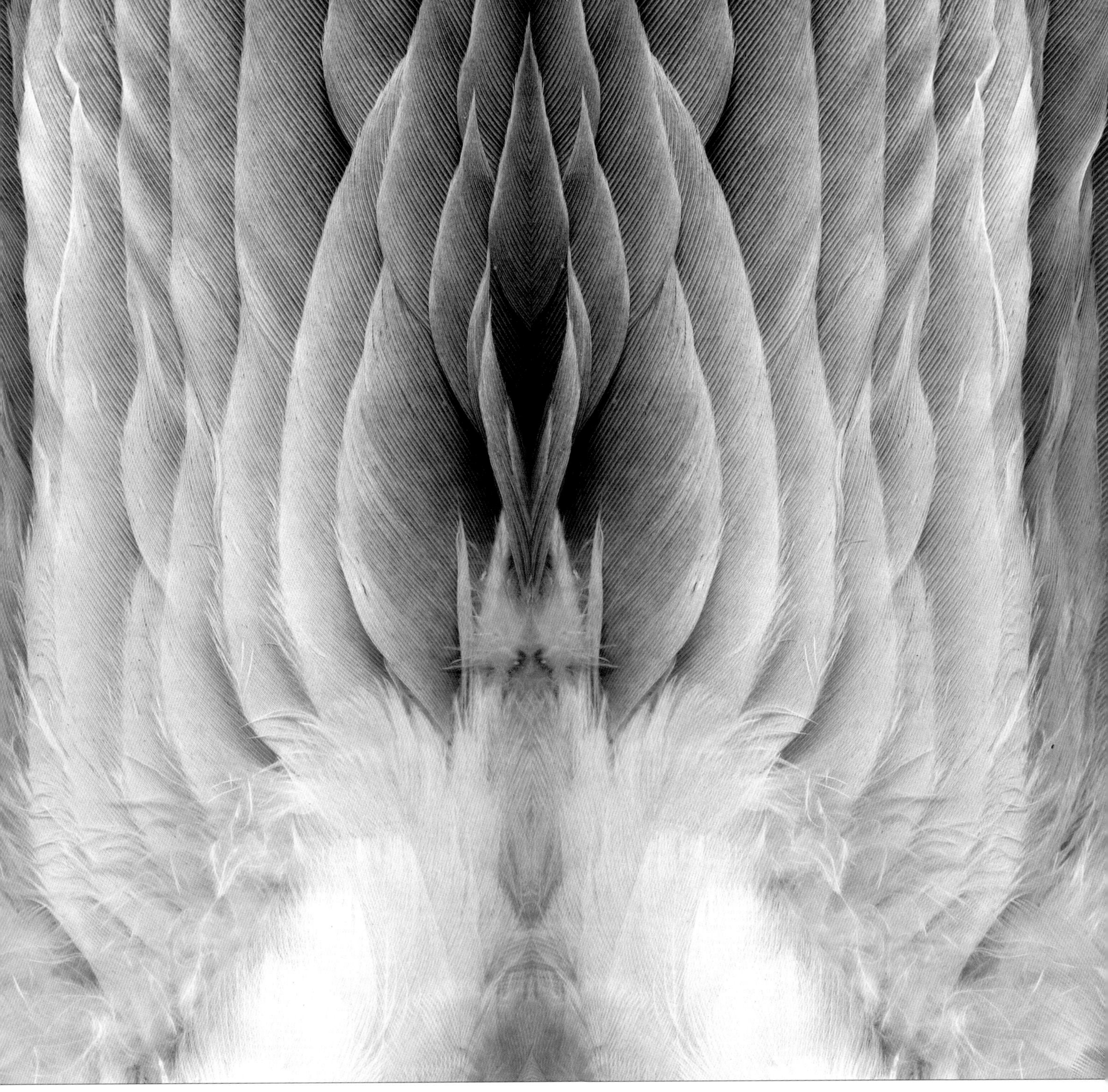

By amalgamating scans from a flatbed with other independent elements using masks and layers, it is possible to construct very personal and beautiful images.

Finally, problems can occur when the colours from one source are fused with those from another; inevitably this results in a cacophony that can appear overwhelming.

One way around this is to desaturate all the colours and then to reconstruct them by using either Duotone or Hue/Saturation. Another alternative is to reduce their intensity by using the Saturation slider – this, of course, can be done selectively.

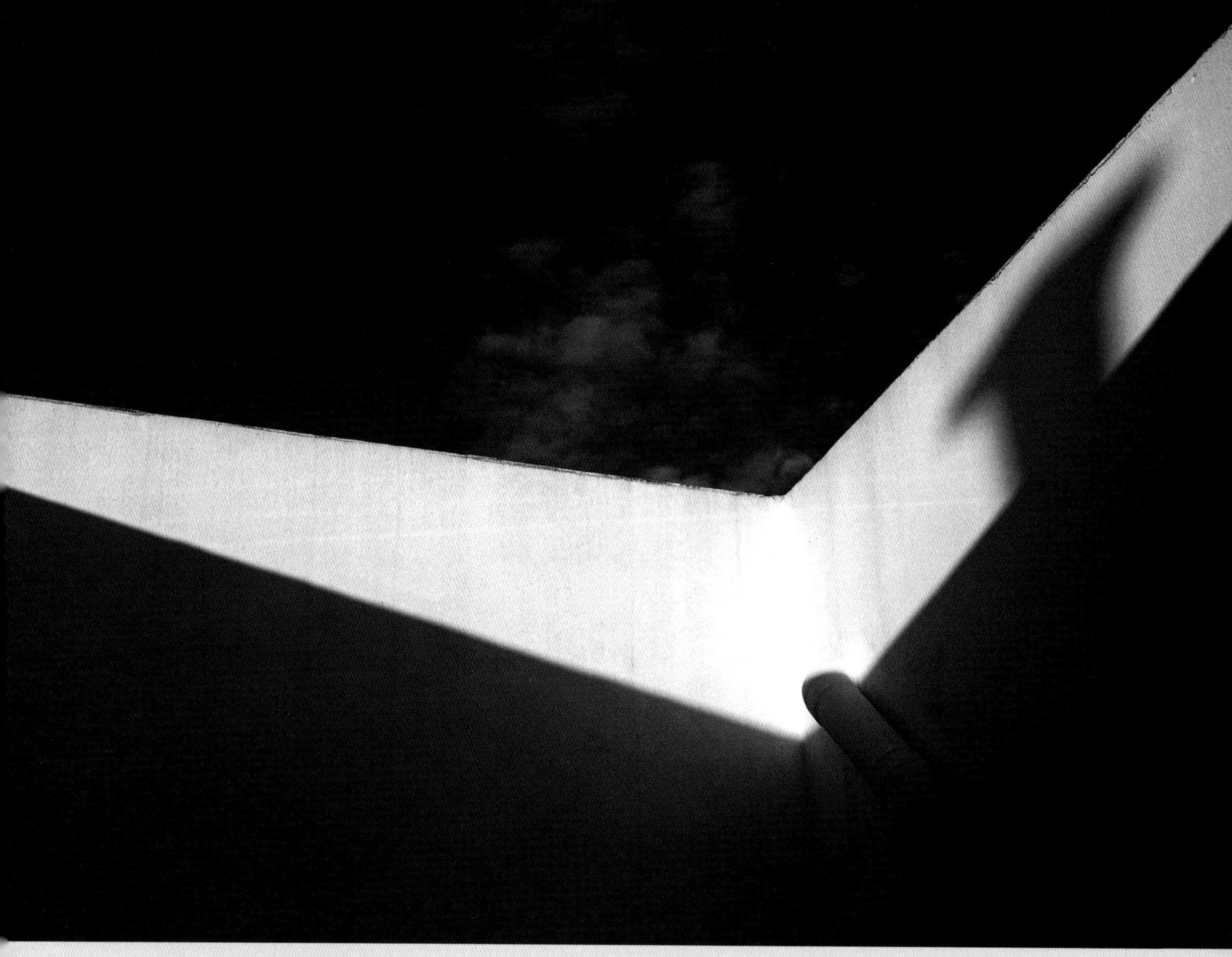

Section 2

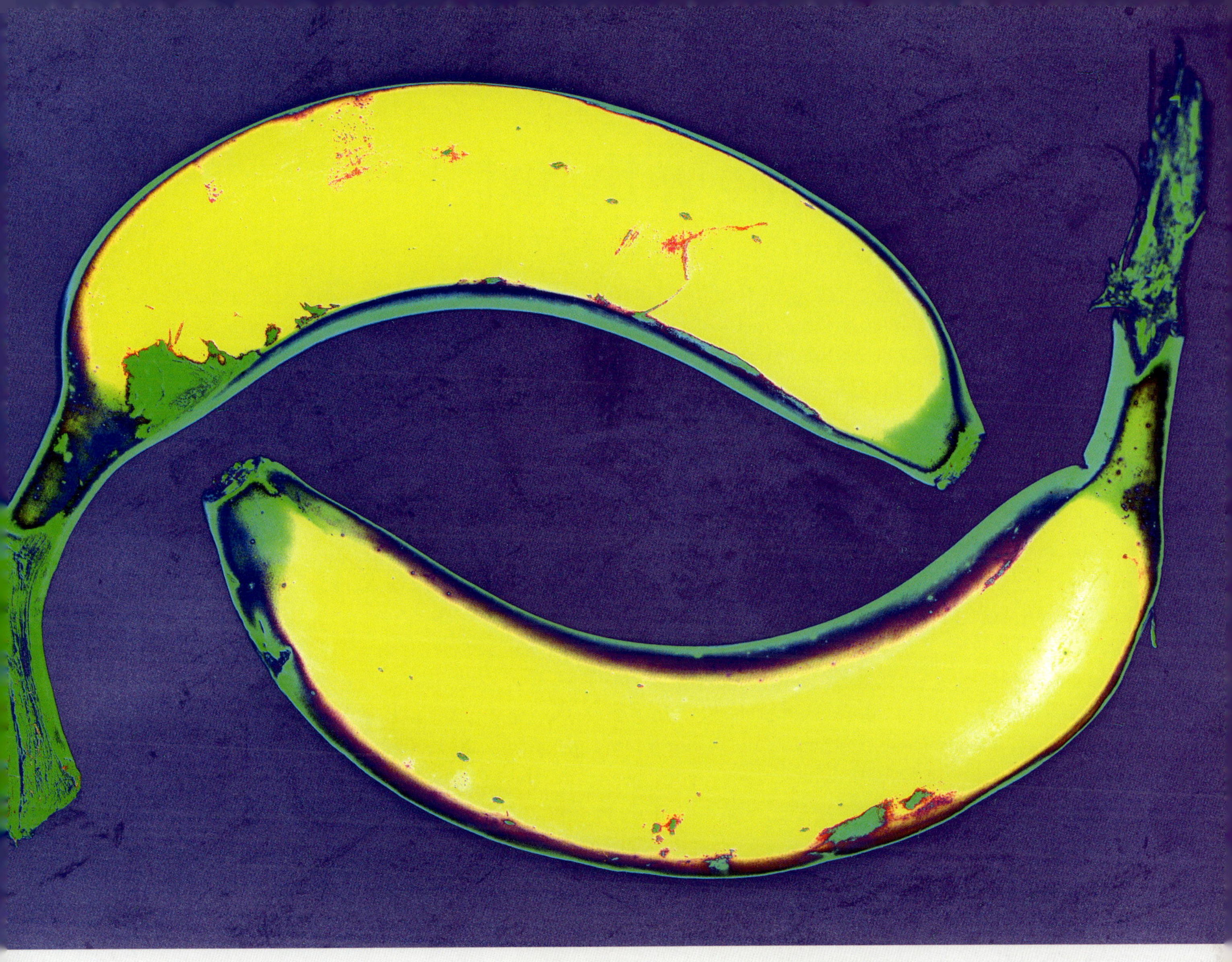

Expanding the conventions

4 Working with text

The cliché goes that "any picture is worth a thousand words", but in reality this is patently untrue – the vast majority of photographic images need captions. Pick up any illustrated book or magazine, and the accompanying text is immediately both evident and necessary. In fact many photographs, although visually compelling, need some help from words; otherwise the viewer is unable to really appreciate their full significance.

ADVERTS AND POSTERS similarly rely on additional text in order to fully get across their message. Mindful of the importance of captions, some photographers even add them to their mounted photographs. But it need not stop there.

Most people recognize that language can add depth to an image, but it is also possible to incorporate text as part of the picture. It is something that artists have done over the centuries – the Bayeux Tapestry is interwoven with text, as indeed is much of Islamic art; the 15th-century Flemish artist Jan Van Eyck would often inscribe little messages on his work, and more recently, contemporary artists, such as Joseph Kosuth, Gilbert and George and Marcel Broodthaers, have also done the same.

Modern words and images

It is the area of contemporary art that offers the most interesting examples, particularly the work of the Dadaists and the Surrealists in the early part of the 20th century. They recognized the subliminal appeal of words within an image and regularly produced collages featuring text – artists such as Hannah Hoch, Kurt Schwitters and Man Ray used language to introduce a corollary to their imaging. More recently, Pop Artists have viewed words as an integral part of the urban environment and amalgamated text into their images in a characteristic deadpan manner. This has not escaped the attention of some contemporary photographers, such as Duane Michals, who regularly enhances his work by the inclusion of the written word.

Undoubtedly the most interesting group is that of the Conceptual artists of the late 20th century, some of whom felt that art should be text-based and that the written word should replace the image. Artists such as the American Lawrence Weiner would

Peeling wall

Text is an important part of our environment. Signs and posters have become so commonplace that they are easily overlooked, but these often have a visual appeal, especially when they are weathered and disintegrated. This painted poster appears to have peeled away from the wall, leaving a haunting shadow of the original message. This makes it more interesting, as we try to make some sense of it.

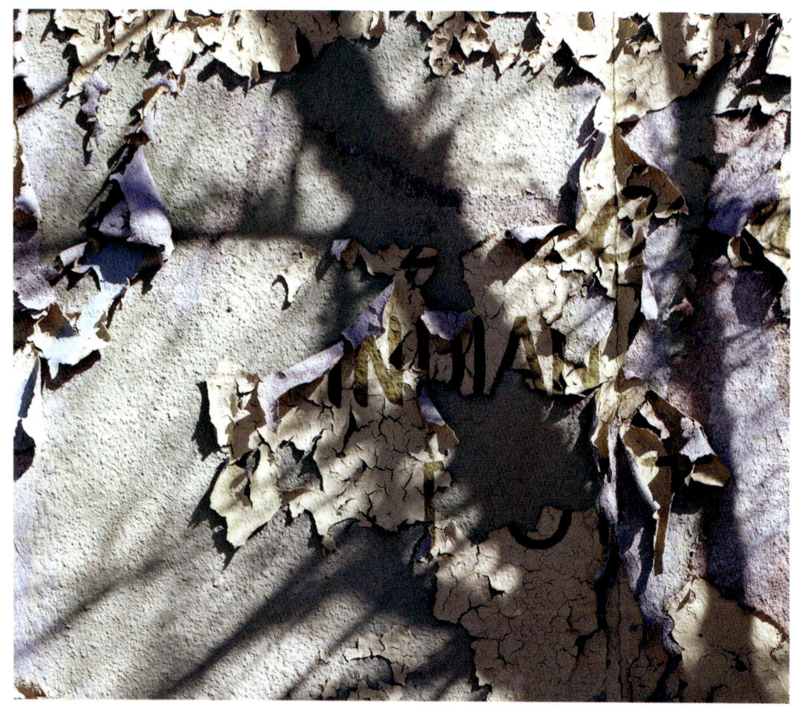

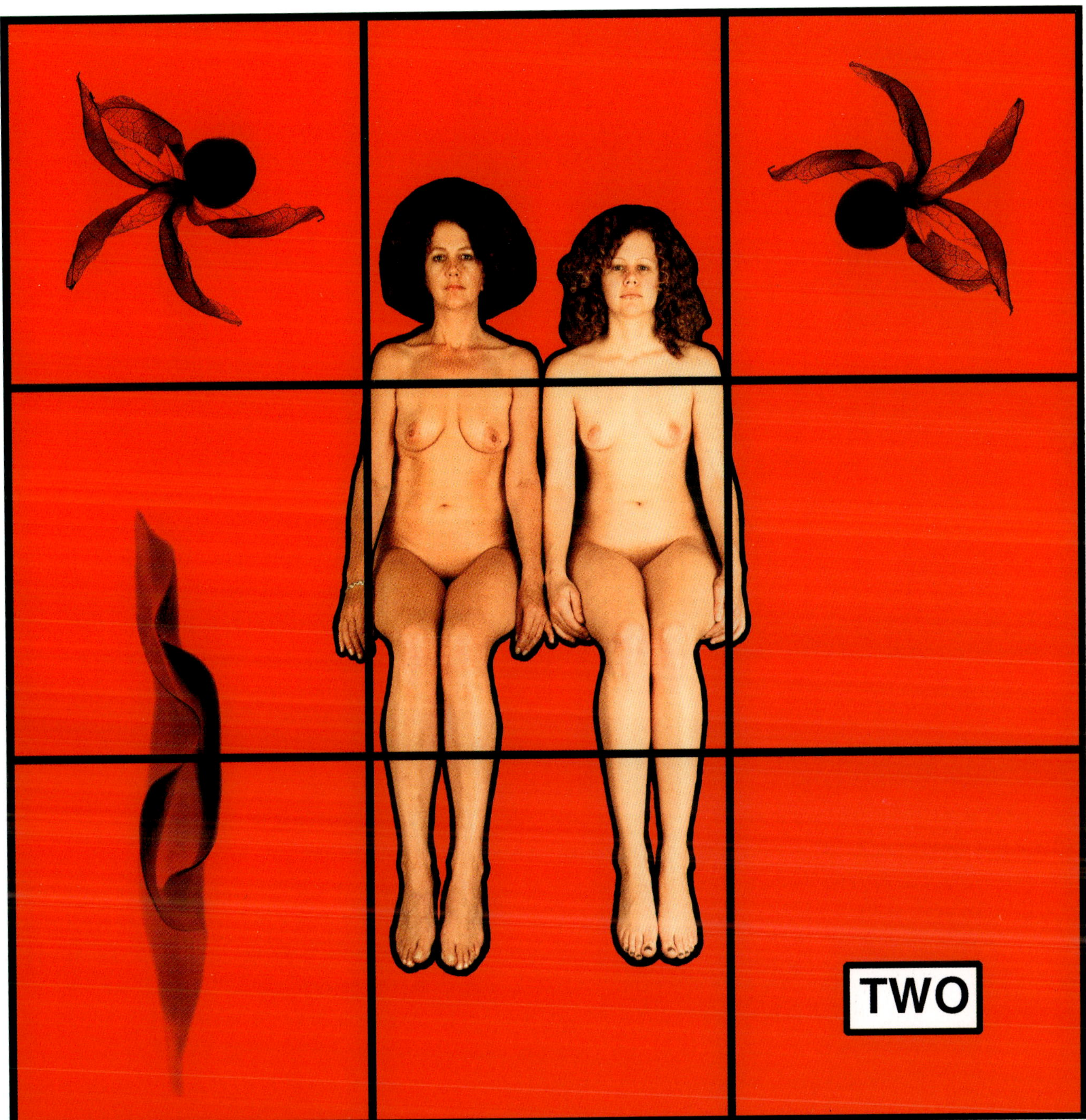

Two

A "homage" to the artists Gilbert and George, this portrait of mother and daughter, Dominica and Joni, was originally photographed with a Fuji S2 Pro digital camera. The figures were desaturated and cut out, and the red background was inserted as a separate layer. The images of the lily flower and physalis fruit were created using a flatbed scanner. The text box was created by using the rectangular Marquee tool and filling the area with white and then using Edit > Stroke to create the black outline. The text was then typed into the box on a separate layer.

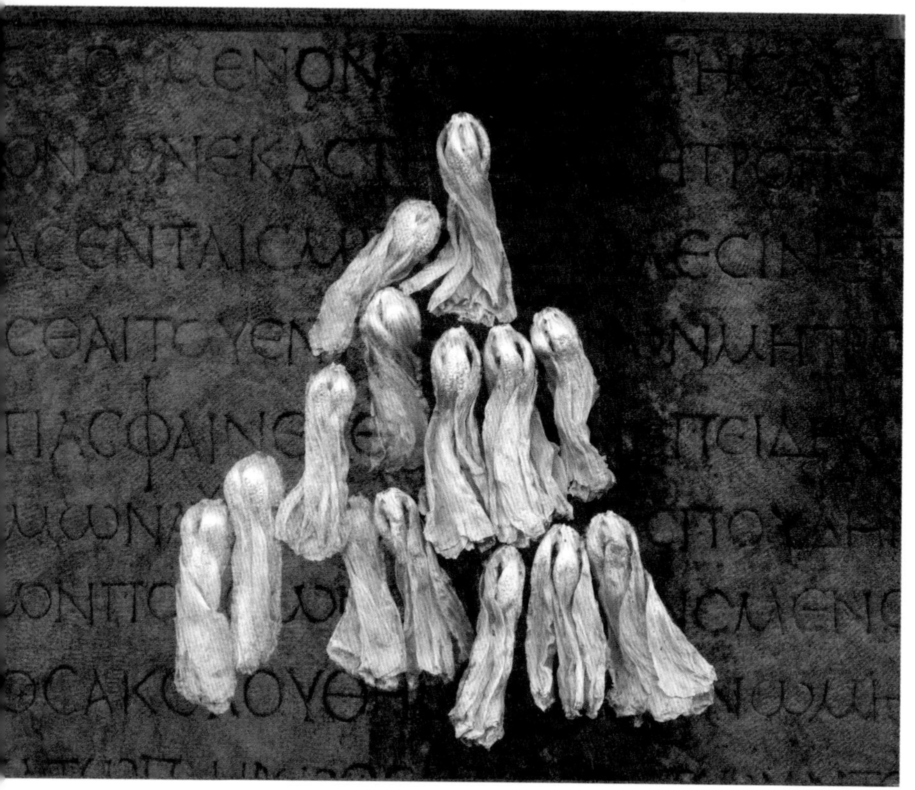

Hollyhocks

Text from another language and culture can introduce a new layer of meaning into an image. In this example a handful of discarded hollyhock pods were arranged on a flatbed and scanned, but as I looked at the pods more closely, I became aware of their figurative qualities. They looked like mythical figures draped in white garments. Using a negative I had taken of ancient text at Ephesus in Turkey, a spiritual dimension has been added to the image.

present their work in the form of text directly onto a gallery wall (although art without images would probably test even the most avant-garde photographer). Artists such as Victor Burgin, John Baldessari, John Stezaker and Stephen Willats, have used written text in conjunction with images in order to more fully explore philosophical, social and political issues.

Ways of using text

Clearly there are within the world of art numerous precedents where text has been used to add further meaning to an image, and this has influenced a number of contemporary photographers. The extent of this can be noted in various ways.

1 Text can become a legitimate subject in its own right, and photographing it is a simple first step. Look at peeling posters on walls, billboards, road signs and petrol stations; they are very much in the style of Pop Artists such as Robert Indiana and Ed Ruscha.

2 The addition of captions directly to work. This can be done conservatively, for example simply by including the text at the bottom of the image, or it can be included as an integral part of the image.

3 Text can sometimes provide an interesting layer in a complex piece of work, particularly when using a strange or unfamiliar language. It is important to appreciate that while the text may have meaning, it also possesses a mysterious visual beauty; reminiscent of the appeal of hieroglyphics, which has been recognized by artists over many centuries.

Creating text using the Type tool

Photography can fulfil many tasks, ranging from technical illustration to fine art, and serve many functions in between. It is particularly widely used in the field of graphic design, which is seen in some eyes as "applied" art.

A simple way of introducing text into a photograph is to use the Type tool, which makes it possible to choose from an infinite variety of sizes, font styles and colours. By double-clicking on the Type tool icon, even more options are made available (see Fig 1).

Editing type

Text can always be changed, using all the facilities available in the Type tool dialog box, providing it remains as a type layer. It is also possible to use some of the Transformation

Creating text using the Type tool

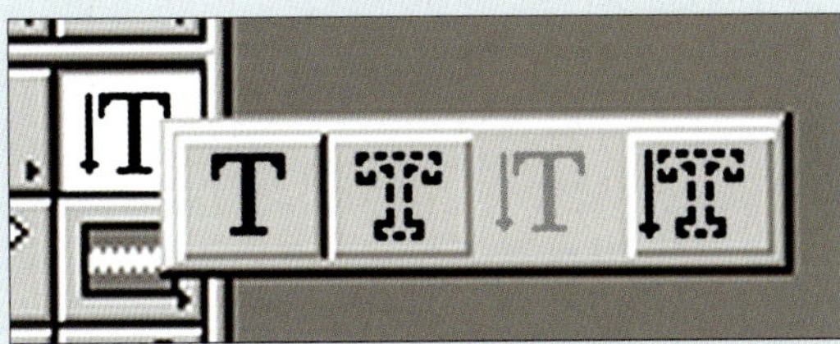

Fig 1

By double-clicking on the Type tool, further options appear. The solid black "T" allows the user to insert text horizontally. The broken line "T" is the horizontal Type Mask tool. The solid "T" with a vertical arrow allows the user to insert text vertically, but this option also allows you to use rotated vertical type. The broken line "T" with a vertical arrow is the vertical Type Mask tool.

Text can be placed horizontally and vertically, or even rotated. The Type Mask tool allows the user to make very sophisticated selections; in this way, translucent text, revealing very subtle tonal or colour variations, can be applied. The permutations here are as varied as you care to imagine, allowing gradients, patterns or overlapping images.

To introduce text, select the Type or the Vertical Type tool. Place the cursor where you want to position the text, although this can easily be readjusted later on. Click, and the Type tool dialog box will appear. In Elements, Photoshop 7 and CS, the following adjustments are made in the Options bar.

1 Select the required font. By scrolling the font box, an almost infinite variety of styles is made available.
2 Select the Color box. The Color Picker dialog box appears, which offers a very comprehensive choice of colour.
3 Only use the Leading option if you intend to apply various lines of text, as this determines the spacing between each of the lines. If a value is not entered, Photoshop will default to 125%.
4 The Anti-Alias option at the bottom of the dialog box should be used if you intend to use large text, as this slightly blurs the edge of the type, which can look jagged if Anti-Aliasing is not applied.
5 Select the type size and ensure that Preview is ticked, as this allows you to see the text in the image window. If you are satisfied, click OK, and the text will appear over the image.

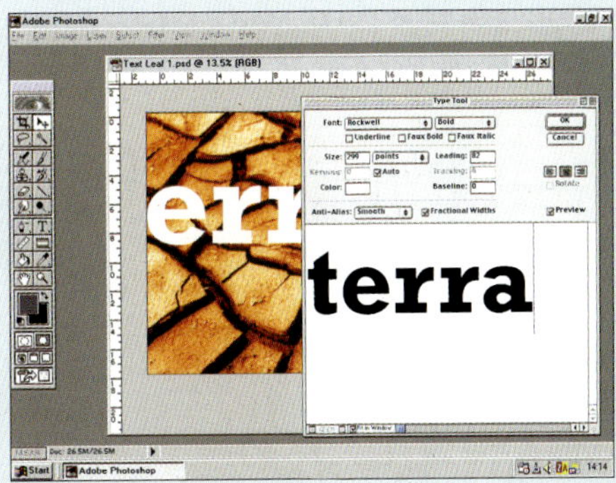

Fig 2

It is important to appreciate that the text represents an independent layer, and can be moved or altered without affecting the picture layer below (see Fig 3). By using the Opacity slider, the text can be made to blend into the image.

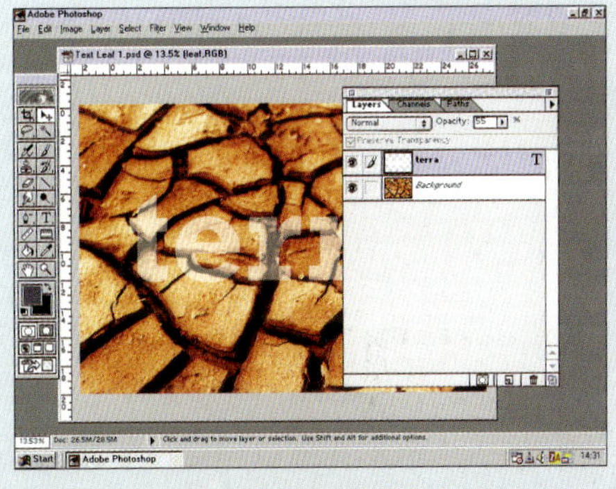

Fig 3

It is also possible to use an Alignment option for centring the text, or aligning it to the left or right. However, it is easier to use the Move tool when repositioning text, but it is important that the Move tool cursor is placed accurately over the text and the Auto Select Layer option box is unchecked, otherwise you risk moving the picture layer.

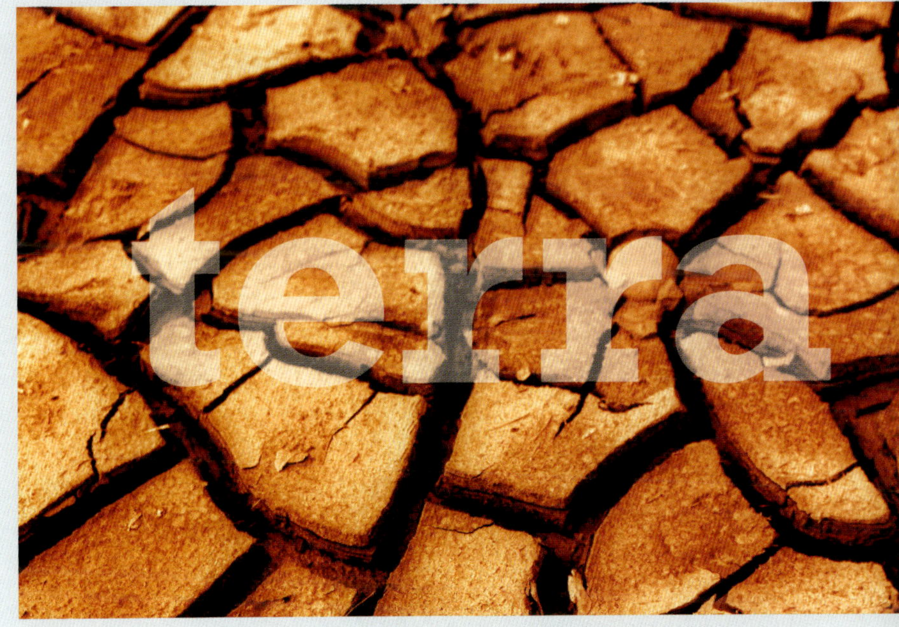

Terra

The fonts in Photoshop are designed to assist graphic designers to accurately introduce text into images. Conceptual artists are increasingly using words as a legitimate means of extending the visual image.

Aqua

This is a composite of two separate scanned black-and-white negatives of water. Using the Type Mask tool, the elements of one of the negatives were imported into the other. The final image was dual-toned using Color Balance.

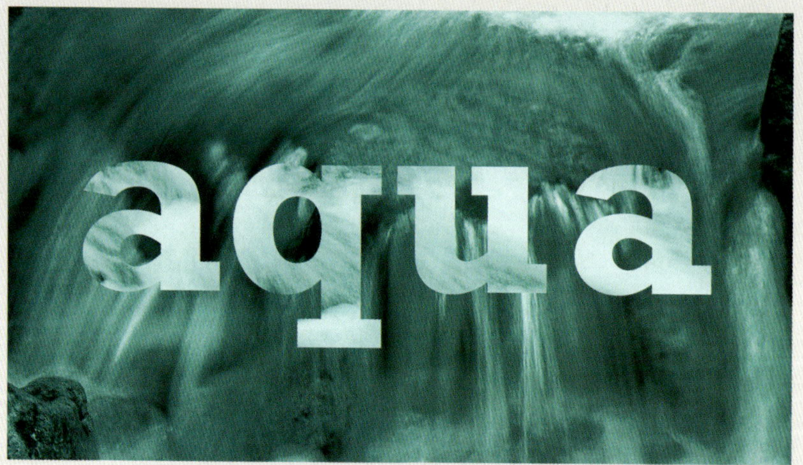

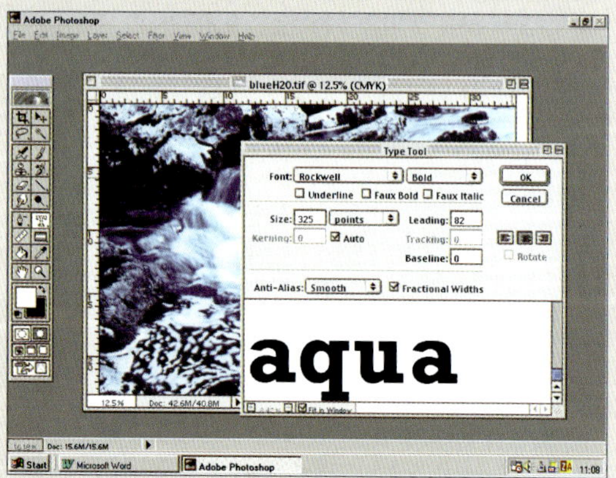

Fig 4

Select the Type Mask tool and place the cursor somewhere within Aqua image 1. Click, and the Type tool dialog box will appear. Select the required font style and size, and then text will appear in the text box.

Fig 5

Click OK and the text will then appear in Aqua image 1, delineated by a broken white line. Call up the file Aqua image 2; place the Move tool cursor inside the text over Aqua image 1, click and drag to reposition it over the new Aqua window.

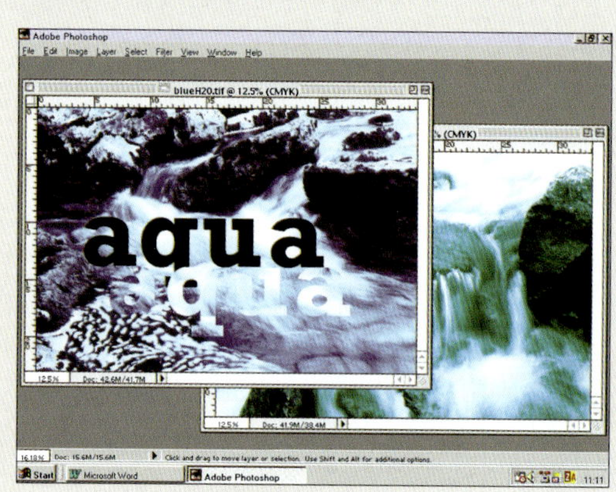

commands available in the Edit menu. If it is necessary to make further changes requiring the other Photoshop commands, the type layer will need to be converted to a standard layer. This is achieved by selecting Layer >Type >Render Layer. At this point, all the other Photoshop commands can also be used.

The Type Mask tool

This is a particularly sophisticated element within the Type tool, allowing images to show through the shape of the letterforms. It is subject to the full range of Photoshop commands, and so some extremely creative uses of applied text can be made.

Using text from other sources

While Photoshop offers a wonderful variety of font styles, the results are predictable; much more interesting outcomes can be achieved by introducing your own text. This can involve importing handwritten notes, text that has been captured on film or scanned using a flatbed. Sometimes the text can have significant meaning; alternatively, it can be used to add texture or decoration to an image. It is worth experimenting with images and text to discover what can be achieved; usually this is done by using layers.

Johnnie Quick

I met Johnnie Quick by chance while he was working in a casino restaurant in Beatty, Nevada. When I spoke to him I learned that he had been the drummer for, and is now the sole survivor of, rock'n'roll pioneers Bill Haley and the Comets. As a straight portrait, this image is hardly worth a second glance, but as soon as the narrative is added, we naturally feel compelled to read it. The text has been deliberately obscured a little to force readers to scrutinize it – the hope is that they casually look at the portrait, then examine the text. As it dawns that the portrait is of a person who featured in the very birth of rock'n'roll, they are encouraged to re-examine the portrait with more care. This is an example where the text is designed to add further meaning to the image.

The image was created by producing two layers, one with the portrait and a second with the text written on a piece of white paper (see Fig 6). I introduced a thick black border around the portrait and then inverted the text layer so that the writing appeared white on a black background. Finally, I merged the two layers using the Blending mode.

Fig 6

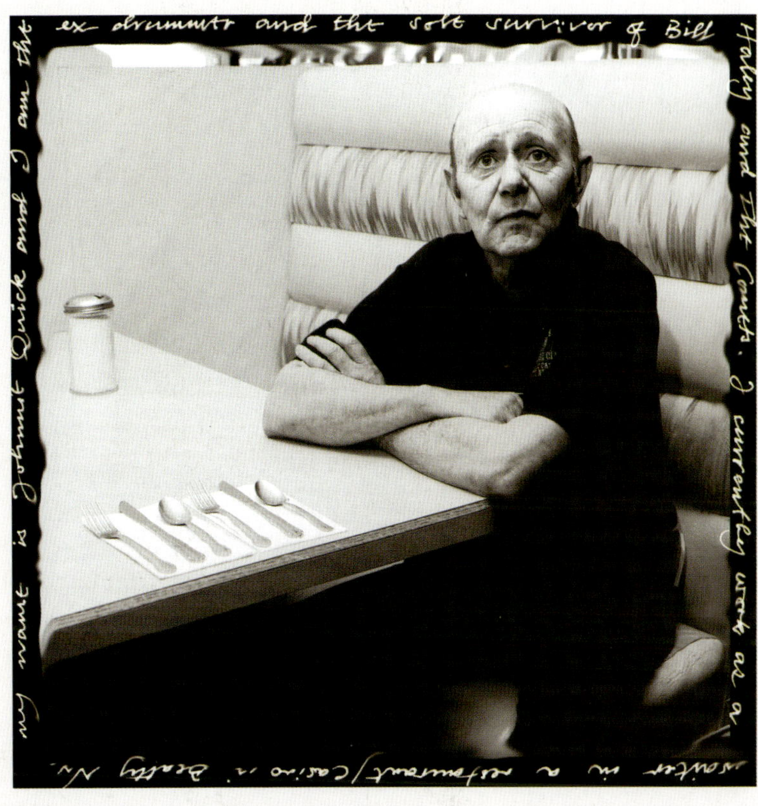

Model with plait

This image comprises three separate layers – the first is a negative of the model, the second is a blank piece of film which had been deliberately distressed and the third was taken from a negative featuring Ancient Greek ruins. By amalgamating the three layers and then using various Blending modes, a more interesting image has been created.

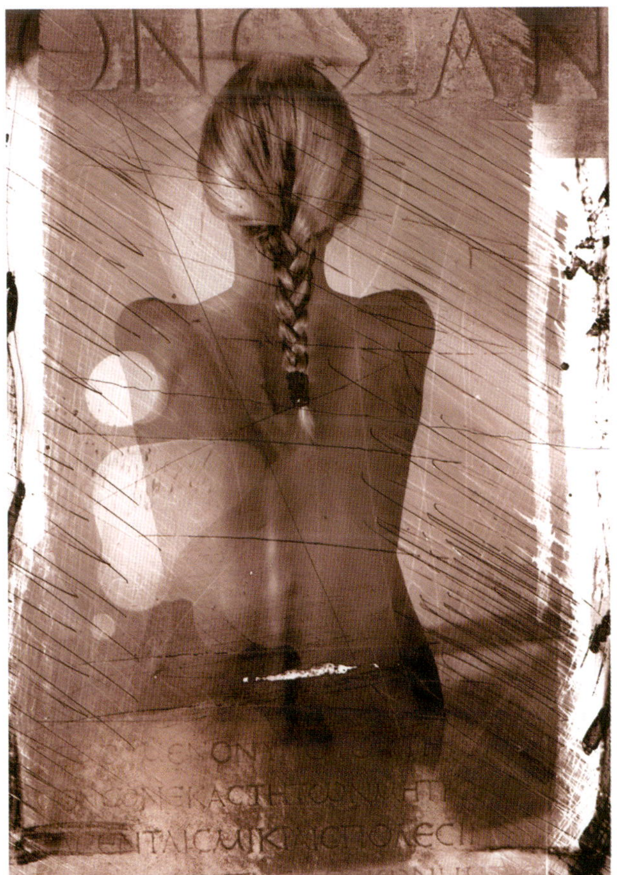

Mixing colour and monochrome

Traditionally, photographers opted to work either in colour or monochrome, and rarely considered mixing the two – hardly surprising, as doing so was very difficult to achieve. When printing colour negative film onto colour negative paper, it really is impossible to select an area that can be translated as monochrome, simply because the dyes within the paper do not allow that.

SIMILARLY, ONE CANNOT reasonably expect black-and-white paper to print colour, although there is currently a fashion for toning and even hand-colouring black-and-white prints, which gives them the appearance of being colour. These techniques are time-consuming and require a fair measure of skill.

Why mix the two?

But is there a need to print colour as monochrome, and black and white as colour? Even if you consider the simple practicalities of having a roll of colour film in the camera, but then encountering a situation that would benefit from being photographed in black and white, being able to exercise a choice does open your opportunities. (If you are capturing your images digitally, clearly this should never become an issue.) If you are shooting colour negatives, it is of course possible to print directly onto black-and-white paper, although as these negatives tend to be denser, the exposures required can often prove to be comparatively lengthy.

Another drawback is that colour film lacks the tonal punch of most black-and-white films, therefore using colour film to print onto black-and-white paper only has limited uses. Working digitally is an entirely different situation. These days many photographers are so confident that they can successfully print black and white from a colour film, that they

Dual Toning with Color Balance

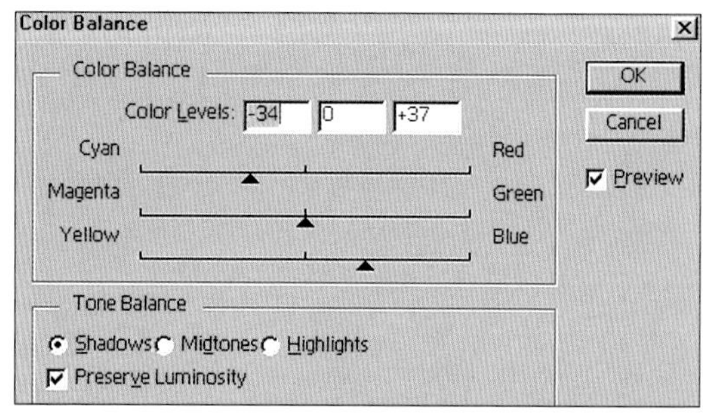

Fig 1

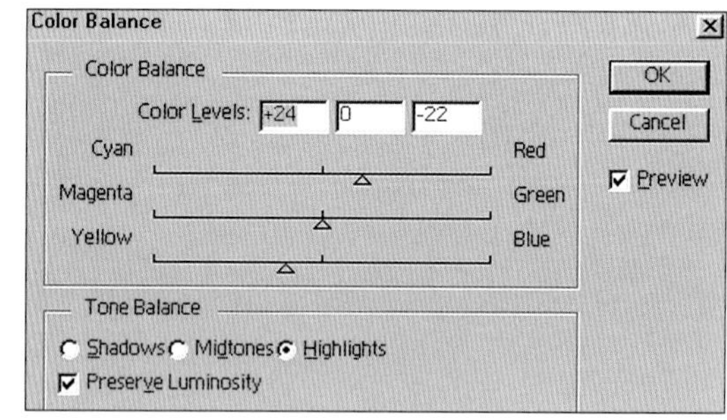

Fig 2

now use it exclusively. When scanning the film, whether it is colour negative or slide film, the image can easily be desaturated and converted to monochrome.

Scanning monochrome

By way of contrast, when using monochrome film it is good practice to scan it in RGB mode in order to maximize the full tonal range. But while the scan remains in this mode, it can be coloured using one of two simple options.

1 An overall colour can be introduced by

Gondolas, Venice 1
A straight black-and-white
image scanned in RGB
(Red, Green, Blue) mode.

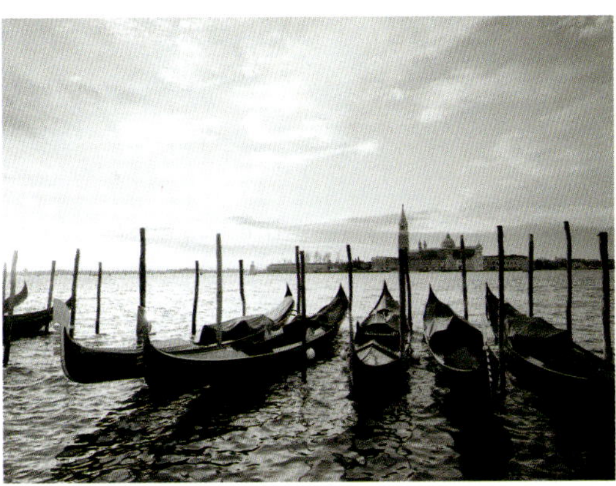

Gondolas, Venice 2
Colour can easily be introduced into a monochrome
image by using Color Balance, providing your file is in RGB
mode. This facility is highly selective, allowing one choice
of colour to affect the highlights whilst another colour
changes only the shadows. In this way, very dramatic
dual-toned images can be achieved.

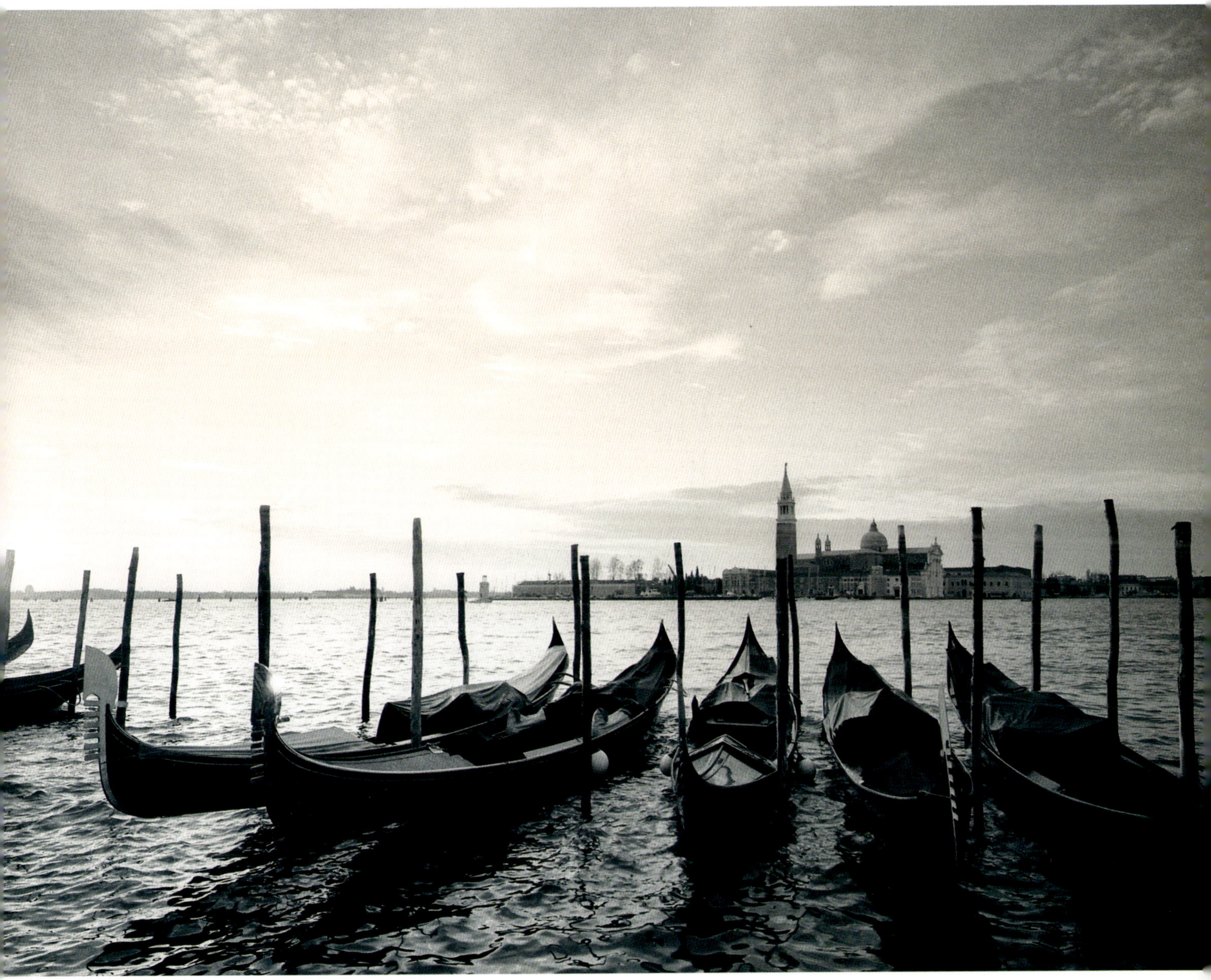

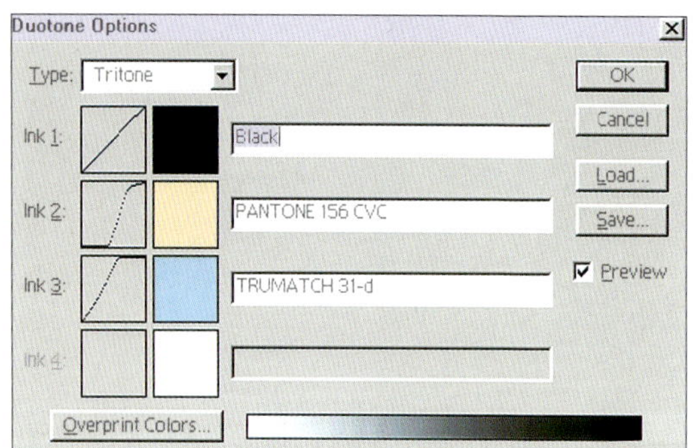

Gondolas, Venice 3

Colour can be added to an image in Grayscale mode by using Duotone. Often the results mimic the effects that can be achieved in the darkroom.

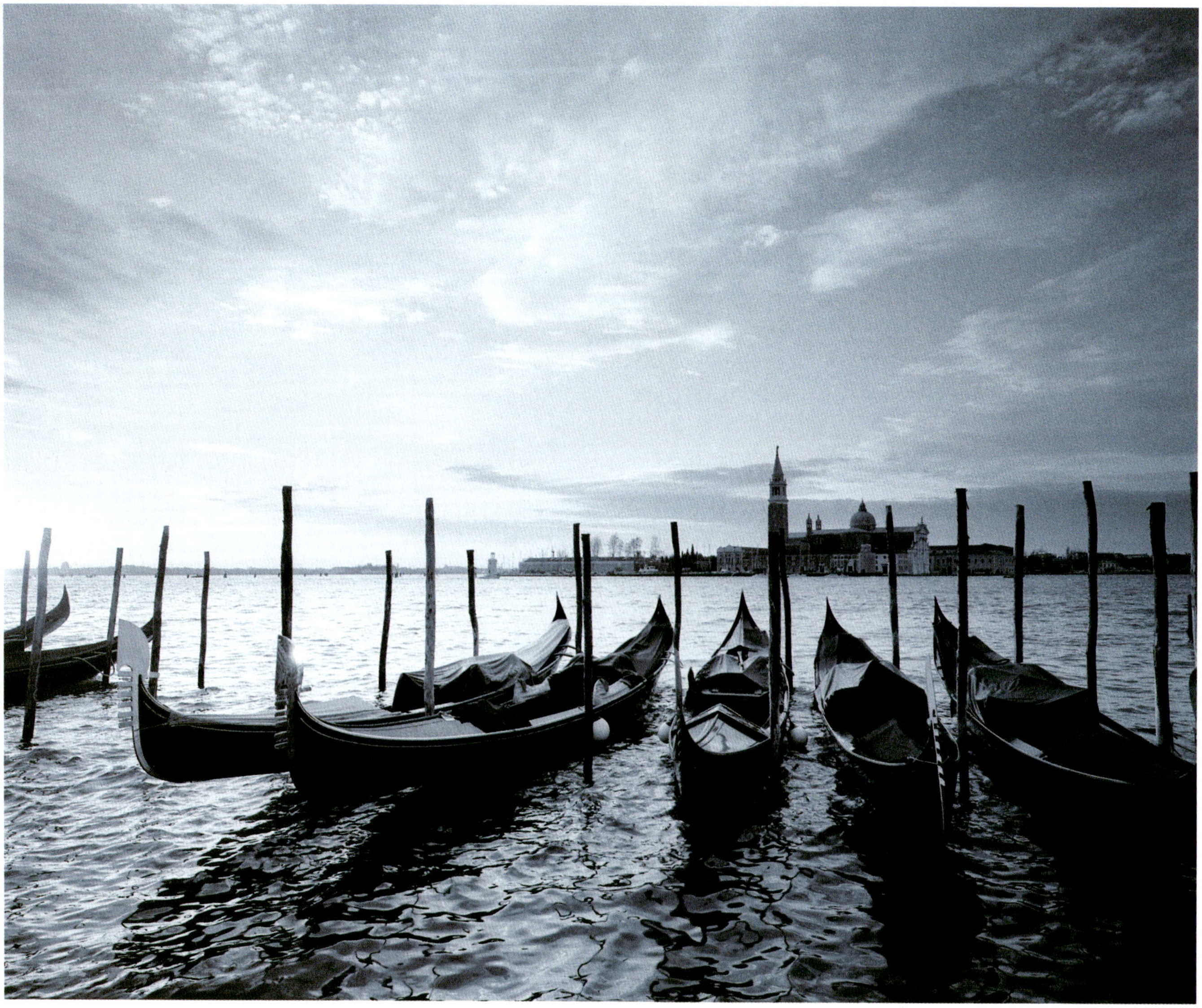

MIXING COLOUR AND MONOCHROME

using Hue/Saturation: Image > Adjust > Hue/Saturation.

2 Two or more colours can be easily introduced by using Color Balance: Image > Adjust > Color Balance. At the bottom of the dialog box there is an option for selecting either shadows, mid-tones or highlights. So, for example, it would be possible to introduce a mixture of red and yellow in the highlights, while ensuring that the shadows were coloured with blue and cyan only (see Fig 1 and Fig 2). If more colours need to be introduced, these can be done selectively by using the many available selection methods.

Duotone

If it is desirable to retain the negative in Grayscale mode, using the Duotone option is the best way of introducing colour. Go to Mode > Duotone (see Fig 3).

This is a remarkably sophisticated facility that offers duotone (the use of two inks), tritone (three inks) or quadtone, (four inks). It is important that this choice is made straight away; and while there is little point in opting for monotone, the choice should be between the other three. Generally the first ink should be black, so the second ink in duotone should be used to create a simple toned image. Using tritone it is easy to create a split tone by placing one colour ink in the highlights while placing a separate colour in the shadows. This is achieved by manipulating the curves to the left of the dialog box. By double-clicking, the ink curve appears, which allows for a very precise placement of the ink within the tonal range. A slightly more sophisticated split can be achieved by using quadtone. There is also a range of ready-made Duotone Curves which can be selected by clicking on Load and selecting from the pre-prepared curves.

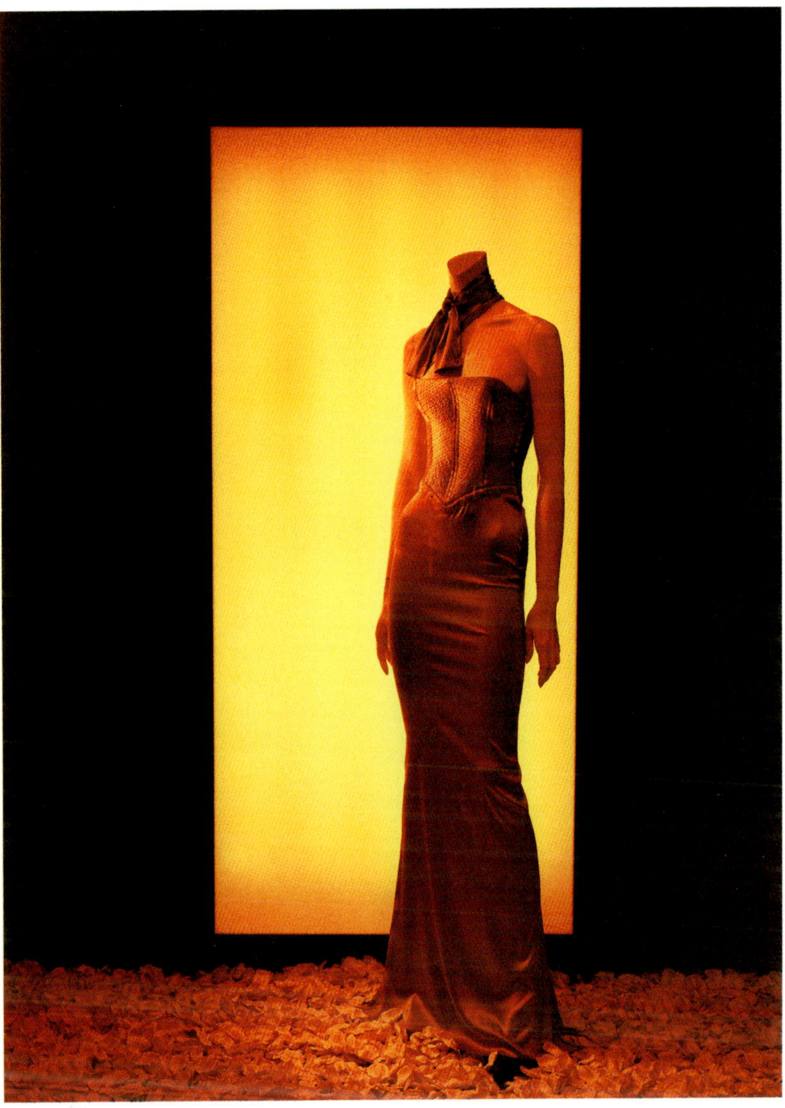

Mannequin

This photograph was taken late one evening using fast black-and-white film. Initially my intention had been to present it as a monochrome, but after it had been scanned in RGB mode, I was struck by its dramatic yet arbitrary colours, recalling the artificial lighting that had illuminating the scene.

Finally, do not always reject the arbitrary colours created when a black-and-white negative is scanned in RGB mode. Occasionally some rather interesting "accidents" can occur.

The legacy

Once we can accept that it is legitimate to present a colour image as black and white and a monochrome as colour, mixing the two should not pose any difficulties. Photography is simply a means of capturing information, and it is what we do with it that really matters. This may have once been seen as heresy, but you have only to observe what is occurring in areas of fine art and graphic design to see that there are practitioners who are comfortable with mixing the two. This is particularly evident in aspects of fine art printing, especially in areas such as lithography, woodcut, silk-screen printing and heliogravure. Artistic luminaries as diverse as Pablo Picasso, Marc Chagall and Henri Matisse regularly produced prints which infused black and white with colour – is this a legacy we can afford to ignore?

How to mix colour and monochrome in photography

■ Starting with a colour image, elements of monochrome can be incrementally introduced by adjusting the saturation slider within the Hue/Saturation facility. This can be done holistically or selectively.

■ By making careful selections, elements from a colour image can be imported into a monochrome negative. Most montages are either monochrome or colour, but there is simply no reason why the two cannot be mixed.

■ By selecting just part of a colour image and desaturating it. This is a ploy often used by graphic designers to add specific emphasis. Try using very blatant selection tools, such as the Rectangular Marquee tool.

■ By selecting part of a monochrome image and selectively colouring it in some way. This very much follows the Victorian tradition of hand-colouring monochrome photographs, except that doing it digitally is far easier. Moreover, once a satisfactory outcome has been achieved, identical images can be repeated again and again, something that is impossible to do using traditional methods.

■ Creating a Background Layer by scanning a colour image and then duplicating it to create a second layer, but then desaturating it. All sorts of new possibilities begin to present themselves; firstly, it is possible to use the many Layers options to fuse together the colour and monochromatic versions. Secondly, by using masks, various parts of the image can be revealed as black and white, while other areas can be shown as colour.

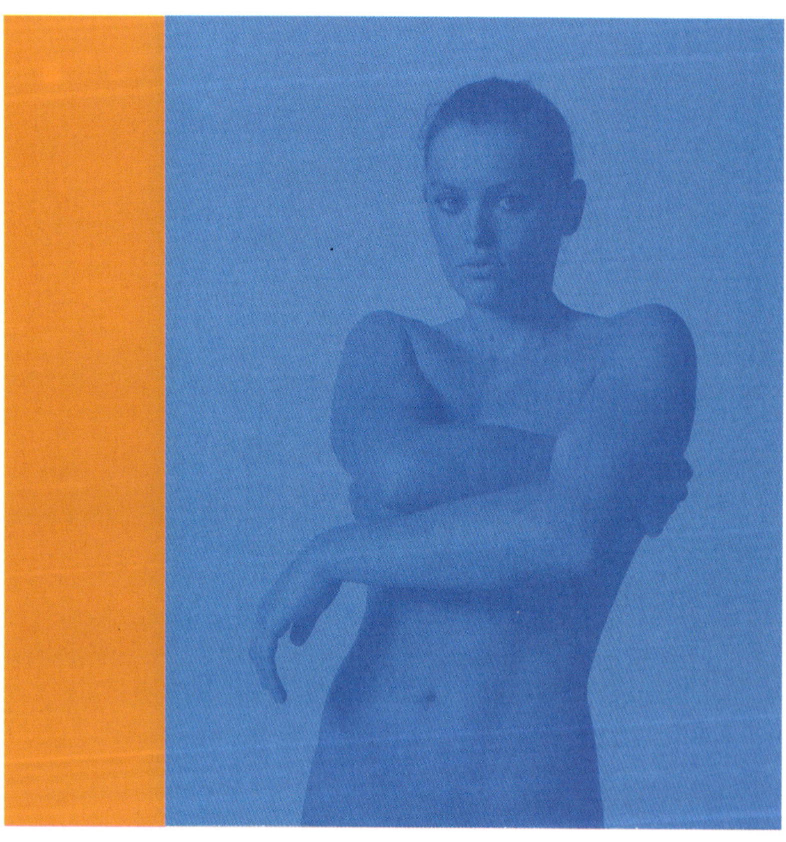

Model with arms folded 2

By colouring the figure blue using Color Balance and then greatly reducing contrast, a strong graphical quality is introduced. This is reinforced by selecting a strip on the extreme left and colouring it orange, a colour opposite blue on the colour wheel. This contrast has the affect of disguising the figure and it is only after several seconds that the model emerges.

Model with arms folded 1

Taken from a black-and-white negative scanned in RGB mode.

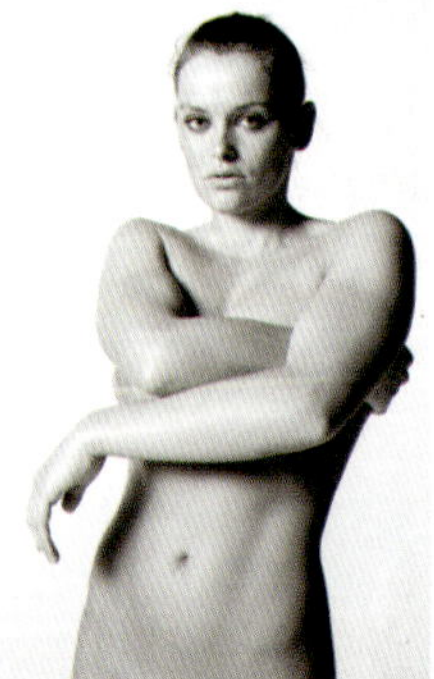

Seecum

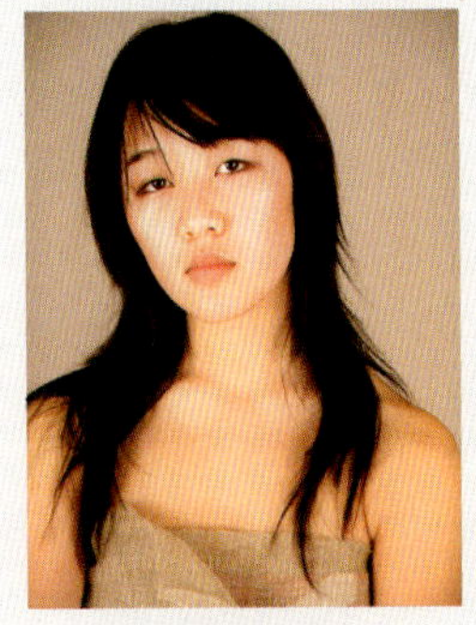

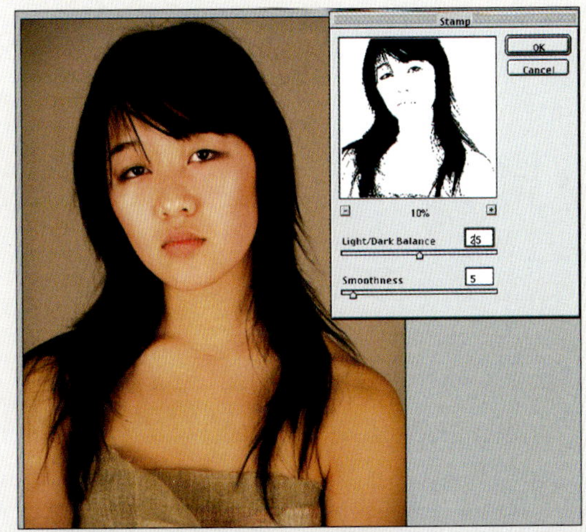

This was an attempt to produce the style of a screenprint. The original image was taken on a Pentax Optio digital camera and was then converted to a graphic black-and-white image by using the Stamp filter, making sure that the foreground colour was set to black. The blocks of colour were then roughly selected and filled on separate layers. The rough selection gave the effect of slight mis-registration, which can be a feature of some screenprints. The colour layers were created on top of the Stamp filter layer, and Multiply Blending mode was used to combine the colour with the underlying black portrait.

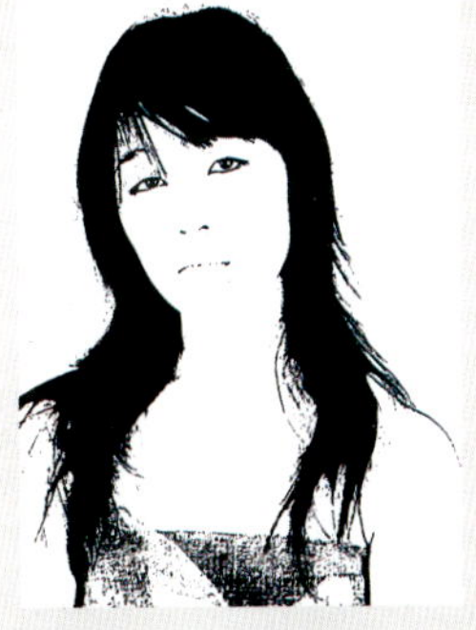

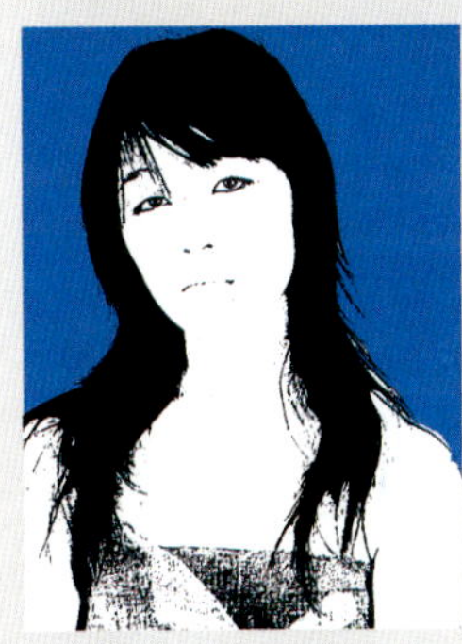

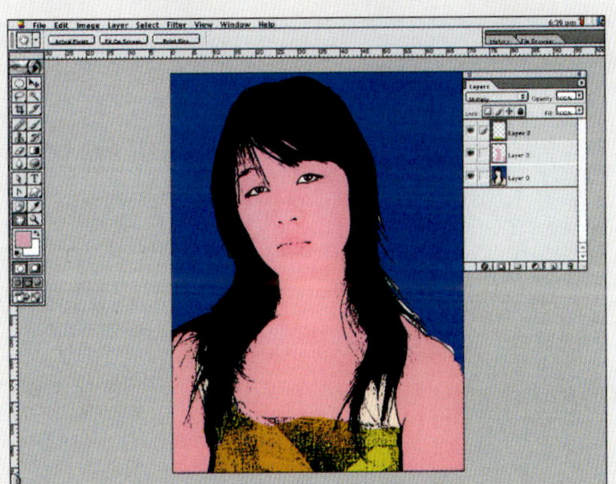

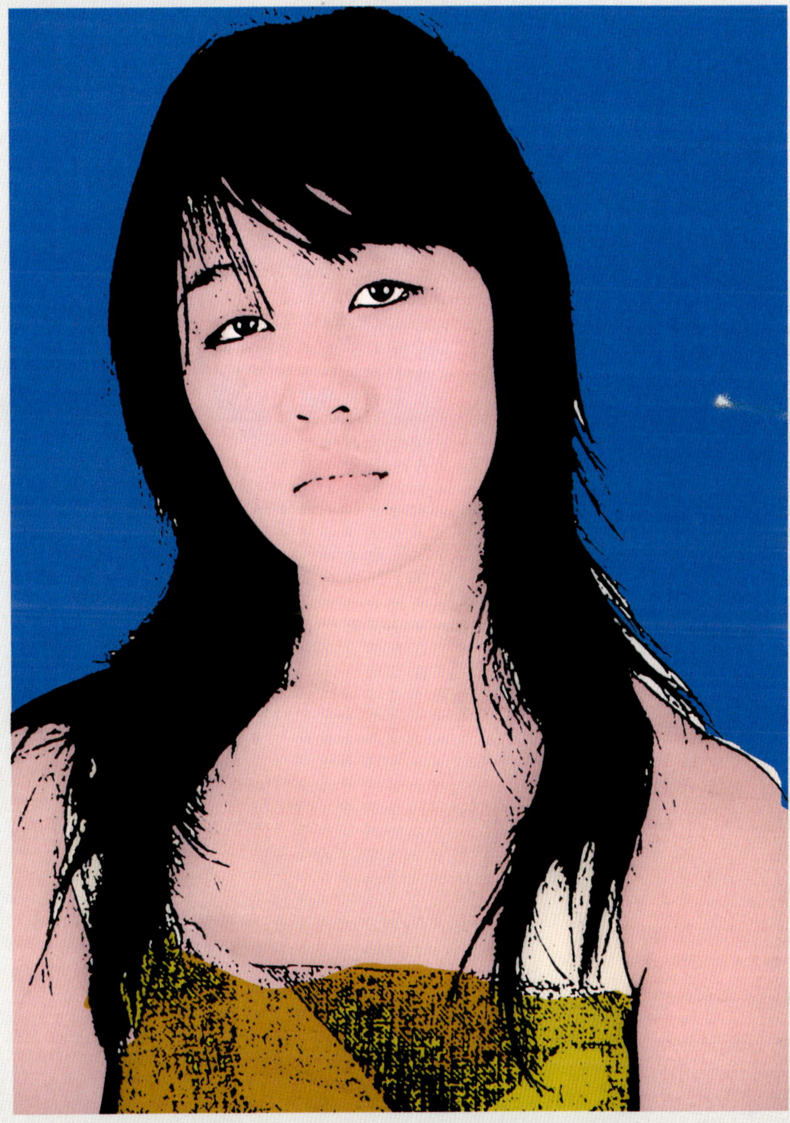

Drive-in cinema

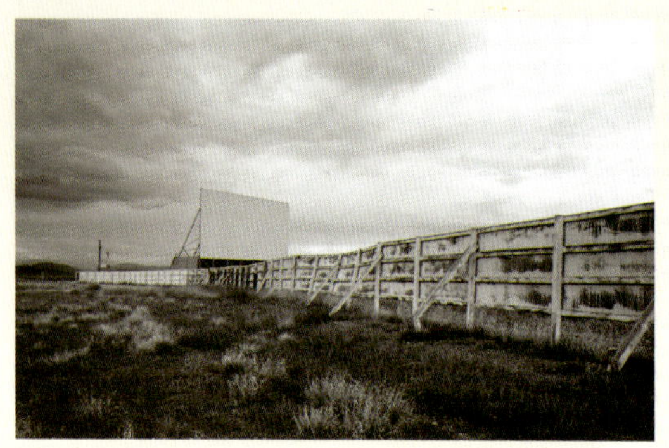

An abandoned and lifeless drive-in cinema that clearly has seen better days. This was taken from a black-and-white film, which was scanned in RGB mode.

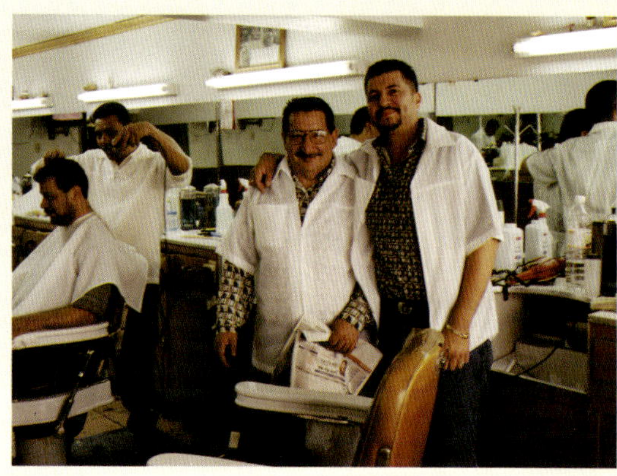

Scanned from a colour negative, this warm and inviting scene offers a complete contrast to the bleak and uninhabited drive-in. As this was only going to occupy a small part of the final composite, it was scanned at a low resolution.

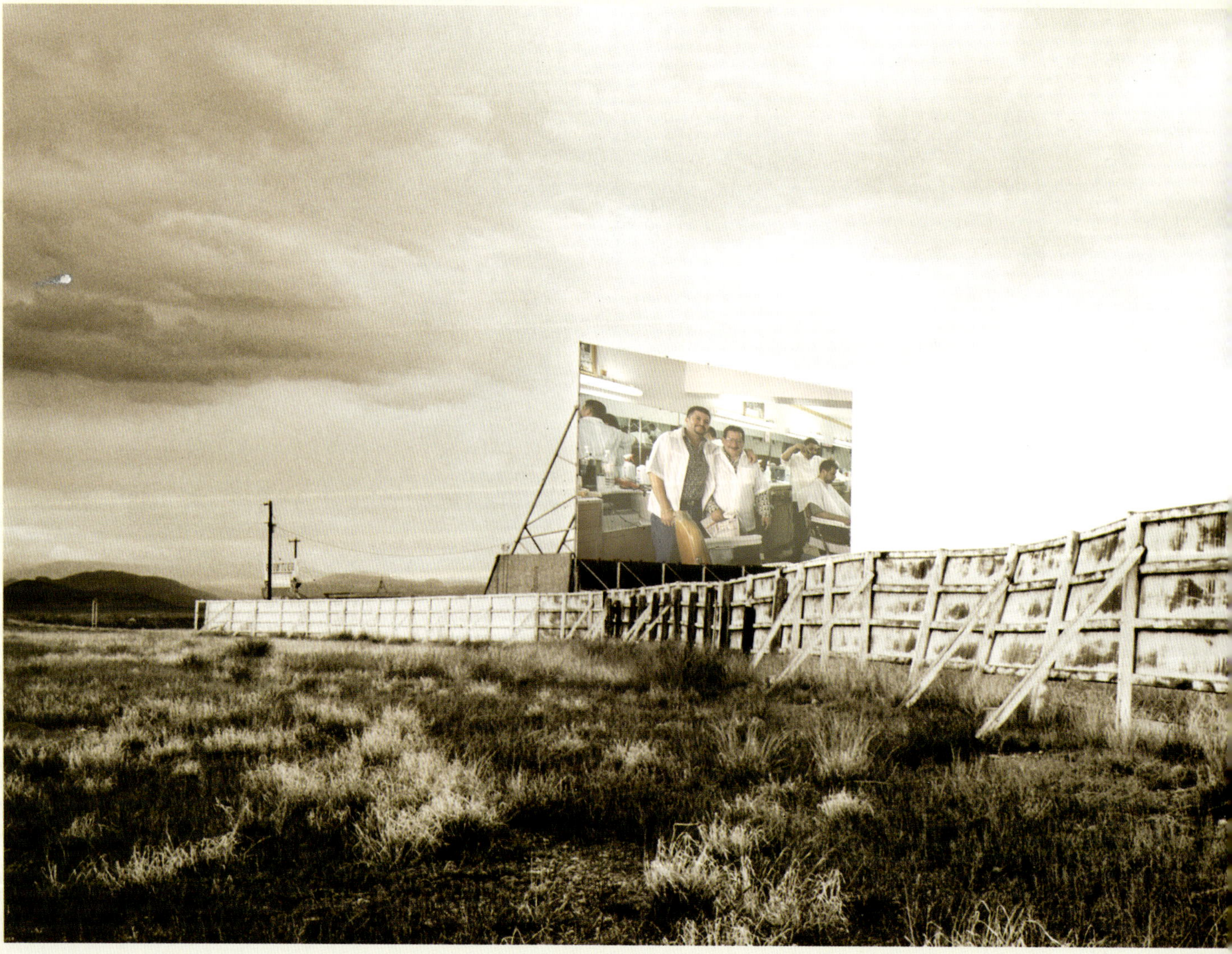

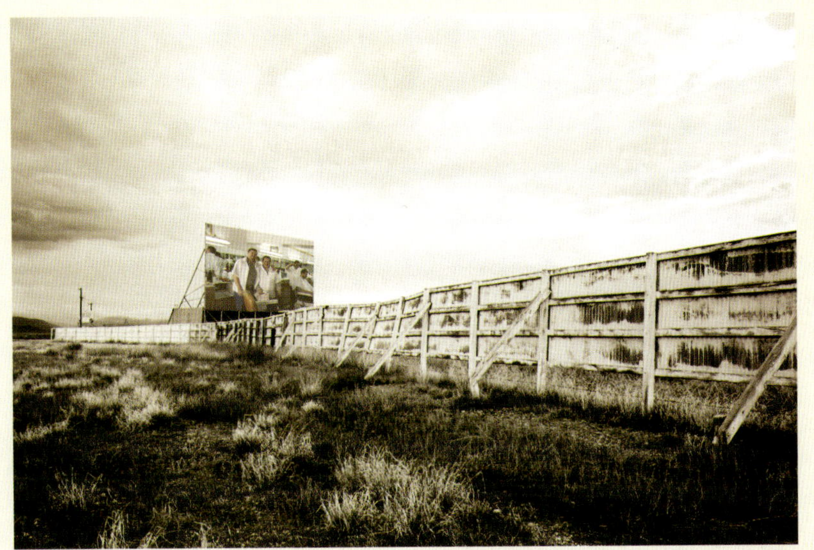

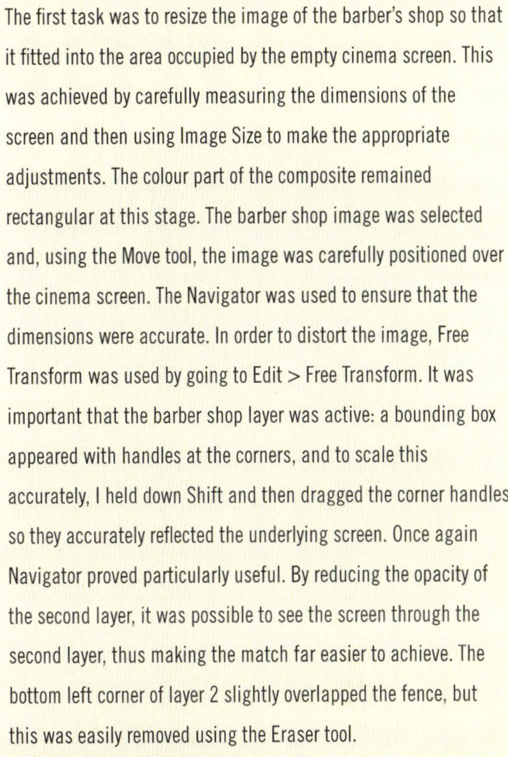

The first task was to resize the image of the barber's shop so that it fitted into the area occupied by the empty cinema screen. This was achieved by carefully measuring the dimensions of the screen and then using Image Size to make the appropriate adjustments. The colour part of the composite remained rectangular at this stage. The barber shop image was selected and, using the Move tool, the image was carefully positioned over the cinema screen. The Navigator was used to ensure that the dimensions were accurate. In order to distort the image, Free Transform was used by going to Edit > Free Transform. It was important that the barber shop layer was active: a bounding box appeared with handles at the corners, and to scale this accurately, I held down Shift and then dragged the corner handles so they accurately reflected the underlying screen. Once again Navigator proved particularly useful. By reducing the opacity of the second layer, it was possible to see the screen through the second layer, thus making the match far easier to achieve. The bottom left corner of layer 2 slightly overlapped the fence, but this was easily removed using the Eraser tool.

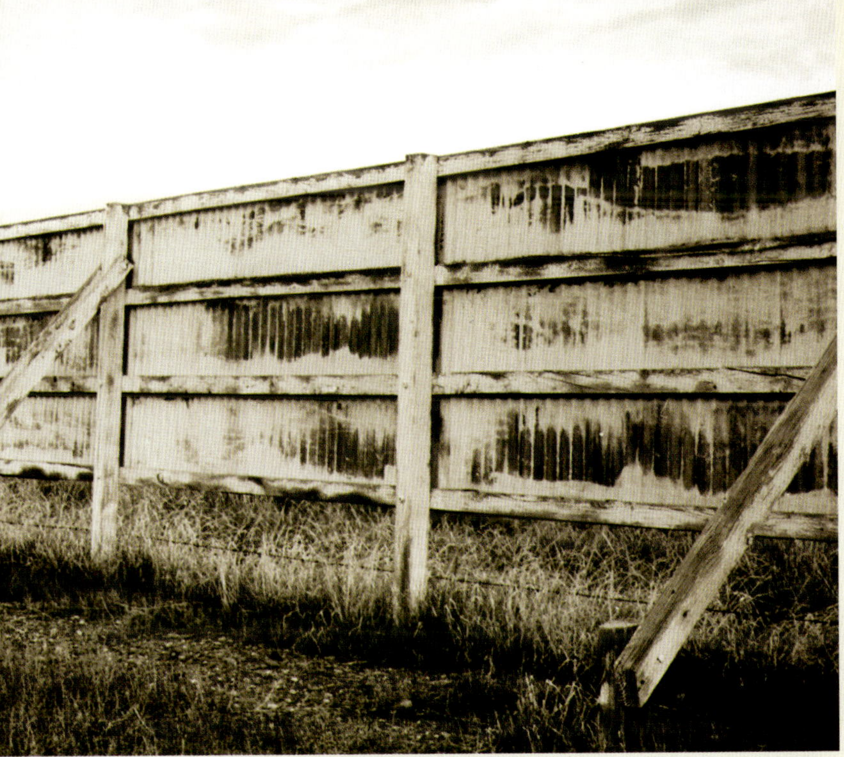

In "Drive-in cinema 2", the scene lacked the atmosphere one would expect when viewing a live cinema performance. By selecting and feathering an area to the right of the screen, then lightening the selection, an illusion of projected light was created.

6   Solarization

Solarization is a process in which a strong source of light causes a partial reversal of tones. This can sometimes be seen when an image of a point source of light appears as a black dot.

EVERSAL OF TONE BY gross overexposure was far more common in historic processes, such as cyanotype or platinum prints, but accidental processes can give rise to creative uses, and at various times different people have experimented with deliberate fogging techniques. Probably the first was Armand Sabbatier, who in 1862 used fogging of partially developed photographic materials to produce a tonal reversal in certain areas of an image.

The "Sabbatier effect" is characterized not only by tone reversal but also by the formation of a distinct line at edges between areas of tonal difference. The effect is usually performed by a brief exposure to light midway during film development – of course there is always the risk of ruining an original negative by this process, and many people use a copy negative. (With digital techniques, however, the original file is always safe.) Probably the most famous artist to make use of this process was Man Ray, who produced a series of portraits and figure studies in the 1930s using the "Rayogram" technique.

The effect

A large number of variables have an effect on solarization, not least whether it is applied at the film-processing or print-processing stage. To emulate a solarized print digitally is a reasonably simple matter, but it is also very easy to get carried away and produce a pig's ear from a silk purse.

To understand and control the process it is probably best to begin with a greyscale image without too much contrast, as in this way changes of tonality are easily recognized. You can start with a positive image or one that can be inverted into a negative (Image > Adjustments > Inverse or Control I). Try to select an image with simple forms, rather than one with masses of minute detail.

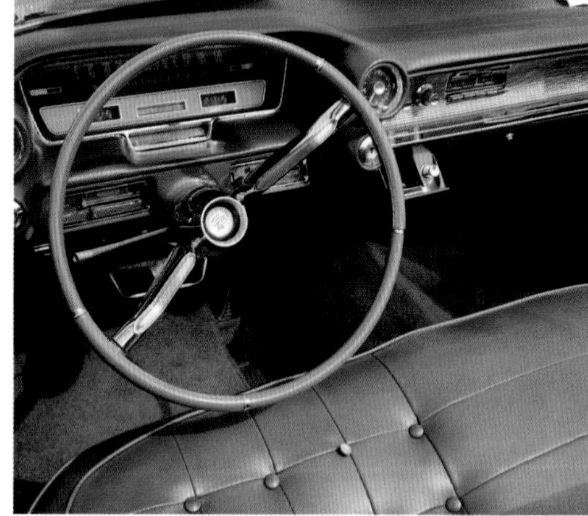

Dash 1

An image scanned from a black-and-white negative in RGB mode.

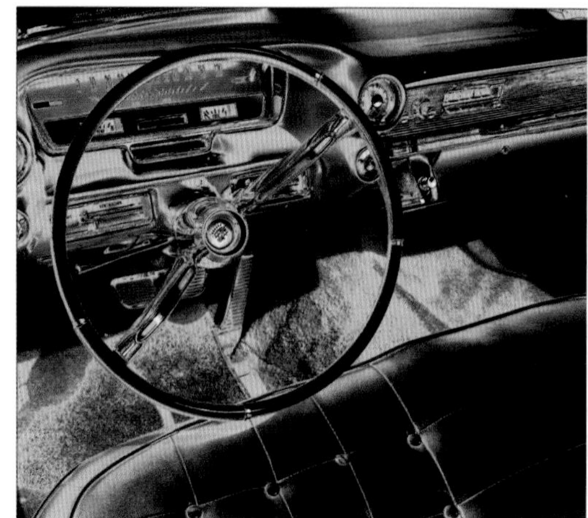

Dash 2

Attempting to solarize a print in the darkroom is a particularly hit-and-miss affair, as it is impossible to see the consequences of exposing the paper to light until the image has been printed. By carefully manipulating the Curves, it is possible to see on screen precisely which parts of the tonal spectrum are being altered. In this example, I particularly wanted to accentuate the key highlights within the image.

Using filters for solarized effects

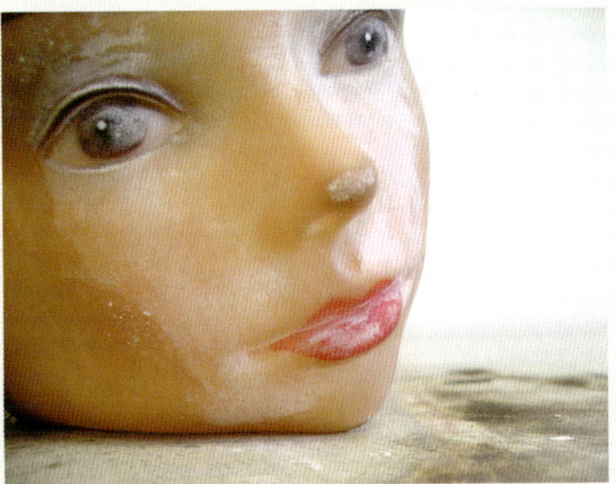

Fig 1

This is the original colour image, taken with a Pentax
Optio digital camera. Before applying the Solarize filter,
the image was desaturated.

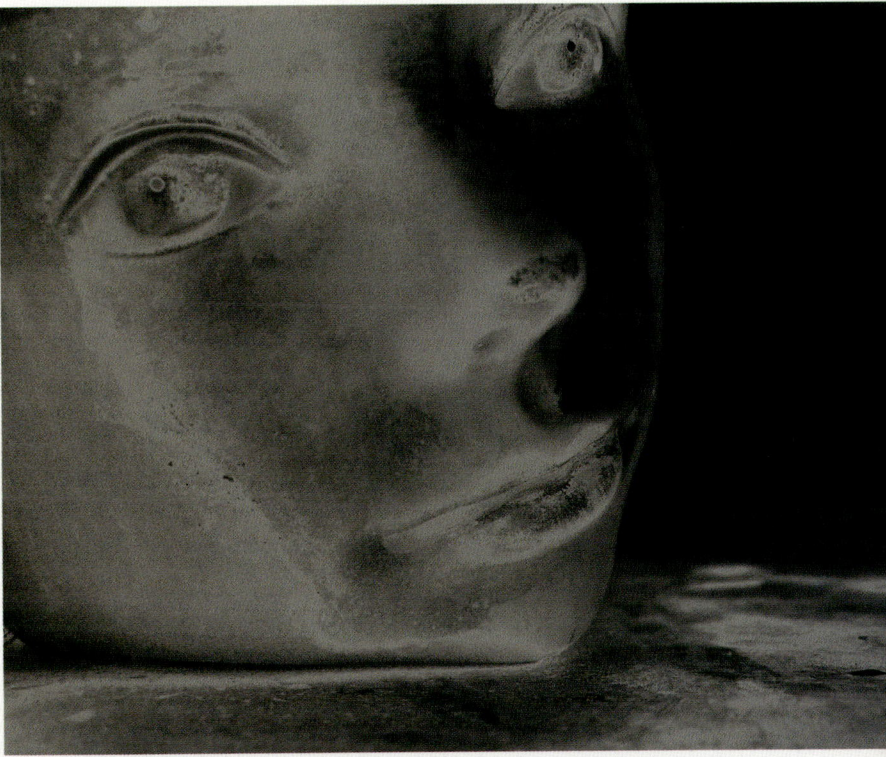

This is the effect of applying the Solarize filter, which has produced a solarized negative image.
This can be inverted (Control I) to produce a positive.

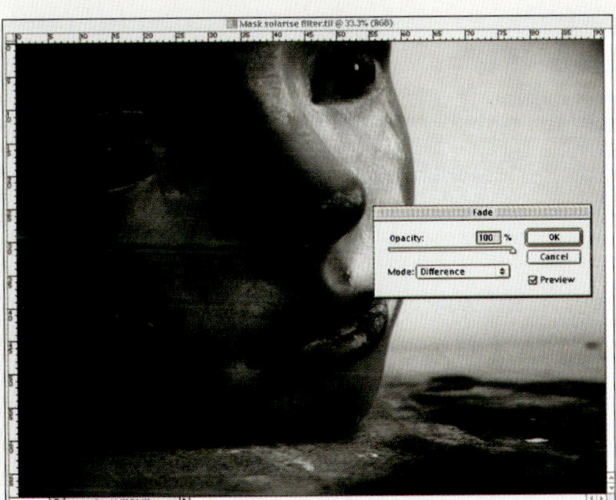

Fig 2

Immediately after applying the Solarize filter it can be
modified by using the Fade filter command: Edit > Fade
filter. An interesting application of this is to apply a
Blending mode.

Here, the image was first solarized with the Solarize filter,
then the Difference Blending mode was applied in the
Fade filter command.

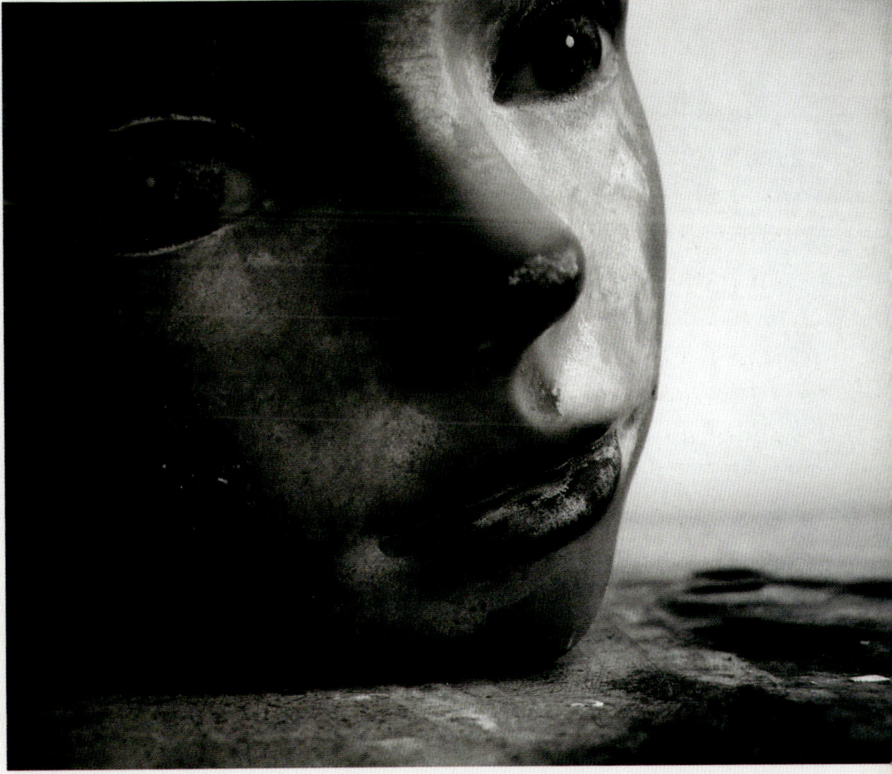

Using the Solarize filter

Filter > Stylize > Solarize is Photoshop's own solarization filter and works pretty well. Using this technique the final effect will be identical, whether you start from a positive or negative image. Remember that the effect of the filter can be reduced using the Fade filter command (Edit > Fade > Solarize) immediately after applying it, so its effect can be fine-tuned. Also in the Fade filter command is the ability to blend the solarized image to produce some interesting alternatives – in particular, the Difference blend can provide a very strong effects.

Use of Gradient Map

Selection of an appropriate gradient map (Image > Adjustments > Gradient Map)

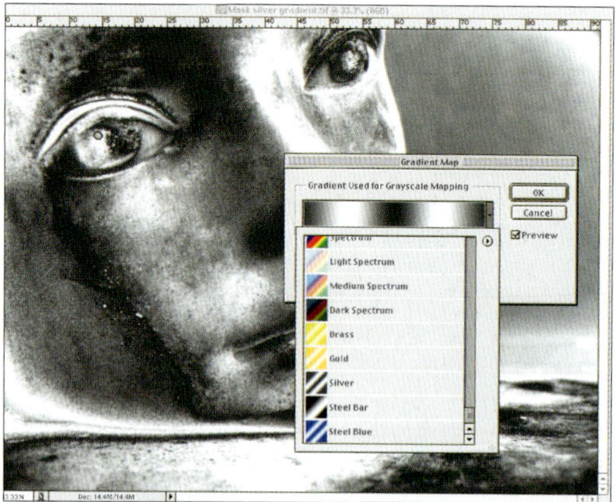

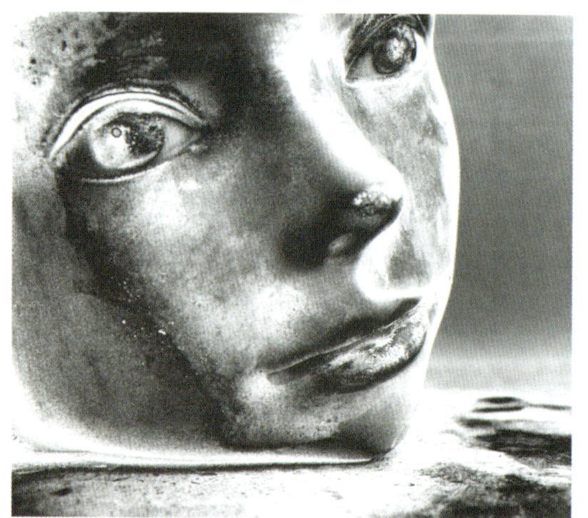

causes changes in tonality, even if one of the supplied colour gradients is used. The Silver gradient is quite dramatic, but you can experiment and make your own.

Using Curves

This is by far the most controllable way to work, as precise tones can be pegged and individual highlights, shadows or mid-tones can be partially or wholly reversed. Work on an Adjustment Layer so that fine-tuning can occur at any stage. There are an infinite number of variations, but the simplest place to start is to peg the mid-grey point and move the white point to the black to produce an inverted "V" shape, which will darken the highlights. Alternatively, move the black point to the white to lighten the shadow areas. Try other shapes: the "M" shape and "W" shape produce particularly strong effects.

By using an Adjustment Layer, the associated mask can be used to selectively apply the solarization effect. Paint with black to remove the effect or white to bring it back.

The effect of solarization by using Curves can be further modified depending upon the image. Often the contrast can be adjusted using another Curve, or colour can be added to a monochrome RGB image using Color Balance or Hue/Saturation.

Solarizing in colour

This is to be approached with caution – it is all too easy to produce images that can only be appreciated by the truly colour-blind or those high on hallucinogens. Major changes in colour are possible by using the type of Curves already described; however, it is far better to use rather more restrained changes that affect specific areas of colour – try using a Curves Adjustment Layer, but apply the change to a specific Channel rather than the

Using Curves for a solarized effect

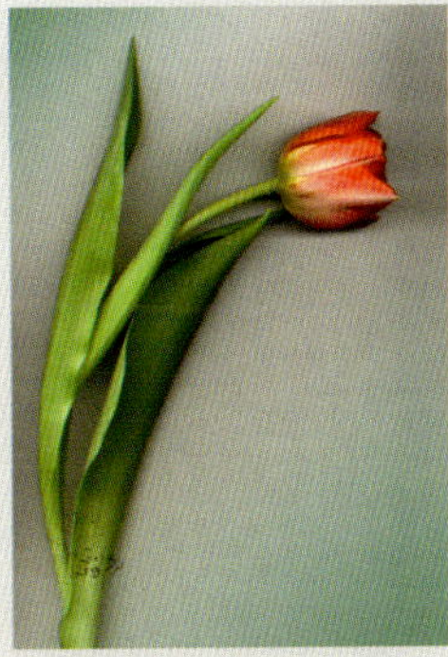

The original colour image, created by scanning a tulip on a flatbed scanner.

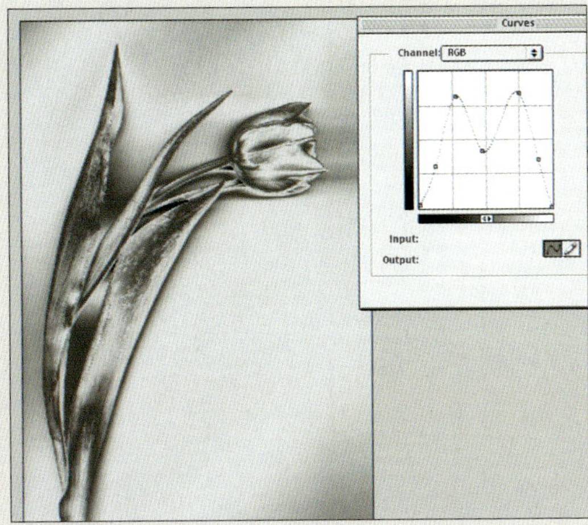

Fig 4
The image was desaturated and an M-shaped curve was then applied.

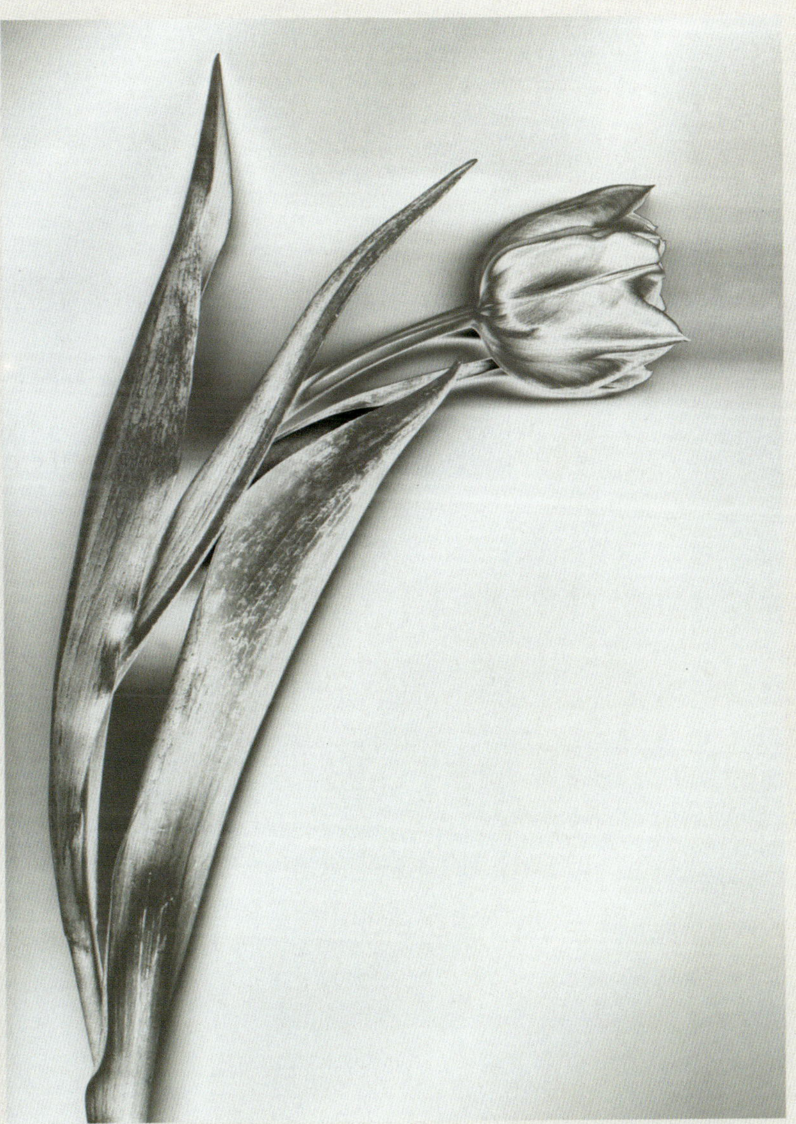

The final solarized monochrome image.

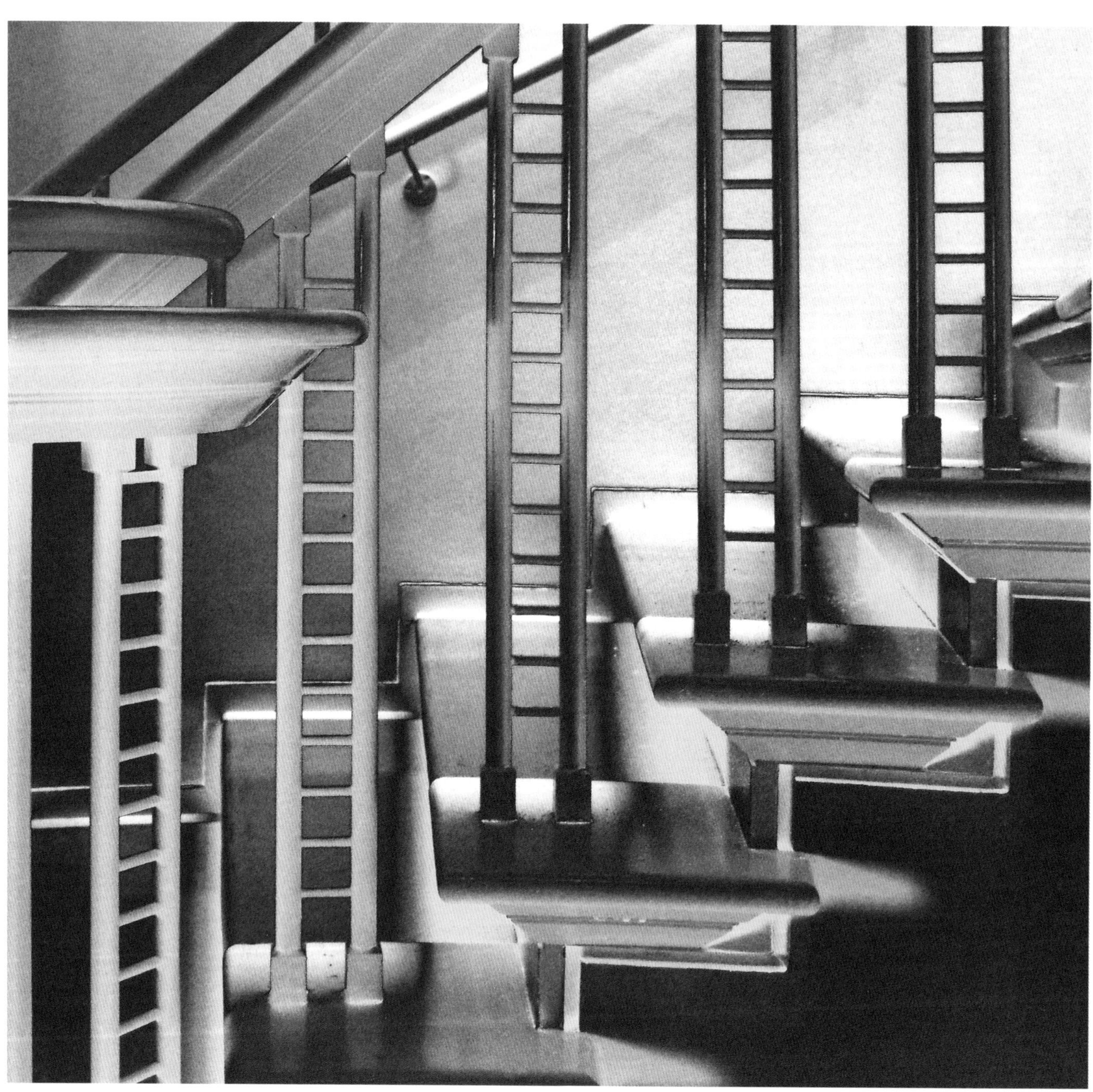

whole RGB range: by pegging the Curve, changes can then be applied to specific areas of the image. Leaving some resemblance to normality often helps.

Use of Blending modes

Another way to produce a subtle colour solarization is to create a copy layer of the original colour image, which is then desaturated and solarized. The original colour image is then placed at the top of the stack in the Layers palette and a Blending mode is applied. By altering the opacity of this colour layer, very subtle effects can be achieved.

Producing a colour solarized effect

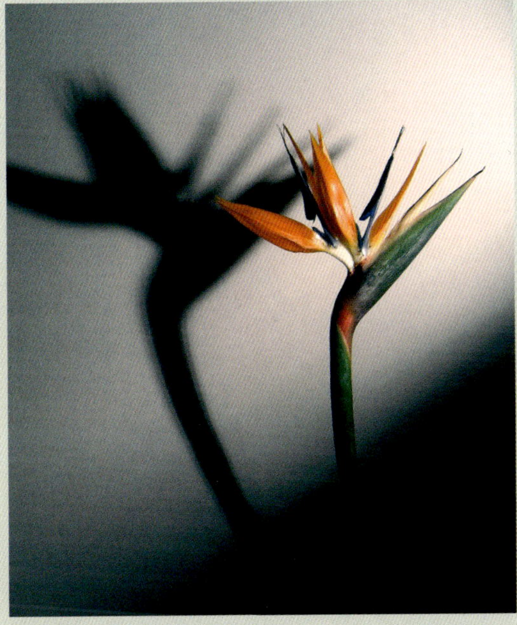

The original colour image was taken on a Pentax Optio digital camera.

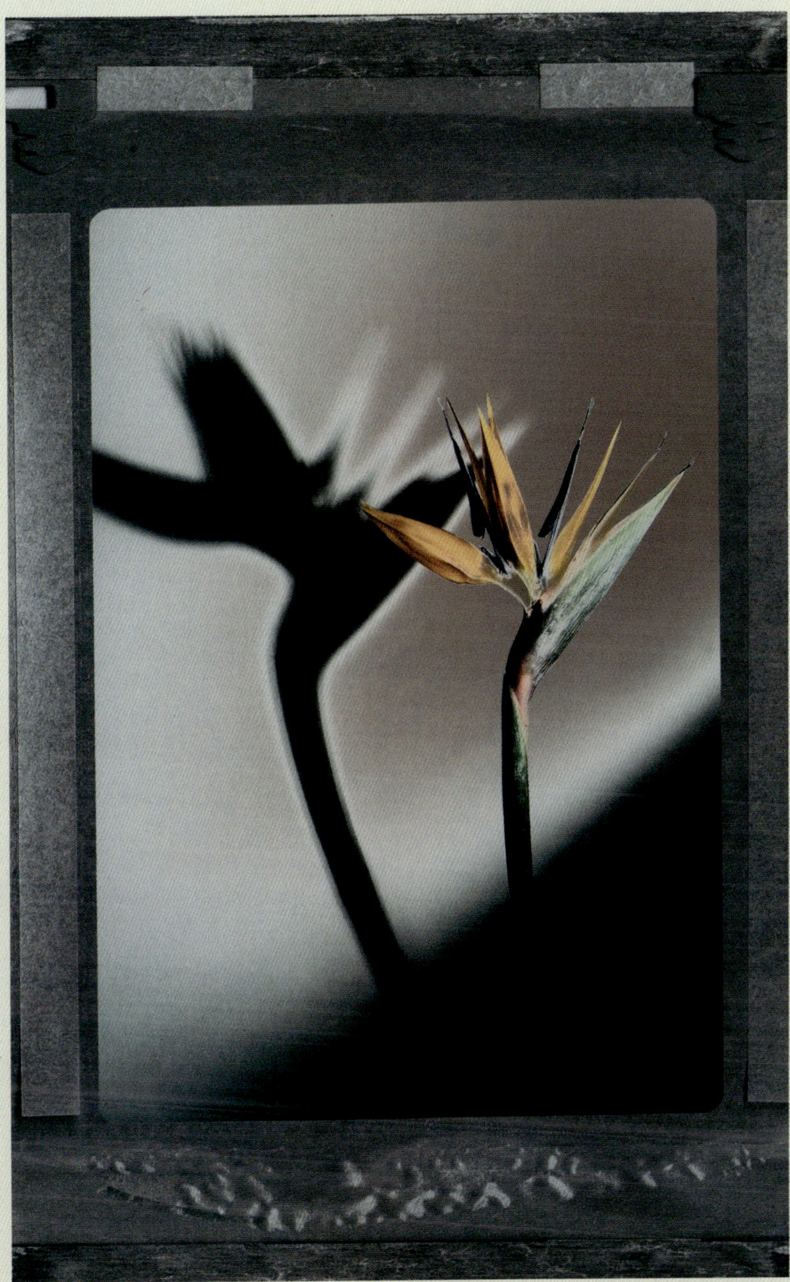

Scanning an old Polaroid film and using it as a separate layer to frame the flower completed the solarized image.

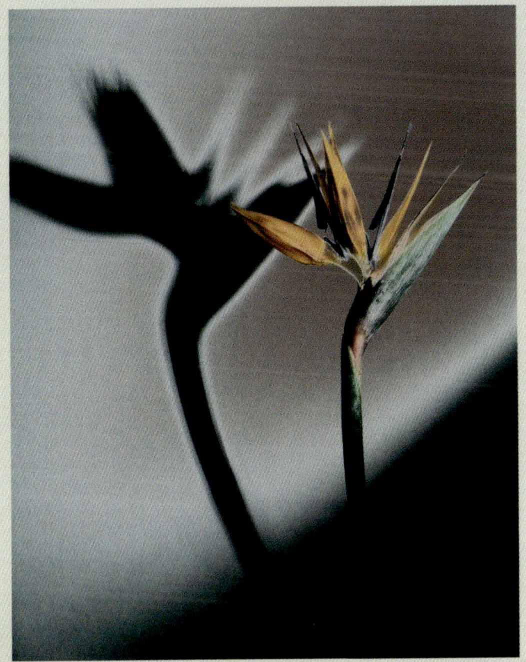

Subtle changes in Curves were all that was necessary to produce a partially solarized effect.

Using Blending modes with colour solarization

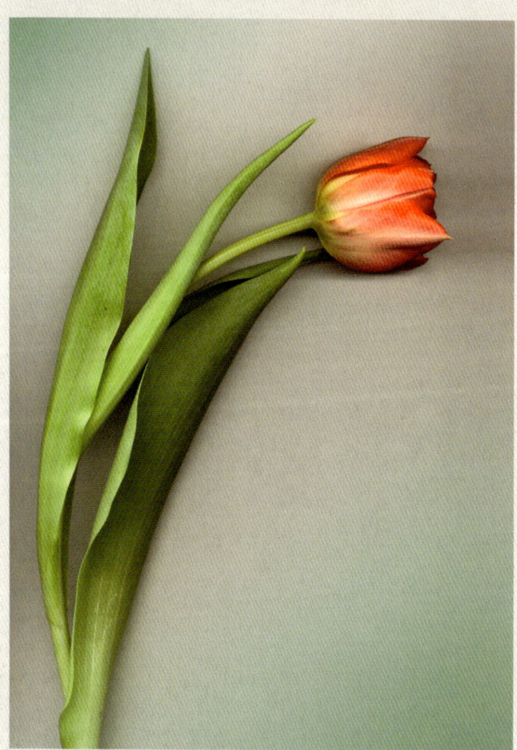

This is the original colour
scan of a tulip on a
flatbed scanner.

Fig 5
The solarized monochrome
layer was blended with
the colour layer using
Soft Light.

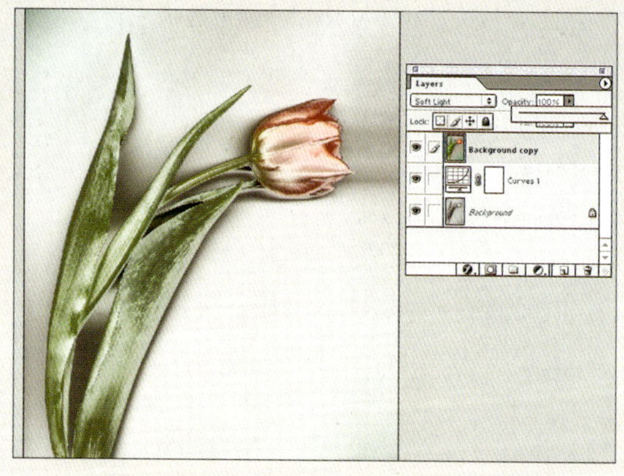

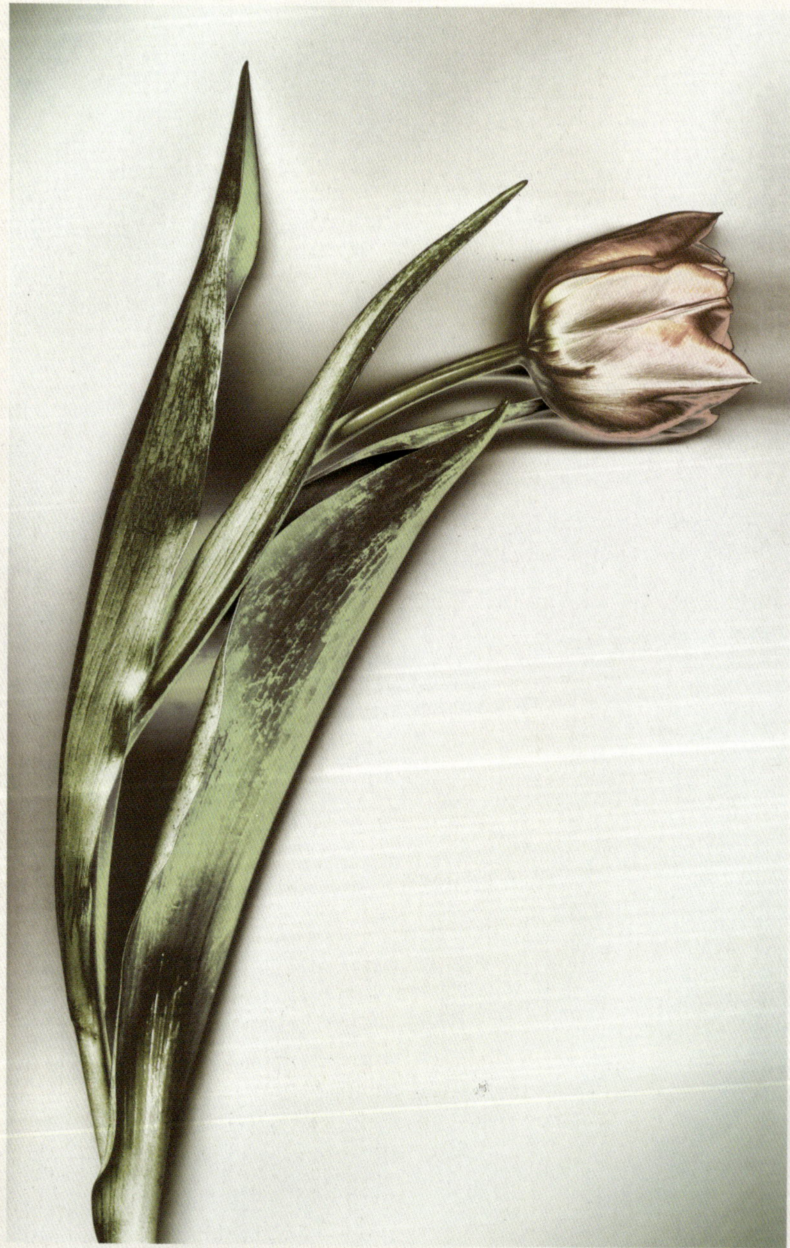

Final image of the tulip
using Soft Light.

Colour Solarisation using Curves

Banana – original ccan

Two bananas were scanned on a flat bed scanner with the lid up to produce a black background.

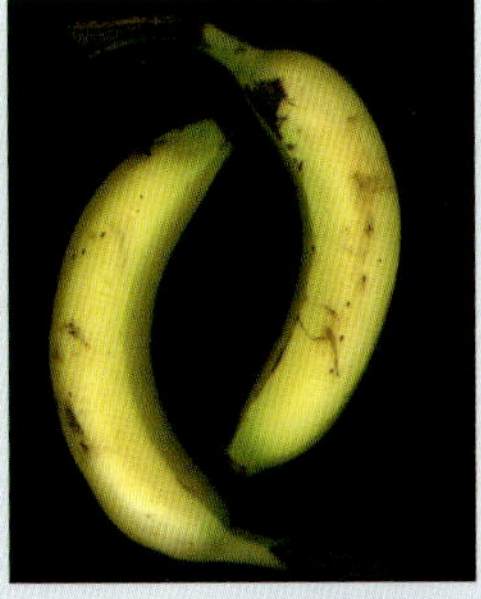

Layers Palette

This shows the original scan layer and the two Curves adjustment layers. By using adjustment layers they can be revisited and changed at any time.

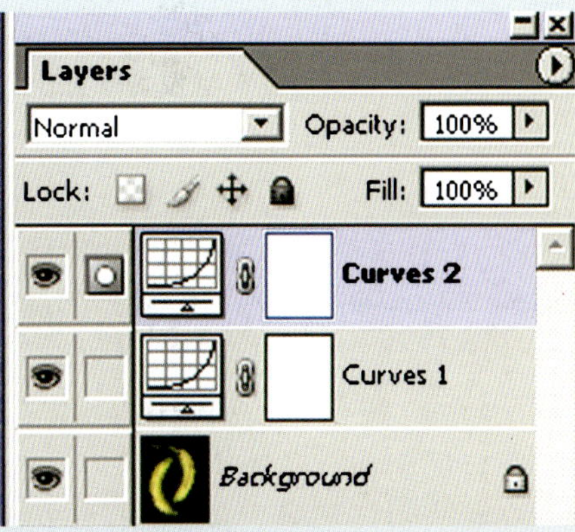

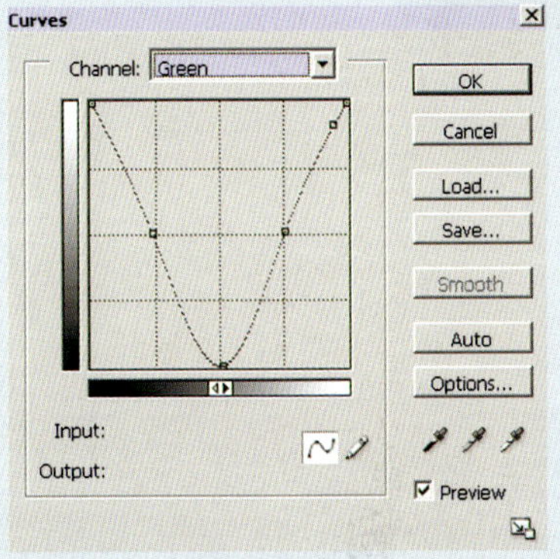

Curve 2

A second Curves adjustment layer was added and the Green channel manipulated to produce a blue background without significantly altering the yellow of the bananas. I like to work with a number of Curves adjustment layers rather than just one as it allows me to concentrate and adjust individual colours more easily.

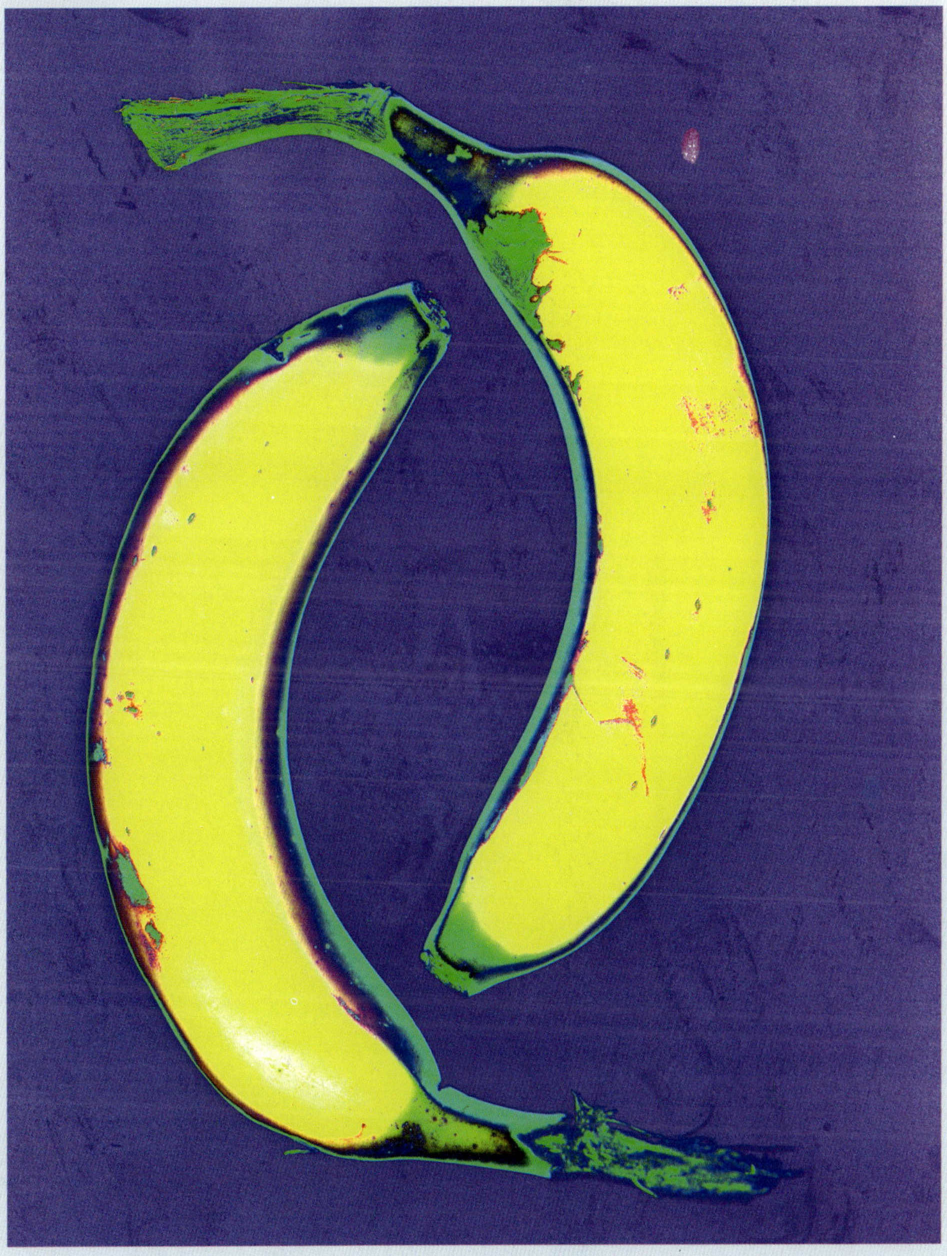

Final image

The finished image is now bursting with colour. A matter of taste but a considerable change from the original and certain to attract attention.

7 Inverting colour and tone

Dandelion and feathers

I captured the intricate detail of this dandelion down using a flatbed scanner, and the detail is overwhelming. However, the down was too delicate to place a white cover over it, so I was left with a fathomless black background. By inverting the image, not only has the background suddenly come into play, but the detail within the fronds has also become noticeably more apparent.

Crouching nude

This is a composite of a single image, although one of the layers has been flipped horizontally and then reduced in size. The negative qualities within the image have been induced partially by inverting, but also by using Difference in the Blending mode.

A colour or black-and-white negative is often seen as a means to an end, and it rarely occurs to the photographer to leave the image in its negative state. After all, we see positively, so what purpose can there be in printing a negative as a negative?

IT'S BY NO means unknown for photographers to become excited when viewing a film in its negative form, then to be equally disappointed when the negative has been printed as a positive and the print turns out to be just a bit too realistic. The image in its negative form often possesses a mystery the positive rarely has, for while we may be able to identify certain elements, others remain an enigma, which is part of the appeal.

Increasingly, contemporary photographers are recognizing the potency of negative images and are working them into their images. This is not a new idea, and can be traced back to the British Pop Artist Richard Hamilton, who in the mid-1960s produced his, *I'm Dreaming of a White Christmas*. Hamilton was very adept at manipulating images, and realized that as he distorted the positive and negative effects of a photograph, this had an emotional impact on the viewer. Various photographers have followed in his wake, including Jeff Weiss, Thomas Barrow, Alice Wells and Robert Fichter.

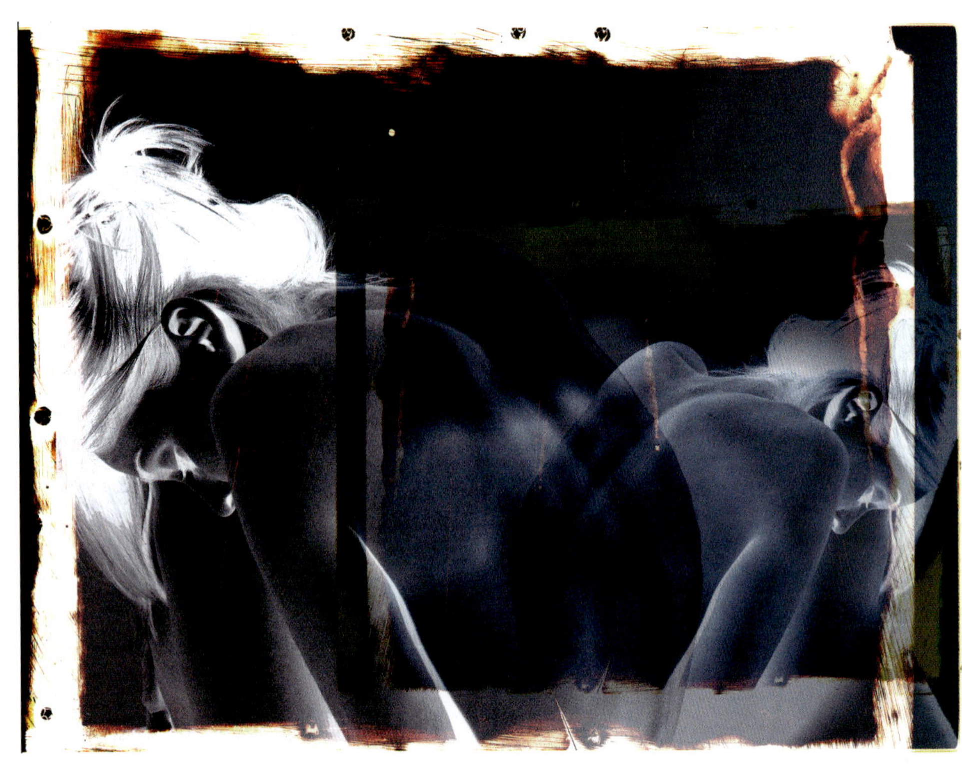

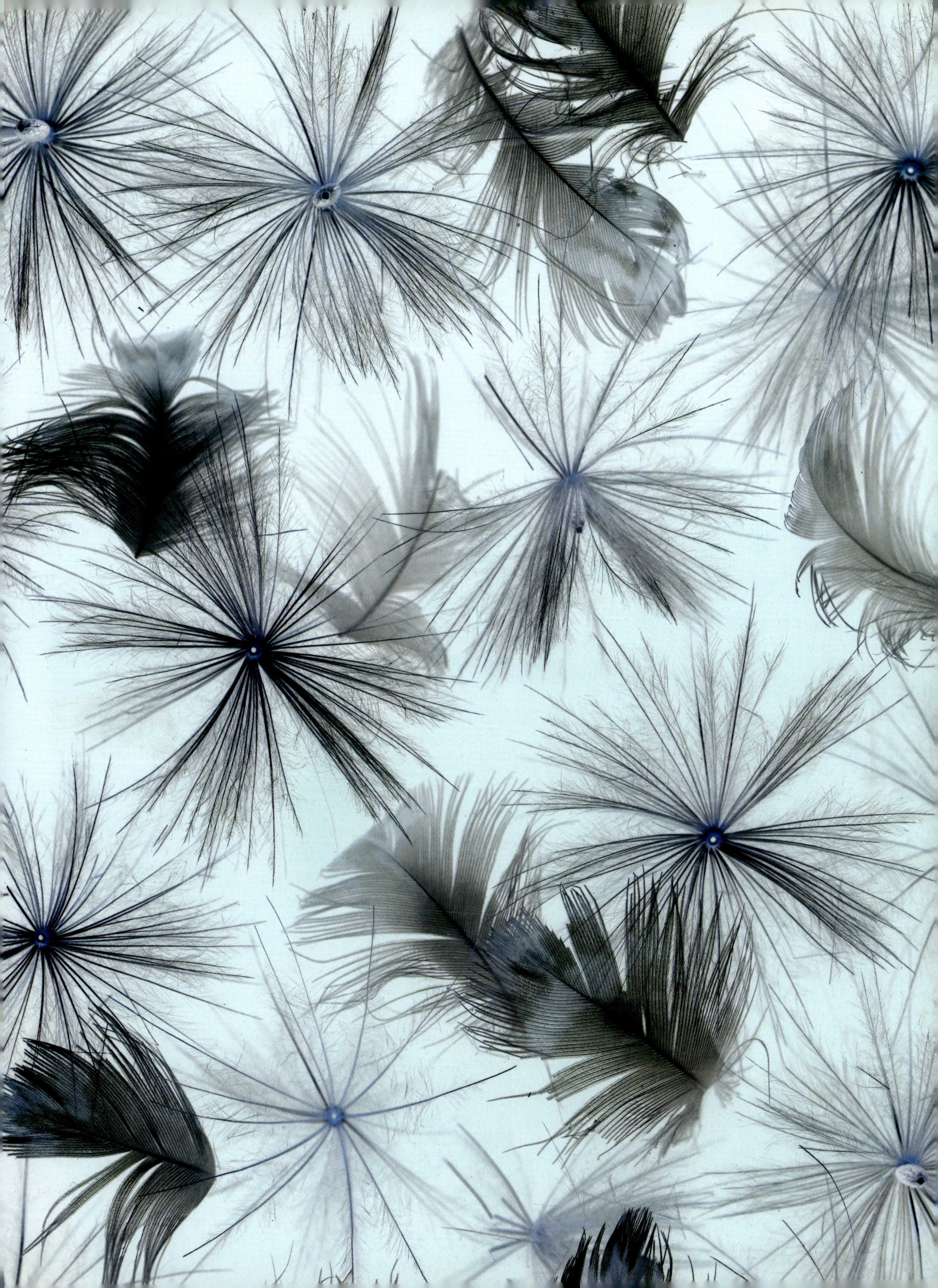

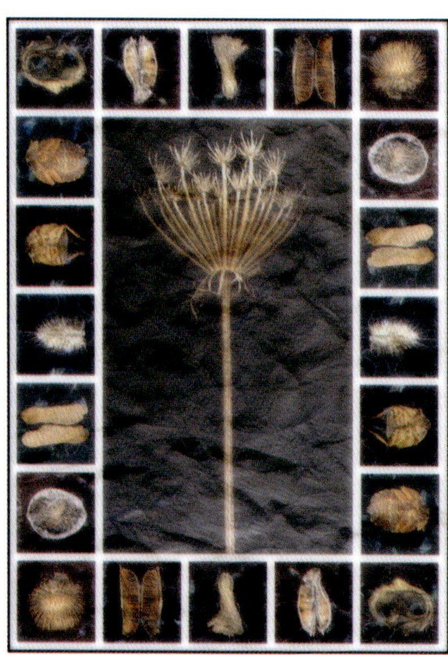

Example 1 Genesis No. 2

Most of the natural forms within this composite were found and collected during a walk. I wanted to express the diversity, yet similarity, of many of the forms. However, when I showed colleagues this print, they often tried to identify individual elements at the expense of viewing the image as a whole.

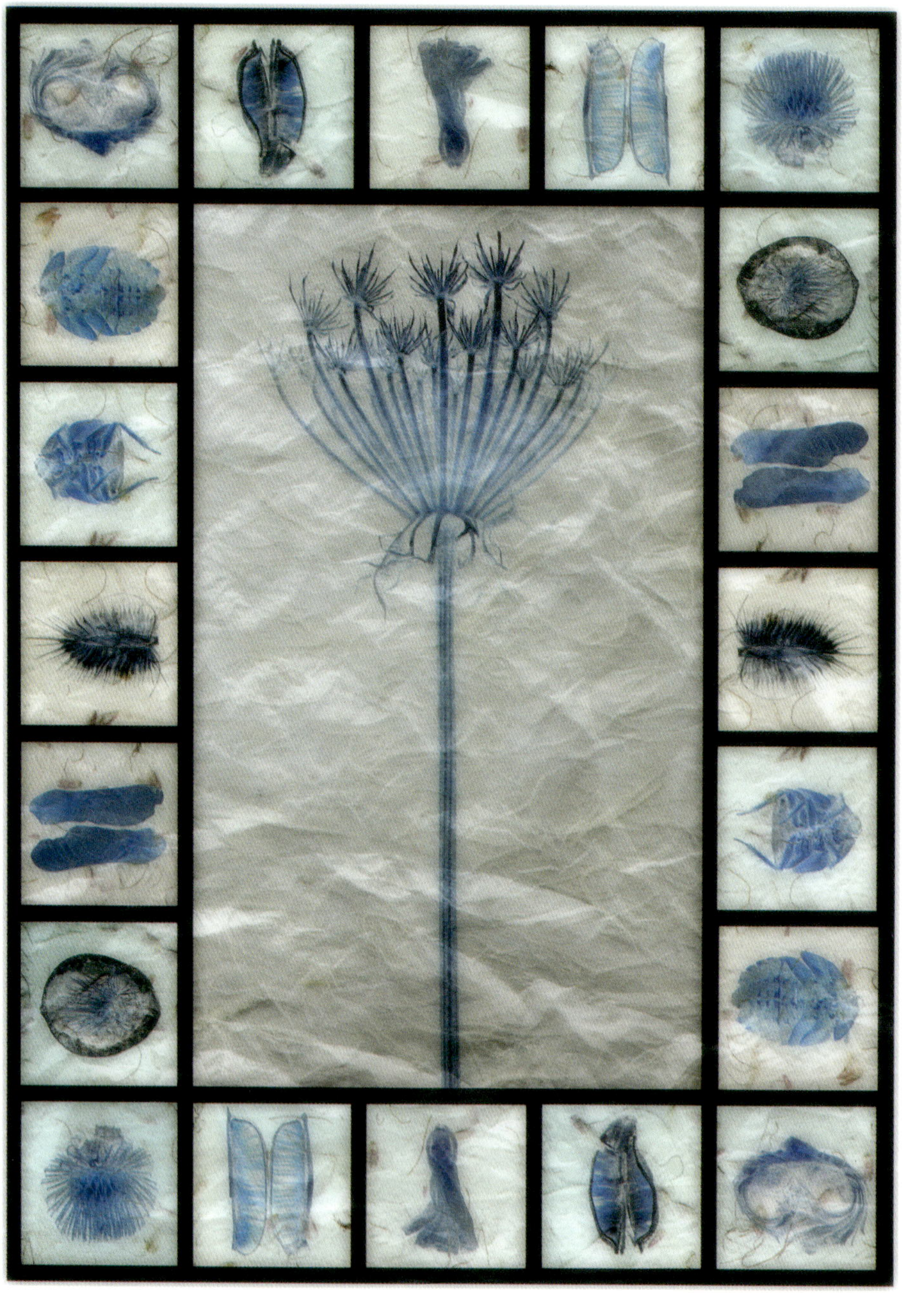

Example 2 Genesis No. 2

The holistic quality I was after became immediately apparent the moment I inverted the image. While it is quite obvious that all the elements comprise small natural forms, their precise nature is difficult to fathom because we are denied both the correct colours and tones; only the shapes give us a clue. Ultimately, this is a much more interesting picture.

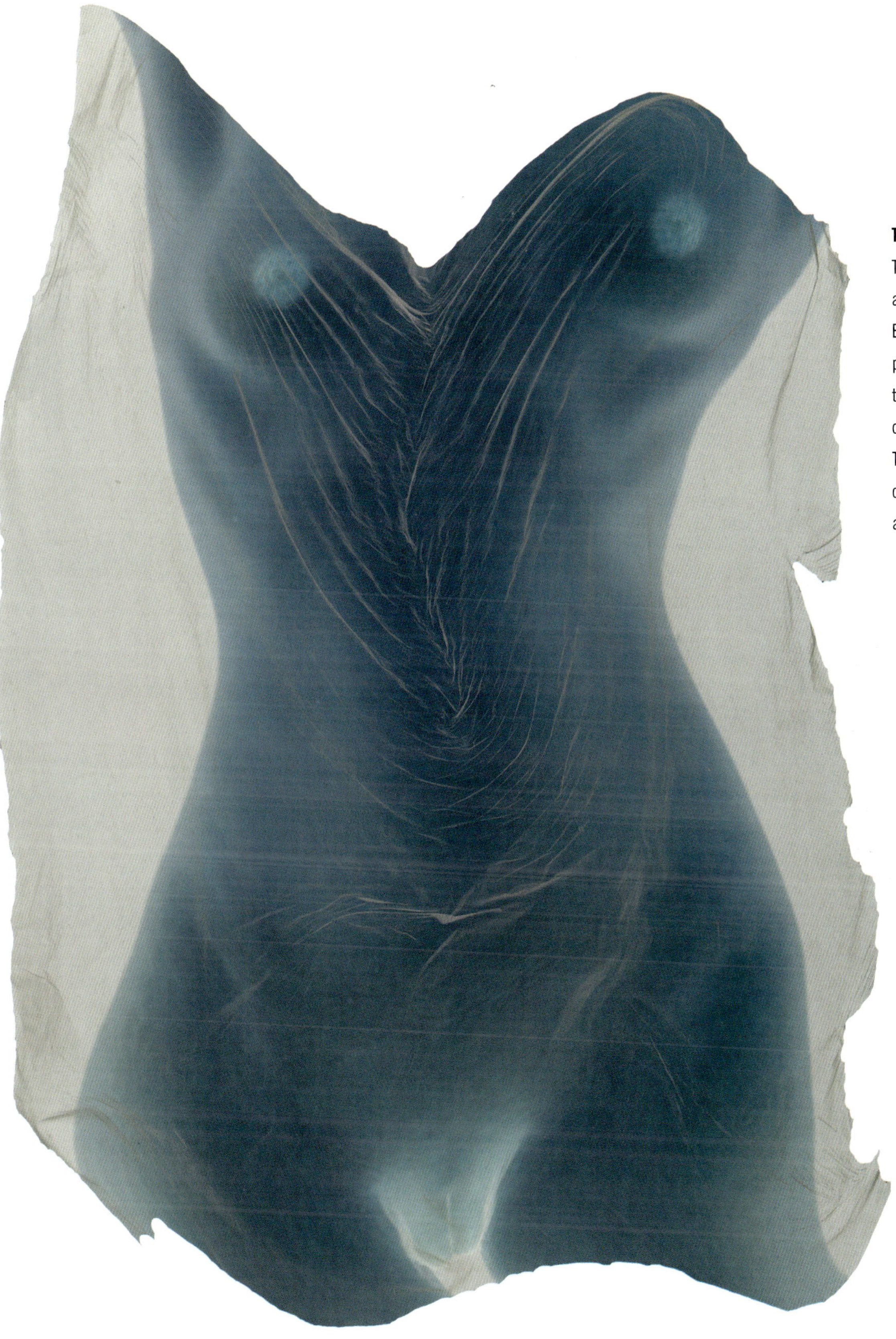

Torso

This reversal effect was achieved by using the Exclusion Blending mode to place a colour original of the torso over a lower layer of a scanned plastic bag. The original positive flesh colour has been rendered as a negative blue colour.

8 Cross-processing

This is not getting angry while developing film – although pre-digitally it would have ranked as the most boring aspect of photography – it is in fact processing colour film in the wrong developer. A technique much loved by fashion and portrait photographers such as Nadav Kander, it involved processing slide film in C41 chemistry or colour negative film in E6 chemistry.

DEPENDING UPON THE film stock selected and the exposure given, colour shifts were produced. This obviously required experimentation with a variety of film stocks and ISO ratings of the film to give consistent results (unless film manufacturers changed the characteristics of the film without telling anyone). This is certainly one of the processes that is far more controllable using digital techniques.

Going digital

Probably the best way to achieve the cross-processed effect is to use the power of Curves. By selecting individual colour Channels, colour shift in any part of the colour spectrum can be accurately controlled. Once determined, the changes in Curves can be stored as an Action or a Droplet, and applied to any image. As this is an Adjustment Layer, minor modifications can be made easily, appropriate to individual images – this is important because the slavish application of an effect such as this is not appropriate for all subjects and must be fine-tuned as necessary.

Colour negative processed in E6

A typical colour negative film processed in E6 chemistry has a bleached effect, especially in skin tones, with creamy white highlights, and shadows with a cyan/blue cast. To achieve this look, the Red and Blue Channels are adjusted as shown in Fig 1. The RGB and Green Channels can be used to make minor alterations, as required, to change the overall exposure.

Slide film processed in C41

To emulate slide film processed in C41 chemistry, the blue and red Curves are moved into an "S" shape, increasing contrast and causing a crossover of colours. The Blue channel has a reverse "S" shape, which causes a reduction of contrast. Again, the RGB Channel can be used to make further adjustments to overall contrast (see Fig 2).

Colour negative processed in E6

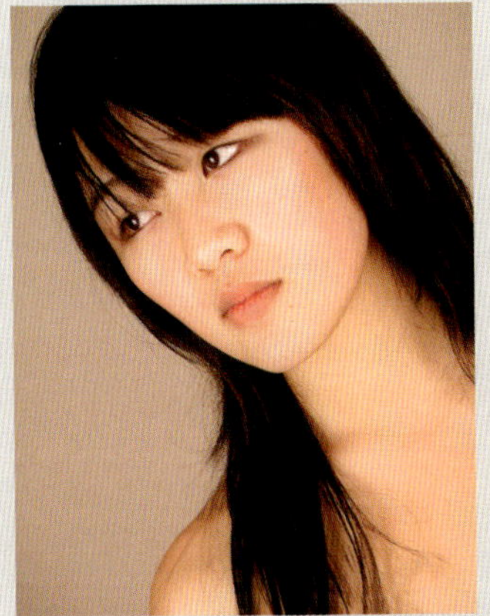

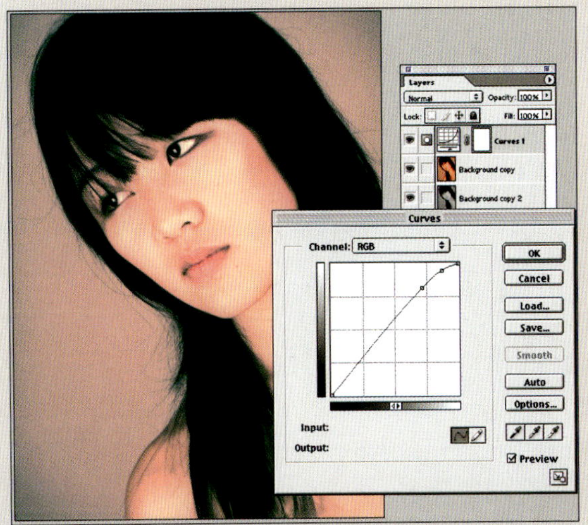

Channel alterations to
produce colour negative
processed in E6 effect.

RGB Channel

This the original colour
image, taken on a Pentax
Optio camera.

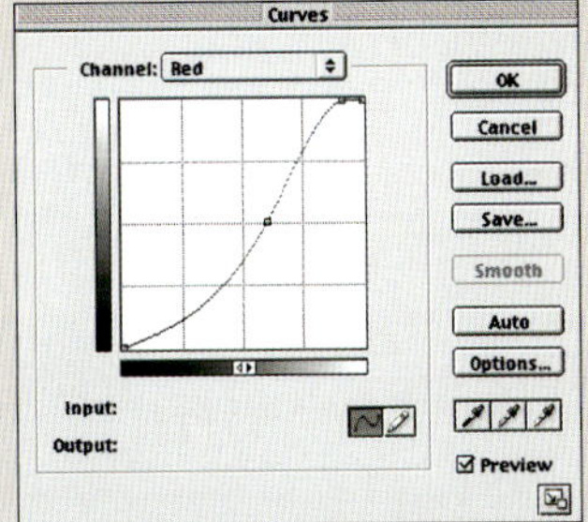

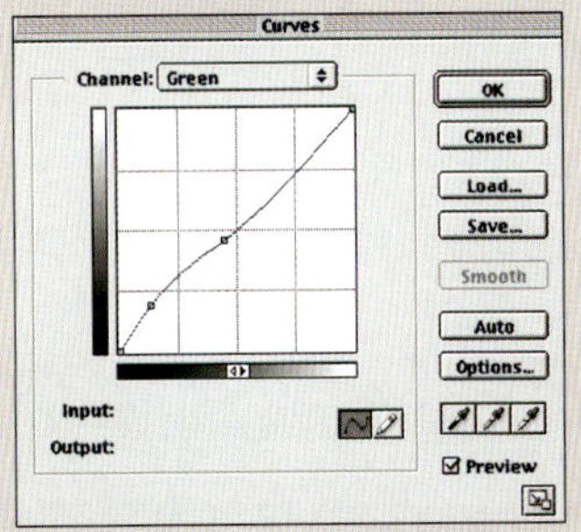

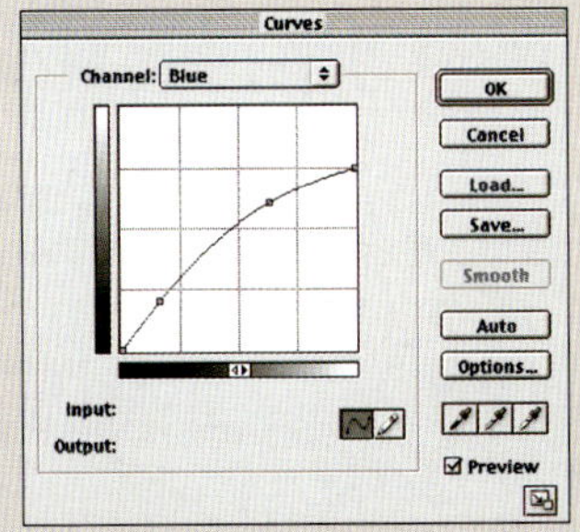

Red Channel

Green Channel

Blue Channel

A copy layer of the original
colour image was made, as
was a desaturated copy
layer. As the original colour
layer was a little saturated,
the Opacity was reduced to
48% to blend with the
monochrome layer beneath.
The Channels were then
adjusted as in Fig 1, using
a Curves Adjustment Layer
at the top of the stack.

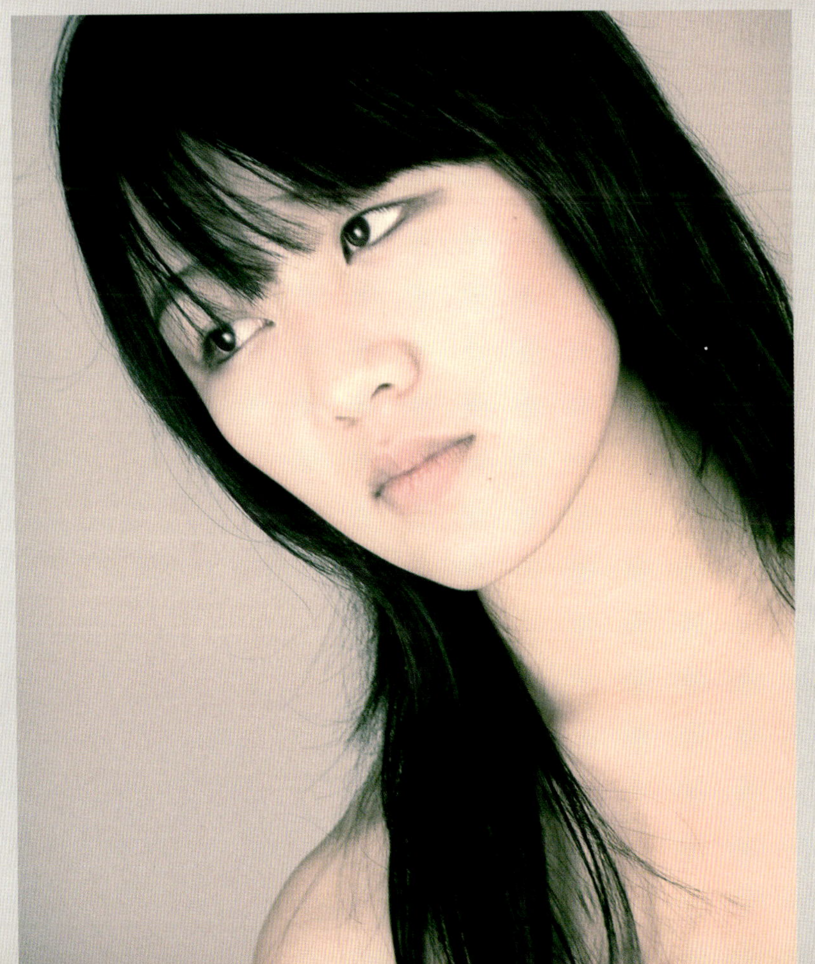

Slide film processed in C41

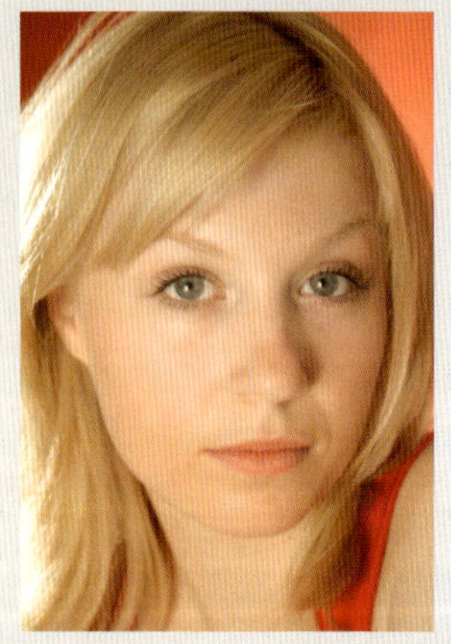

Original colour image taken on a Fuji S2 Pro camera.

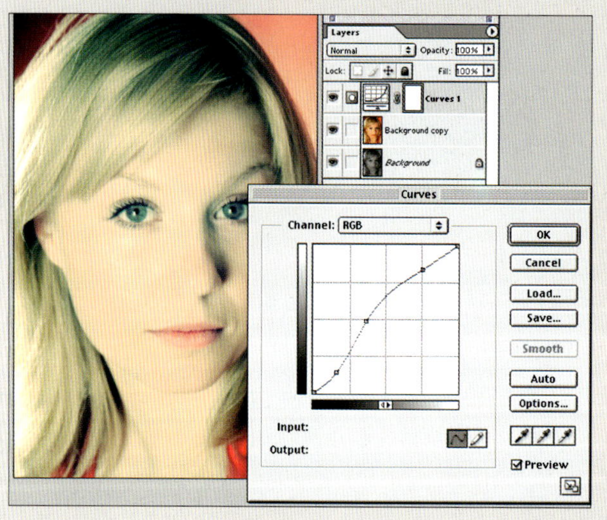

Fig 2
Channel alterations to produce slide film processed in C41 effect.

RGB Channel

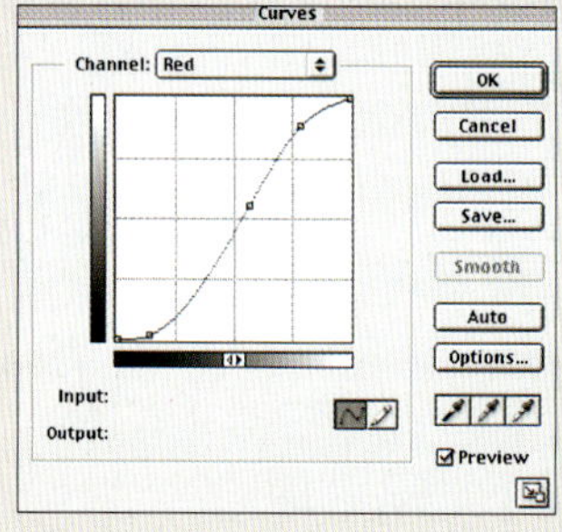

Red Channel

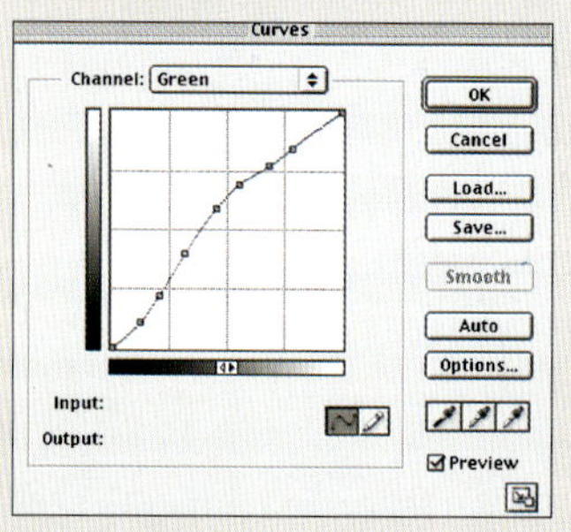

Green Channel

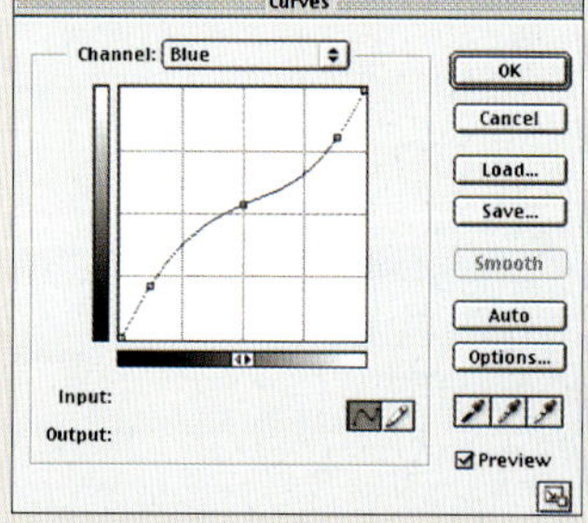

Blue Channel

A copy layer of the original colour image was made and a desaturated copy layer produced. As the colour layer was still a little saturated, the Opacity setting was reduced to 72% to blend with the monochrome layer beneath. The Channels were then adjusted as in Fig 2, using a Curves Adjustment Layer at the top of the stack. A second Curves Adjustment Layer was then made to fine-tune the contrast.

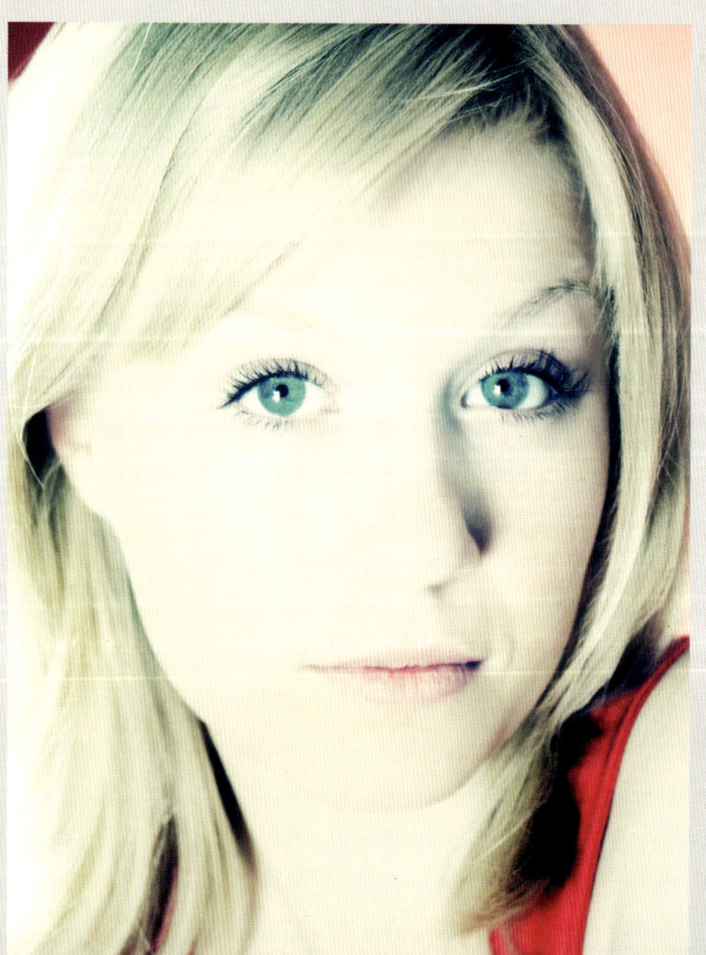

Cross-processing slides as negatives

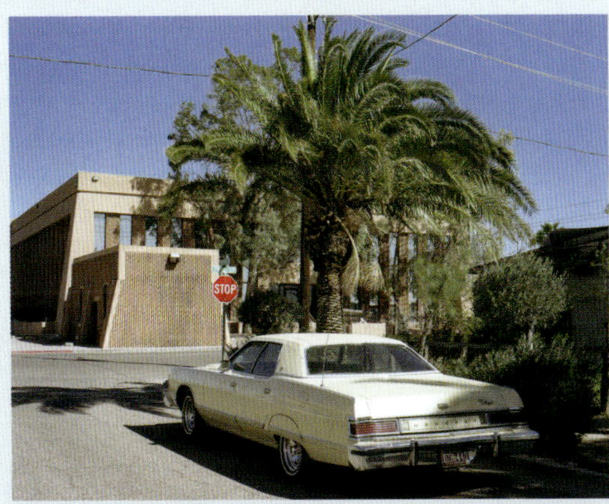

Example 1 Stop

A straight print taken from a scanned slide. Whilst this photograph is contrasty, the final image shows full highlights and shadow detail.

Example 2 Stop

Processing colour slides in C41 chemistry induces a heightened reality as the resulting print shows very high contrast, often in burnt-out lights, and deeply saturated colours. The same effect can easily be mimicked by Curves. The results are not dissimilar to the deadpan images favoured by the Pop Artists.

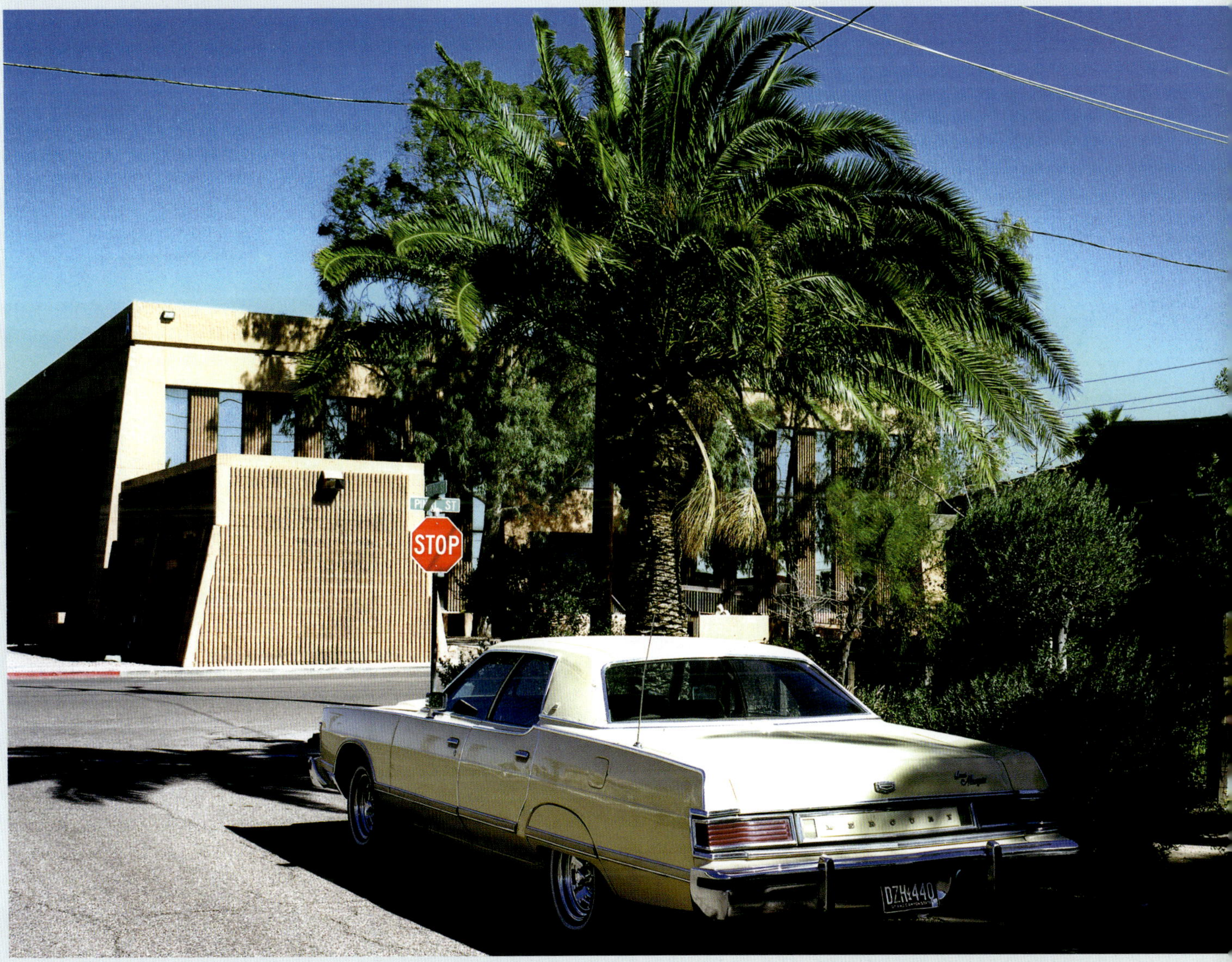

Creating lith prints

One of the concerns some committed darkroom workers have about working digitally is that they feel they need to abandon some of the beautiful printing techniques that have been developed over the years. One of the most revered of these is the wonderful process of lith printing – but this can easily be simulated digitally.

MOREOVER, EVEN THE most experienced darkroom worker would concede that lith is an especially fickle process, which is subject to a number of potential problems: unpredictable staining, uneven toning and pepper fogging are a constant threat to those wishing to produce lith prints in the darkroom; and in addition, it is virtually impossible to produce two identical images. Working digitally, all of these problems can be resolved easily.

In order to successfully mimic a lith print, it is important to replicate its characteristic tonal profile. The unique quality of a lith print is determined by very delicate highlights countered by powerful and gritty shadows. As the lith process accentuates the warm quality of a chlorobromide paper, the prints assume a characteristic warm hue, ranging from a gentle caramel colour to a dramatic pinky-red, depending on the paper used.

Reducing contrast and toning the image

Once you have scanned in a black-and-white negative, convert it to RGB (assuming that you have not already scanned it in RGB mode). The first task is to create the

Rusting oil container 1

A black-and-white print scanned in RGB mode.

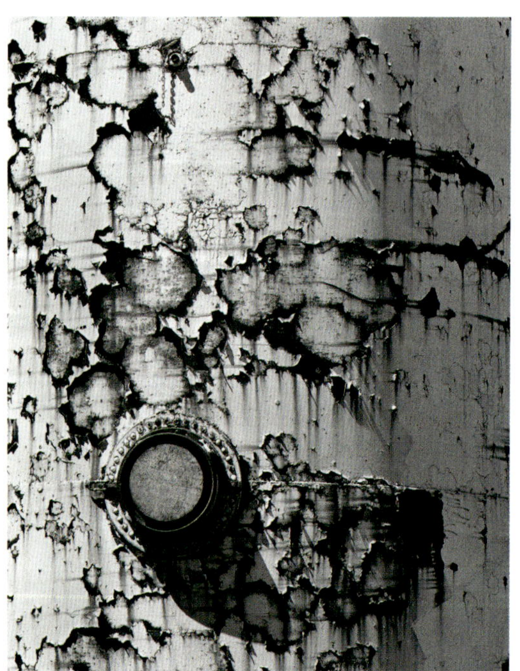

Rusting oil container 2

One of the main reasons why so many monochrome workers opt to produce lith prints is because it is a procedure that opens up other equally beautiful toning processes. One of these is to dual-tone a print first in selenium and then in gold, which introduces a rich tan-brown in the shadows while rendering the highlights a delicate pale blue. This effect can easily be done digitally by using Color Balance.

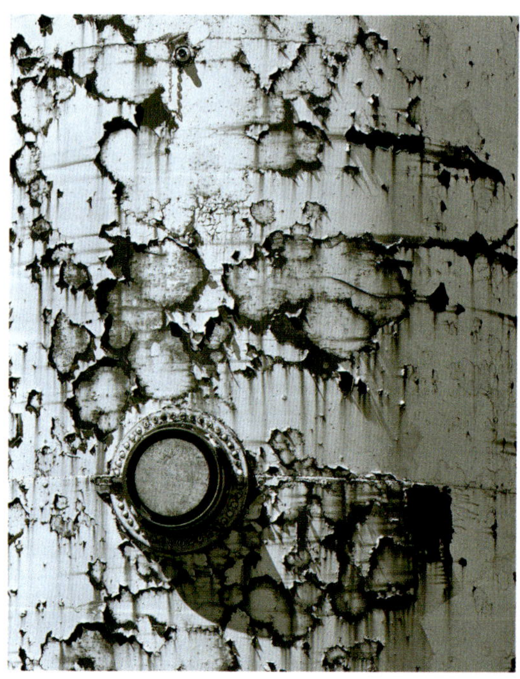

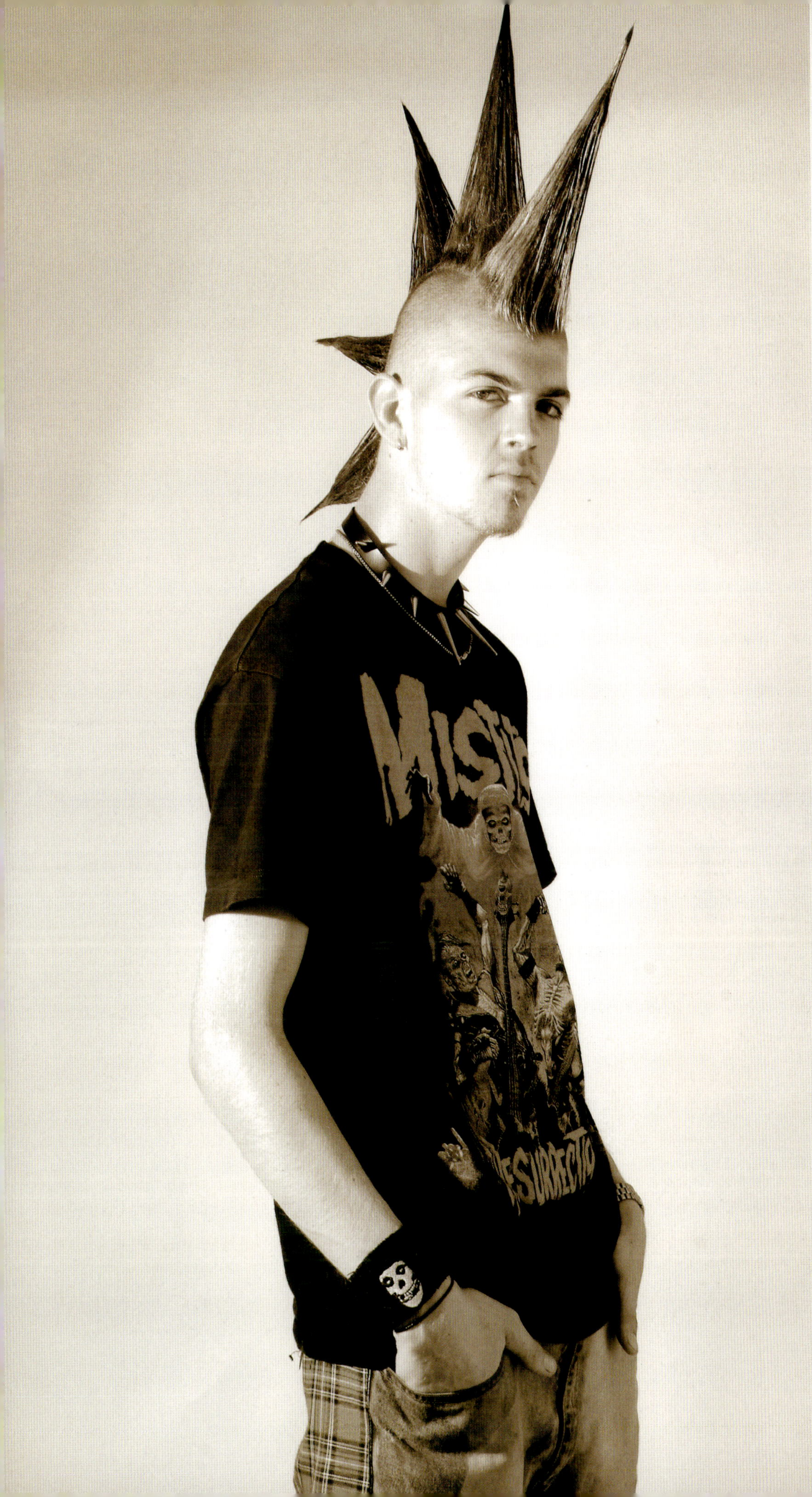

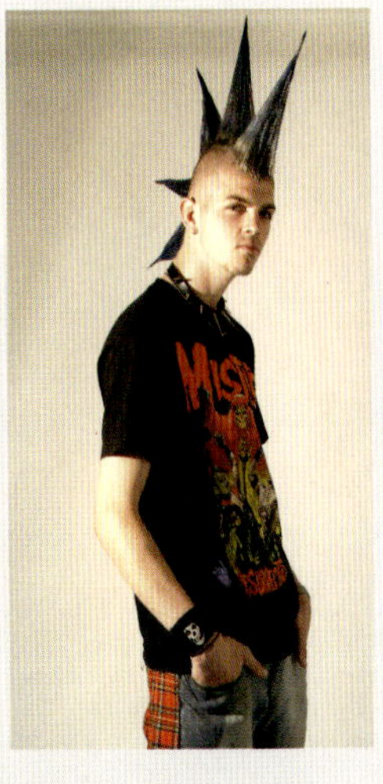

Matt

One of my students is an impressive figure — he stands at about 1.93m (6ft 4in), and his choice of hairstyle takes him way over 2.13m (7ft). A talented junior athlete, his image is more reflective of his taste than of any anger towards society. The original image was taken with a Nikon Coolpix camera. By carefully adjusting the Curves, it is relatively easy to dramatize the shadows, whilst retaining delicate highlight details — qualities that are the hallmark of a lith print.

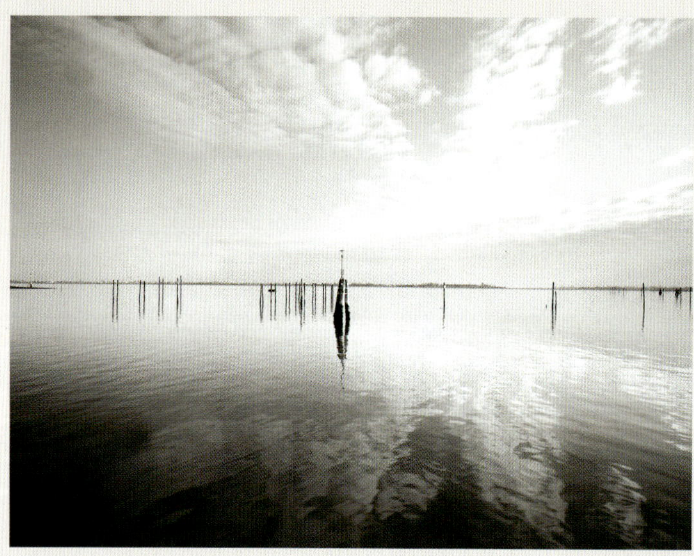

This image was coloured using
Hue/Saturation, and the contrast
was then greatly decreased in order
to flatten the mid-tones.

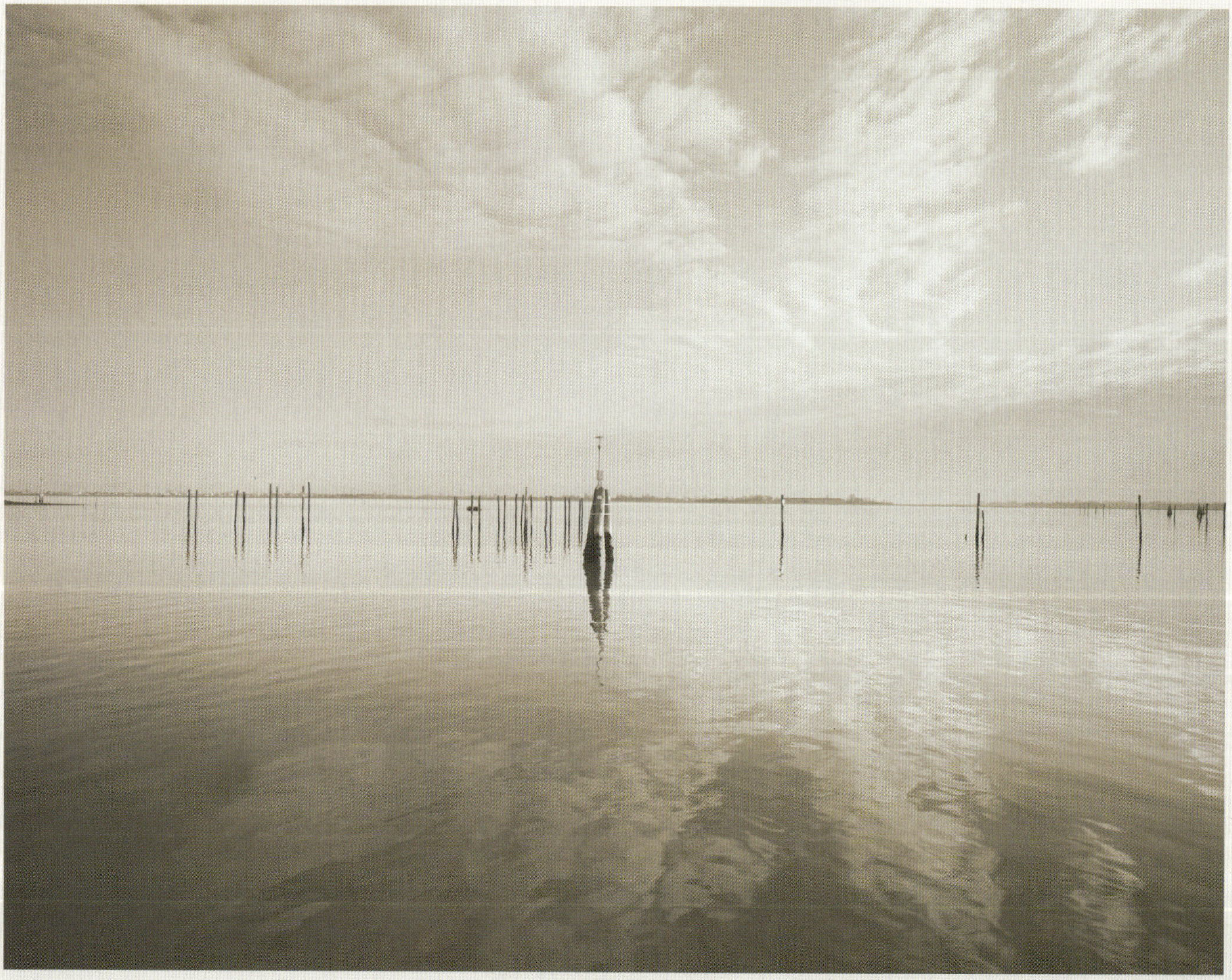

Fig 1

Pegging the shadows while pulling the mid-tones towards the highlights, is an important element when trying to mimic the characteristic lith tonal profile.

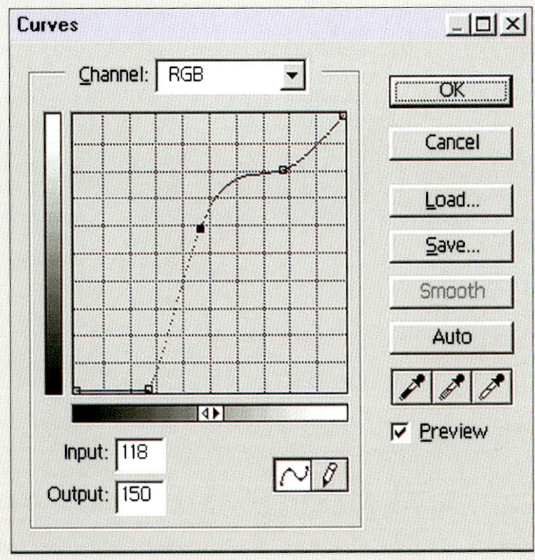

By adjusting the Curves, a very convincing lith tonal profile is now suggested.

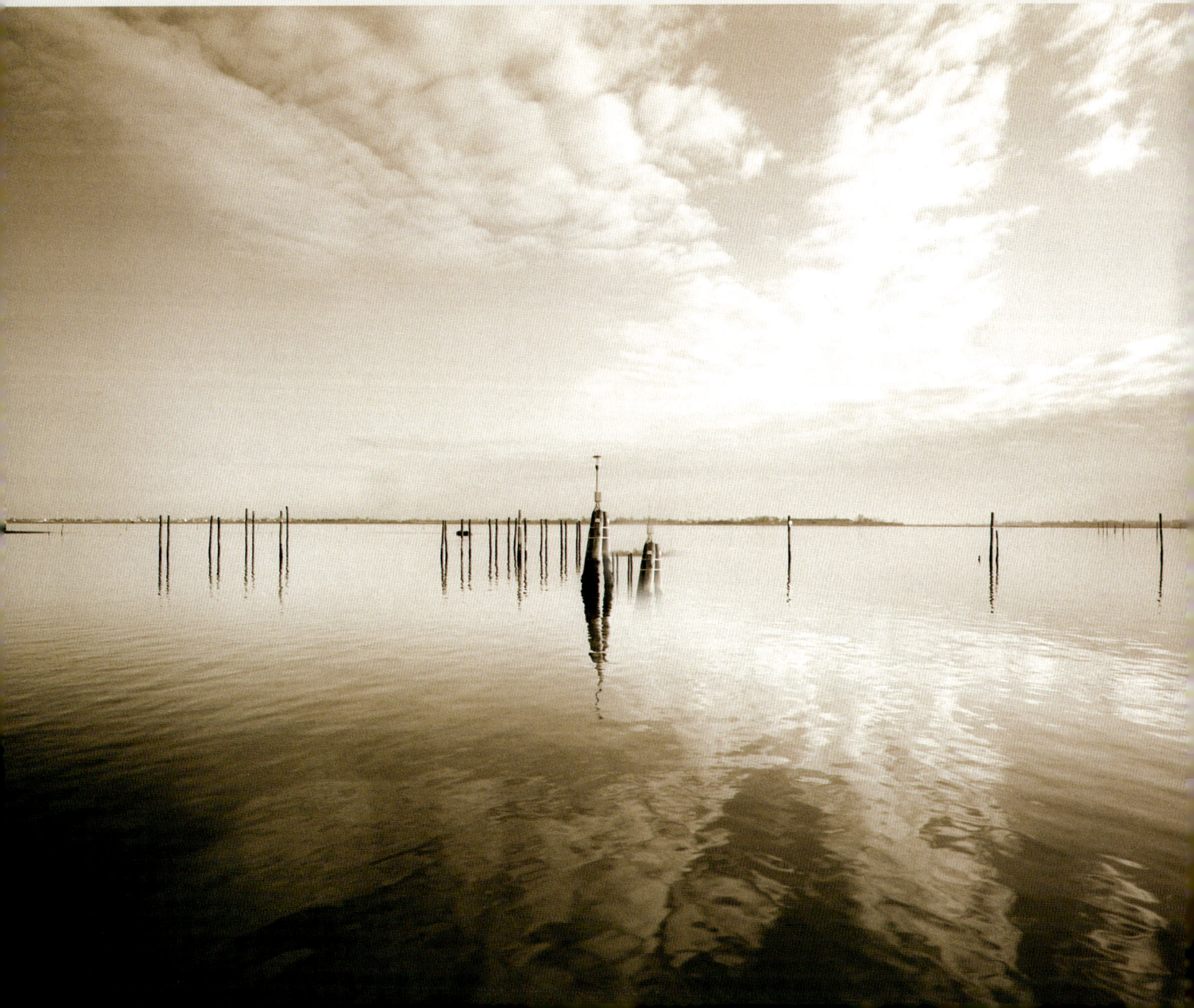

characteristic flat mid-tones of a lith print. This is most easily achieved by using the Brightness/Contrast command. Go to Image > Adjust > Brightness/Contrast. Substantially reduce contrast anywhere between –35 and –50. It is helpful to "tone" your image at this stage by using Hue/Saturation: go to Image > Adjust > Hue/Saturation. Push the slider in a band between 8 and 36, depending on the colour you wish to achieve. Don't be tempted to overdo the Saturation – a reading of 25 normally suffices.

Controlling contrast using Curves

Make a Curves Adjustment Layer, which is the key to establishing the characteristics of a lith print.

1 As it is important that the highlights are retained, peg the first quarter to ensure no further changes are made.

2 Pull the mid-tones towards the highlights, but make sure that the hues do not start to solarize (see Fig 1).

3 In order to mimic the characteristic sooty blacks of a lith print, drag the Curve along the baseline; the further you move it, the more obvious the appearance of "infectious development" will become. This part of the procedure needs to be done with great care; if it is underdone, the image will not look like a lith print, but if it is overdone, the shadows can clog up. Use the Navigator to monitor the adjustments.

Toning a lith print

One of the undoubted joys of producing lith prints in the darkroom is the wonderful results that can be achieved when these prints are subsequently toned, particularly in selenium and gold. Once again, this can be done easily in digital mode.

Achieving a selenium-toned lith print

Selenium toner works most aggressively on darker tones and takes a little while longer to affect highlights, a characteristic that is exploited by lith workers to produce some exceptionally beautiful split-toned images. This can be achieved digitally using Color Balance.

Go to Image > Adjust > Color Balance. To achieve the characteristics of a selenium-toned lith print, you require a pinkiness in the highlights and a blue-grey in the mid-tones, while the shadows should appear brown.

1 Go to the Tone Balance box and select Highlights, then move the Cyan/Red slider towards red and the Yellow/Blue slider towards yellow, attempting to achieve a fleshy pink colour. Click OK.

2 Call up the Color Balance again. This time select Midtones and move the Cyan/Red slider towards cyan and the Yellow/Blue slider towards blue with the aim of achieving a blue/grey. Click OK.

3 Select the shadows, and try to achieve a chestnut brown by once again moving the Cyan/Red slider towards red and the Yellow/Blue slider towards yellow. With a bit of luck, the shadows will turn out a rich chestnut colour.

Creating a dual-toned selenium and gold lith print

This is one of the most beautiful dual-toning processes, which can easily be mimicked digitally. Again using Color Balance, apply the Blue and Cyan sliders to colour the highlights, and the Red and Yellow sliders to create brown in the shadows.

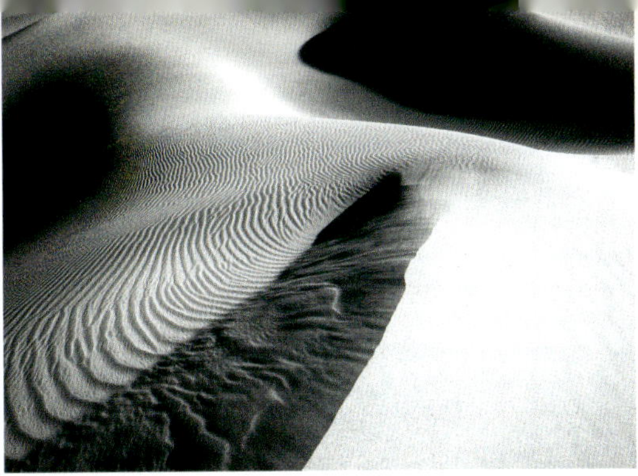

Dunes 1

Scanned from a black-and-white
negative in RGB mode.

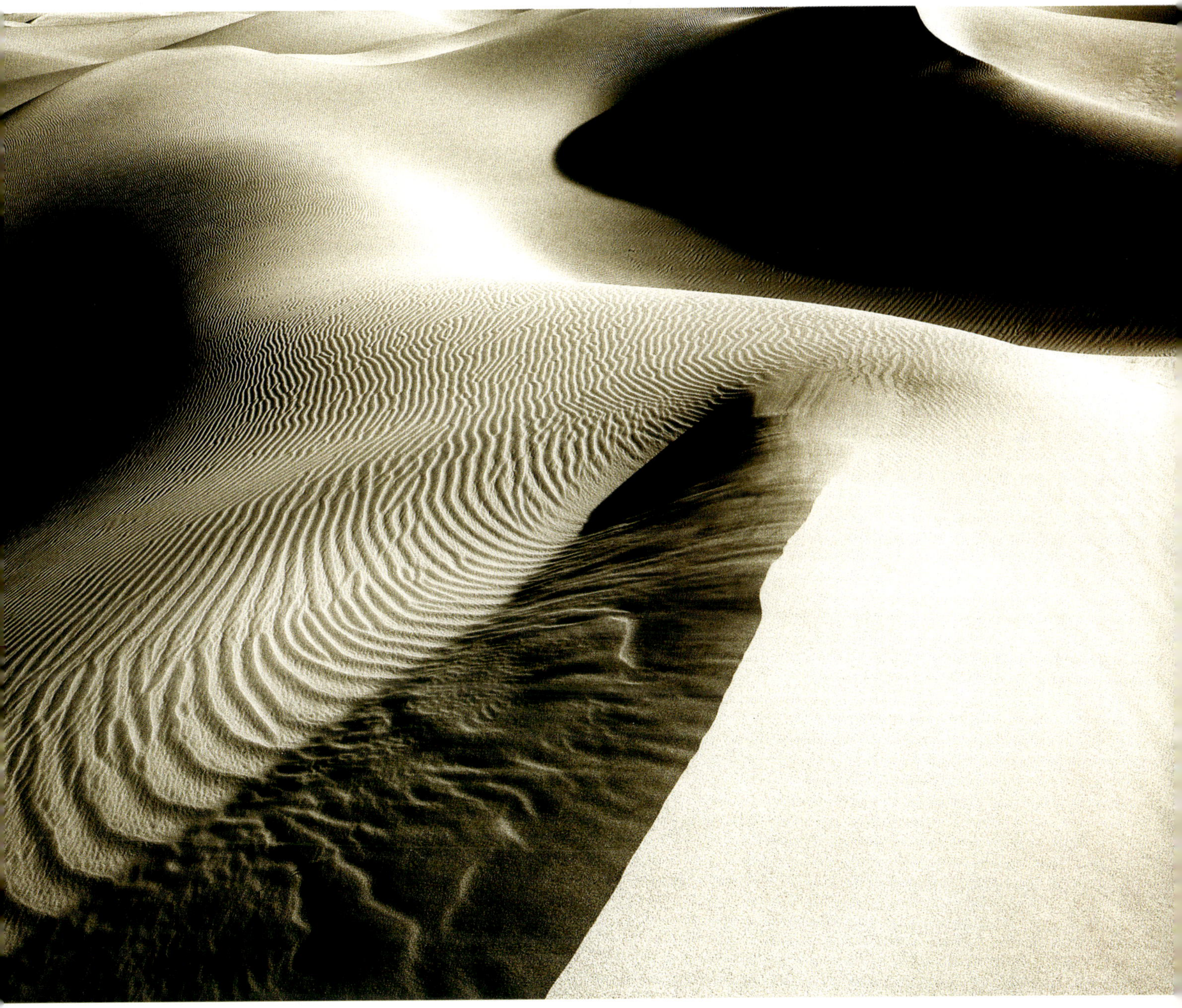

Dunes 2

It is a simple task to create a lith-like print digitally, without having to endure the
staining and pepper fogging that blights so many prints in the darkroom.

10 Polaroid effects

The photographic world has much for which to thank Dr Edwin Land who, in 1948, introduced the first commercially available instant camera, the Polaroid Model 95, which used Type 40 instant film to produce a sepia print in 60 seconds. This heralded what is probably the most exciting and creative era for photographic experimentation by photographers and artists alike.

Nowadays, most people think of Polaroid as a convenient way of producing an instant print without having the bother of time-consuming processing and printing. Commercial photographers routinely use it as a "proofing" material to check composition and exposure. However, a quick look at any Polaroid product guide reveals a vast array of different materials, each with its own unique characteristics. In addition, a number of artistic photographers have found ways to subvert the materials, and some of their creative techniques have become almost standard.

Polaroid edges

Though it is usual to think of the Polaroid print, some materials also produce a negative which can be printed later in the traditional darkroom. One such material is Polaroid Type 55 film, introduced in 1961 and still going strong; it has become hugely popular, especially when the distinctive edges of the negative are included in the printed image to create a type of frame. Of course such Polaroid negatives can also be scanned on a flatbed scanner with a TPU (transparency unit) and printed digitally. From there it is

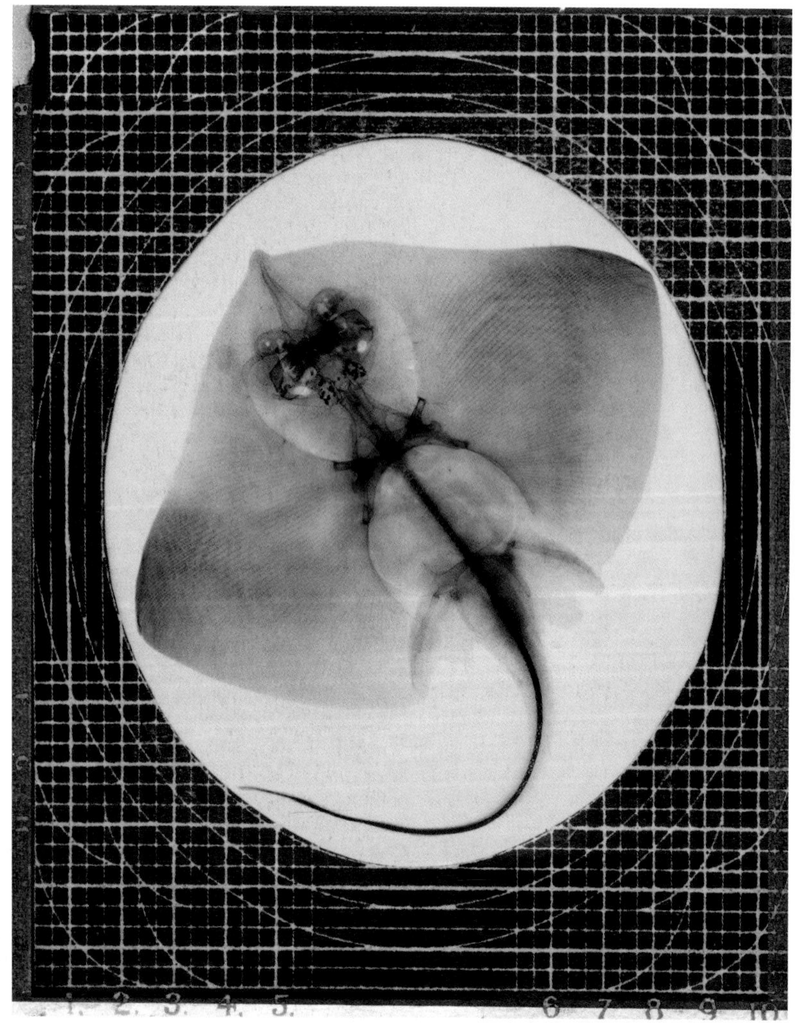

Spotted ray

An X-ray of a spotted ray was combined with a paper mask from an old biological lantern slide. The 'edge' effect was produced by scanning an old Polaroid Type 55 negative and combining it as a separate layer.

Polaroid edges

Type 55 negative scanned at 300 dpi in RGB mode.

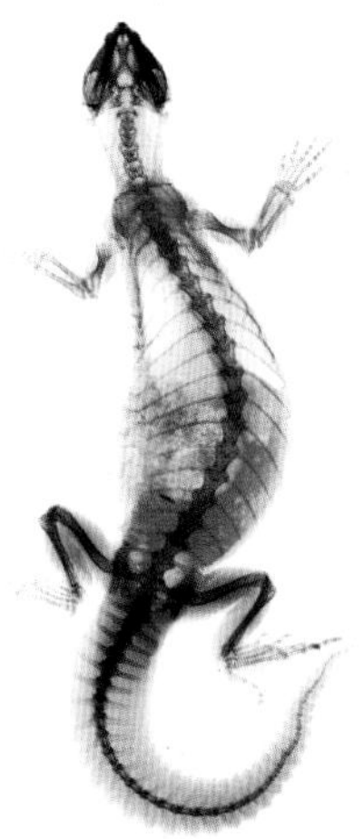

This is a scan of an X-ray of a spiny-tailed lizard, scanned at 300dpi in RGB mode.

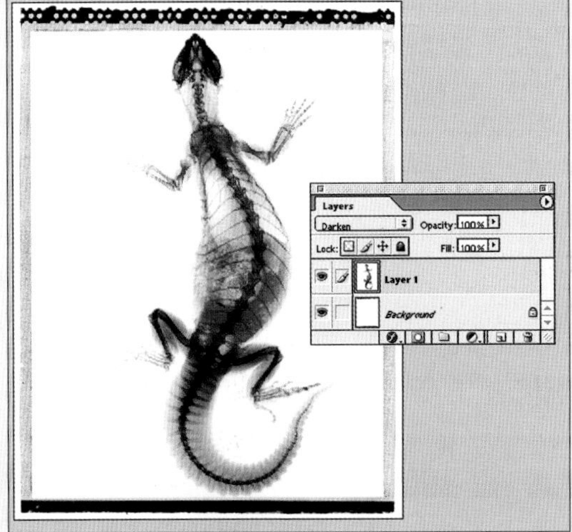

Fig 1
Drag lizard image on to the Polaroid layer and set to Darken mode.

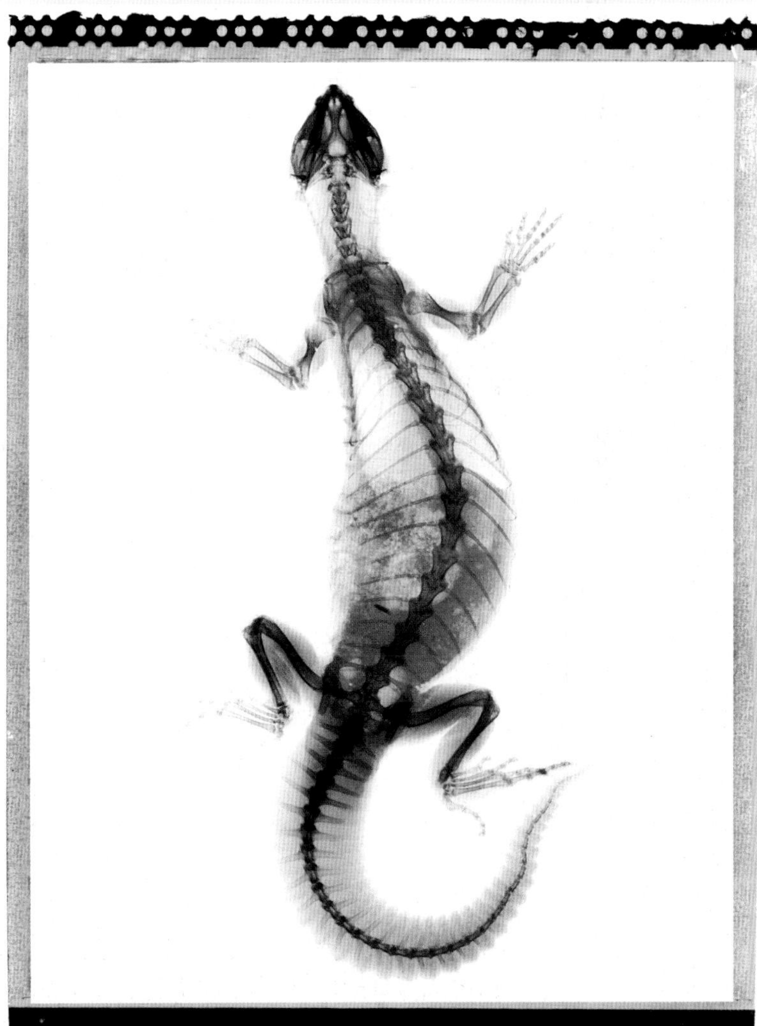

The final image can now be flattened and digitally toned if required.

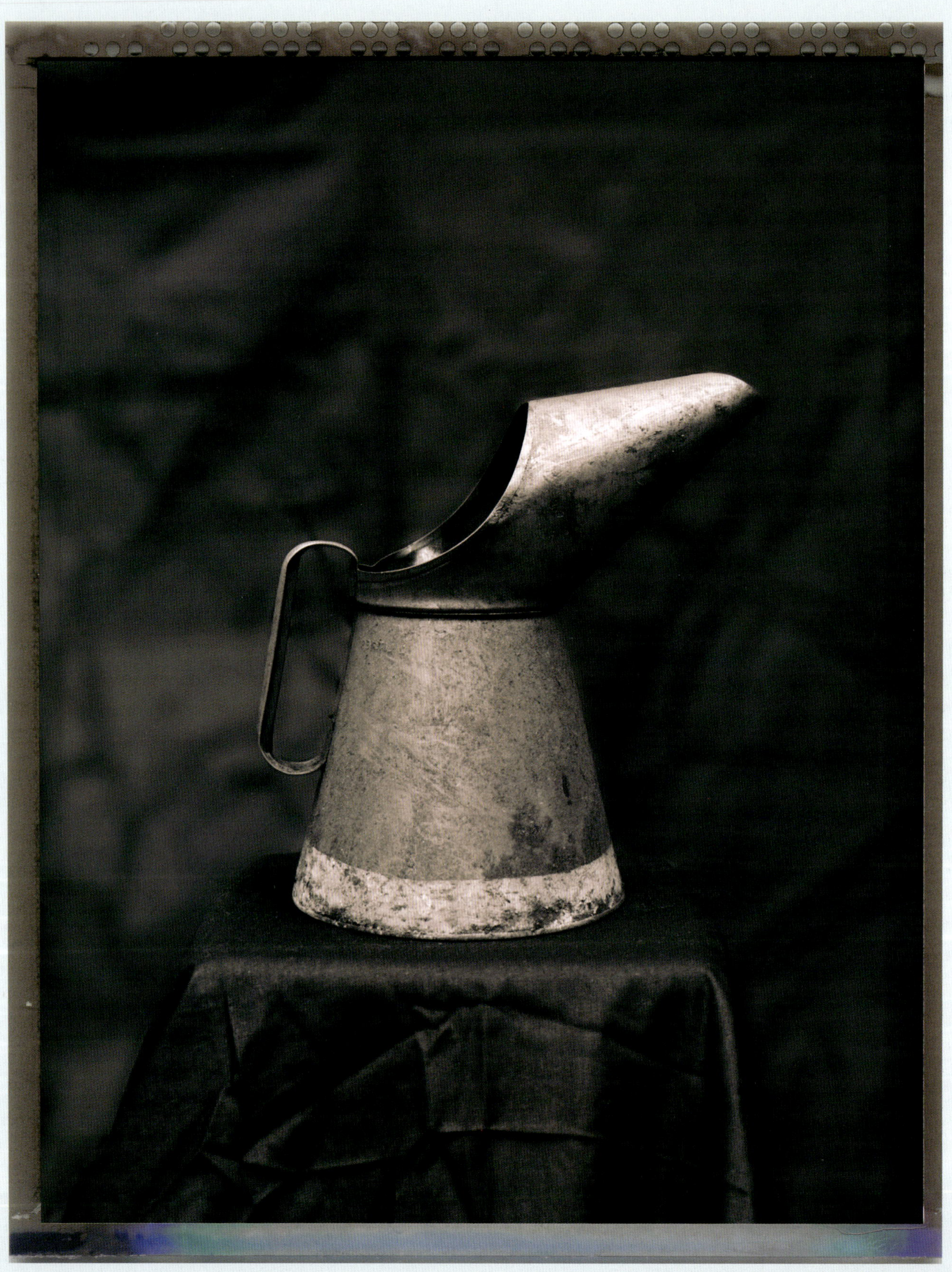

only a small step to take to take the edge from one negative and transplant it onto an image taken on conventional materials, or a digital negative.

1 Make a digital scan of a blank Polaroid Type 55 negative.

2 Select an image from file – the simple example of an oil can was chosen because the edges were obvious.

3 Drag the image on to the Polaroid scan to create a new layer, adjusting the image size if necessary. This image will initially obscure the lower layer containing the Polaroid edge, so use must be made of the Blending modes. The one you choose will depend on the image you select; in this case the background of the image was white, so Darken mode revealed the underlying darker Polaroid edges (see Fig 1). You can experiment with the Blending modes – a quick way to do this is to use the Shift key and the + and – keys to scroll through the options.

Polaroid emulsion lift

This is a technique that works well with Polacolor ER materials such as Types 59, 669

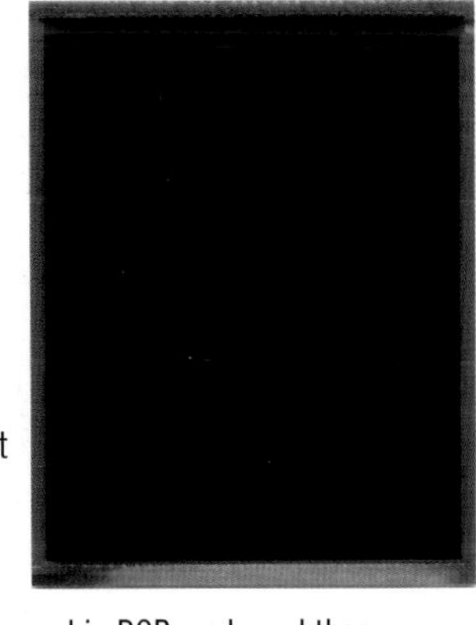

Oil can

A discarded 5x4cm Polaroid negative was scanned on a flatbed, then the picture area was selected and considerably darkened. This was used as the first layer. The oil can was photographed using black-and-white film, scanned in RGB mode and then dual-toned using Color Balance. It was then carefully resized to ensure that it fitted the Polaroid scan. A second layer was created, and then both were merged using the Screen Blending mode.

This was the result of scanning various pieces of a clear plastic rubbish bag, roughly cut and creased (see page 84).

and 809. It is very simple in essence. A colour Polaroid print is soaked in hot water, which releases the image emulsion from its backing. The loose emulsion can then be transferred to another surface. This is usually easier to achieve while the emulsion is still underwater, and the flexible image can be manipulated, stretched or creased. Creases and folds in the emulsion give it a unique appearance.

To simulate an emulsion lift, some creased cellophane or plastic can be scanned on a flatbed scanner.

Creating distortions

Because an original Polaroid emulsion lift is inevitably distorted by the folding and creasing of the emulsion, it is a good idea to apply slight distortions to the image you are going to use – this can make the deception more believable. In fact, it can be a good idea to specifically create creases and tears in the original scans that will harmonize with the image.

Creating distortions and blending images

The original image of hands
and feet, taken with a Nikon
Coolpix digital camera, was
cleaned up and adjusted
for levels and contrast,
and then desaturated.

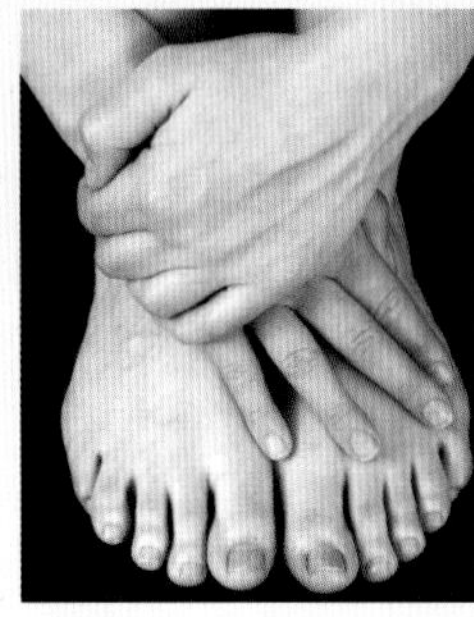

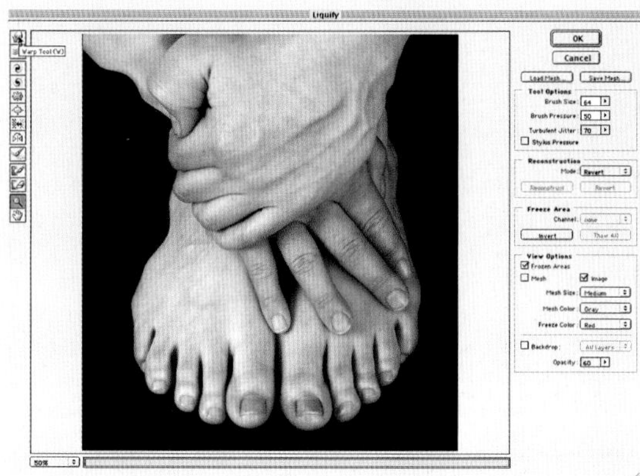

Fig 2

The Liquefy palette, showing
the many options available.
In this instance, only the
Warp tool will be used.

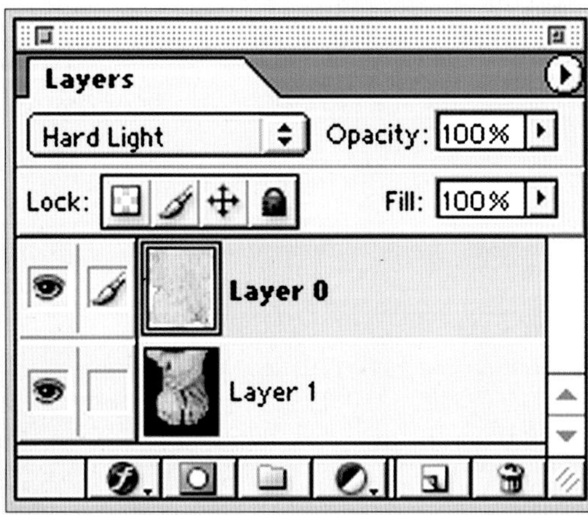

Fig 3

A scan of a plastic bag was merged with the image using
Hard Light Blending mode

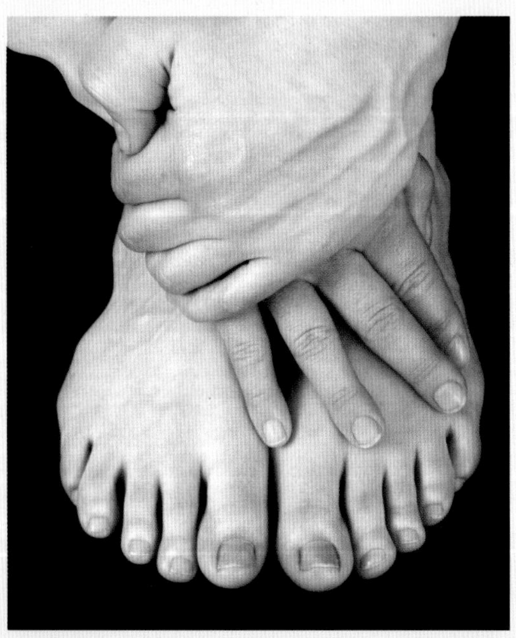

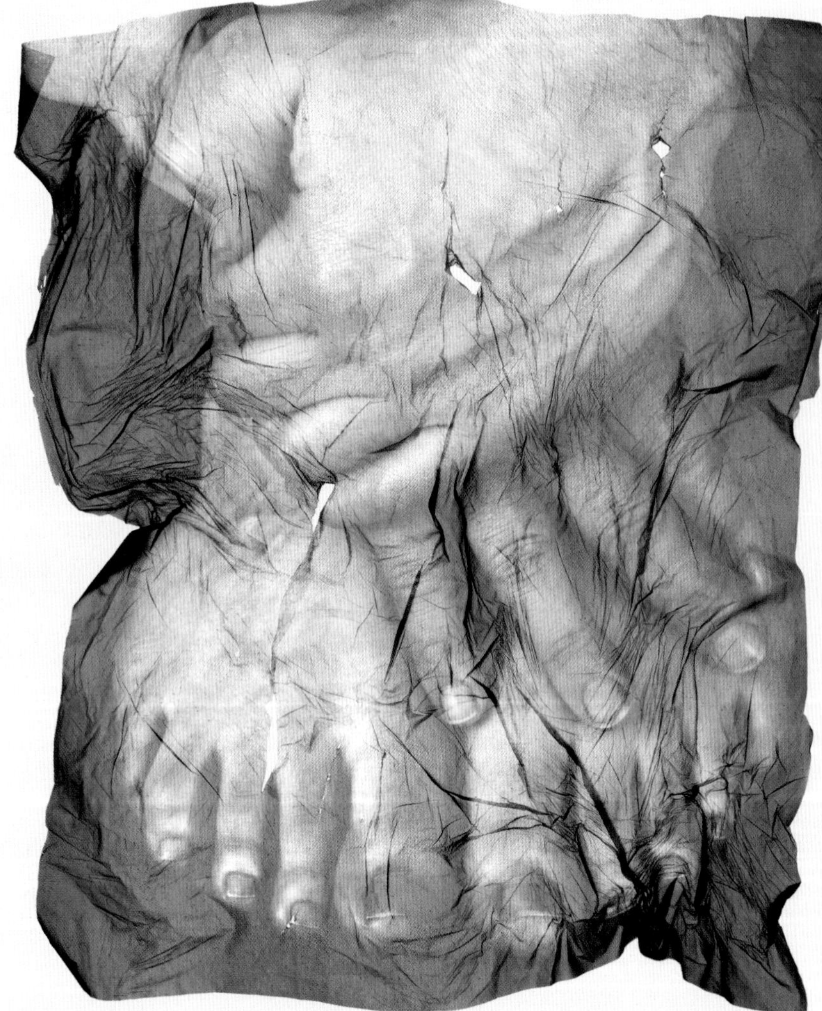

The original image distorted using the
Liquefy filter. Care was taken to match the
distortions with the creases in the original
"Polaroid emulsion lift" scan.

After the image had been blended, it
was flattened. In this case, a slightly
warm colour was added using
Color Balance.

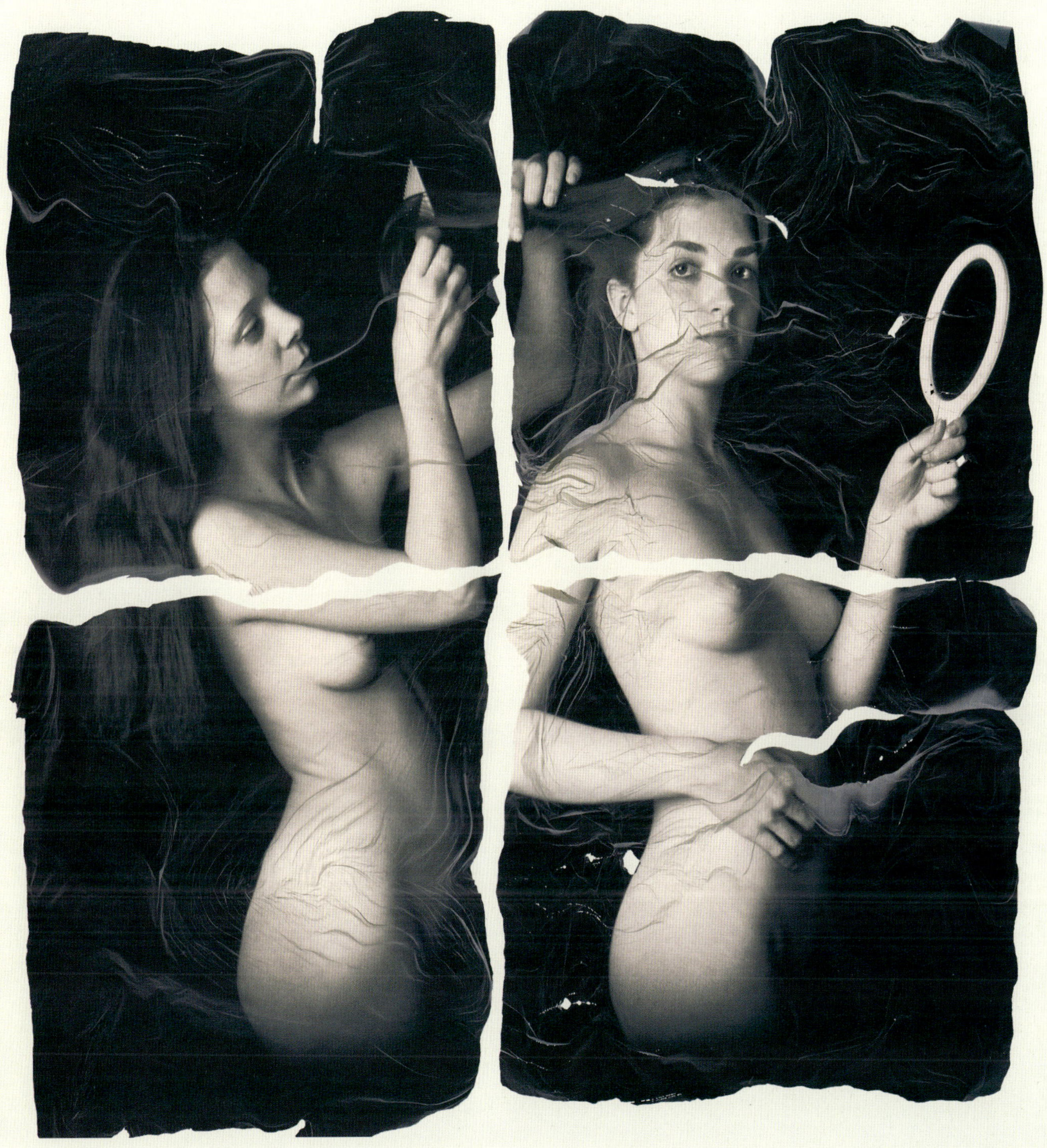

Here, four scans of "emulsion lift" have been used to create a joiner effect (see page 118). The original image was taken on a Mamiya RB 67 camera on Ilford FP4. The 6x7cm negative was then scanned on an Epson flatbed scanner using the TPU. The scans of the "emulsion lifts" were then blended with the image of the models using Lighten mode, and the image was toned using the Red Channel in Curves.

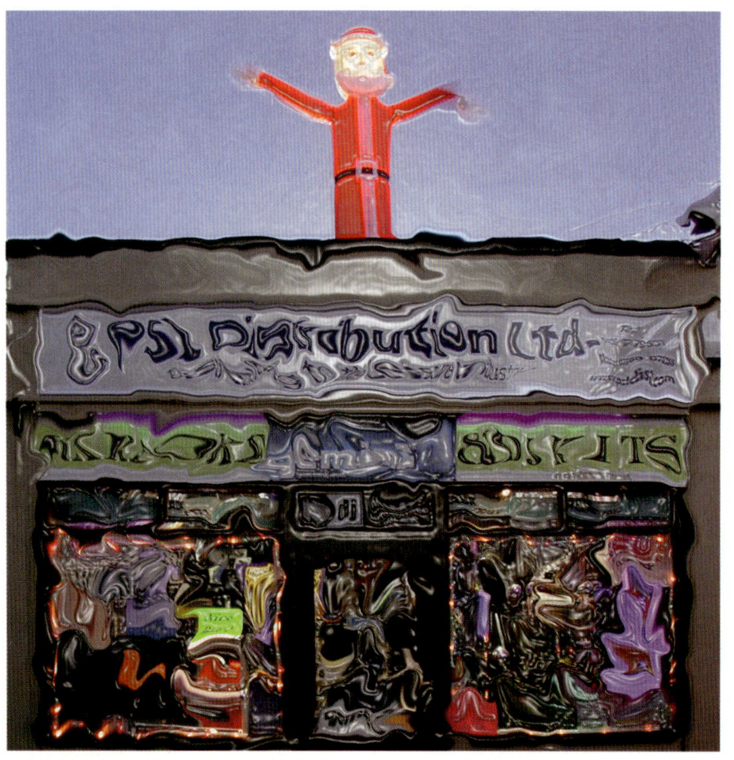

Father Christmas

A night-time shot of a shop display has been converted to an emulsion manipulation effect, as described on page 87.

To create distortions, the Liquefy filter is an ideal option. When opening the Liquefy option – Filter > Liquefy – a large palette appears. The toolbar on the left contains many options for manipulating the image by moving pixels around – it is as though the image has become molten and can be moulded. The first tool, the Warp tool, is probably the most useful in this instance. By choosing an appropriate Brush size, parts of the image can be "pushed" around, but don't overdo this, as the effect needs to be quite subtle. If you do go too far, there is a very handy Reconstruct tool, which can be used to magically restore the image to normal.

Blending the image

Once the image has been distorted, the "emulsion lift" image is moved onto it to create a new layer, and the Blending modes can then be investigated. In this case, Hard Light Blending mode gave the best result (see page 84).

SX 70 emulsion manipulation

SX 70 Polaroid film is a truly unique medium, long in favour with fine artists since its introduction in the 1970s. The tiny images produced lend themselves to various forms of manipulation from scratching and drawing on the final SX 70 print to a rather unusual manipulation of the emulsion layer. Unlike later Polaroid films, the emulsion of an SX 70 film can be moved around by applying pressure with a blunt instrument whilst the film is still developing. This is very similar to using the Liquefy tool as described above, and it will come as no surprise that this tool is a simple way to create the effect of an SX 70 emulsion manipulation.

The overall appearance of an SX 70 manipulation is unique and has a rather "plastic" quality. This can be emulated by first applying the Plastic Wrap filter. The settings of the filter will depend upon the file size of your image – as original SX 70 prints are small, your file size can also be small.

Polaroid transfer

A creative technique that has been employed by contemporary artists and photographers alike is the use of Polaroid transfers. This involves transferring a developing Polaroid image to fine art paper or other substrate. Normally, a Polaroid image is developed to finality before a print is pulled. But if the Polaroid is pulled apart about 10sec into development, it can then be pressed or

Emulsion manipulation

An original colour image taken with a Fuji S2 Pro camera.

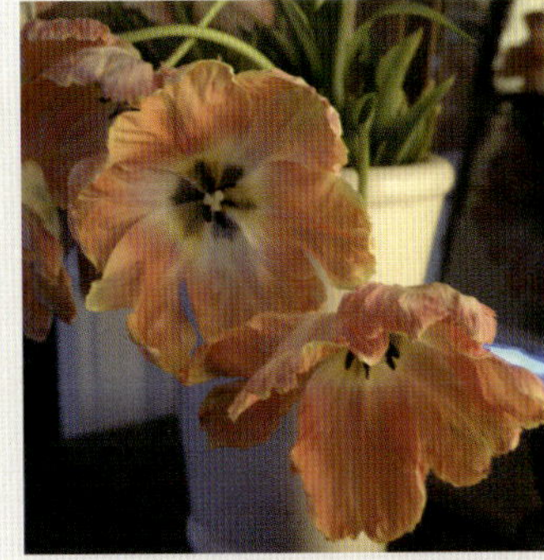

The effect of the Plastic Wrap filter is now visible.

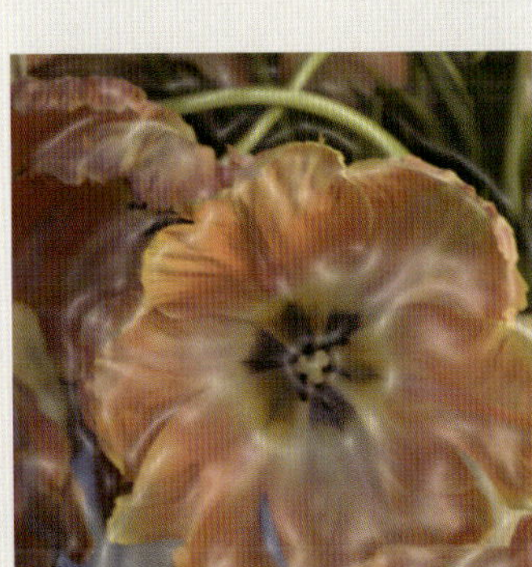

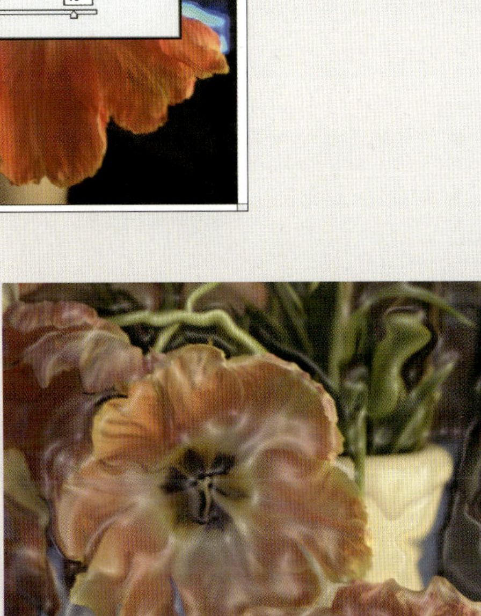

Fig 4

With a small image like this, the Plastic Wrap filter was set at Highlight Strength 7, Detail 5, and Smoothness 13.

The image "emulsion" was manipulated using the Warp tool in the Liquefy filter.

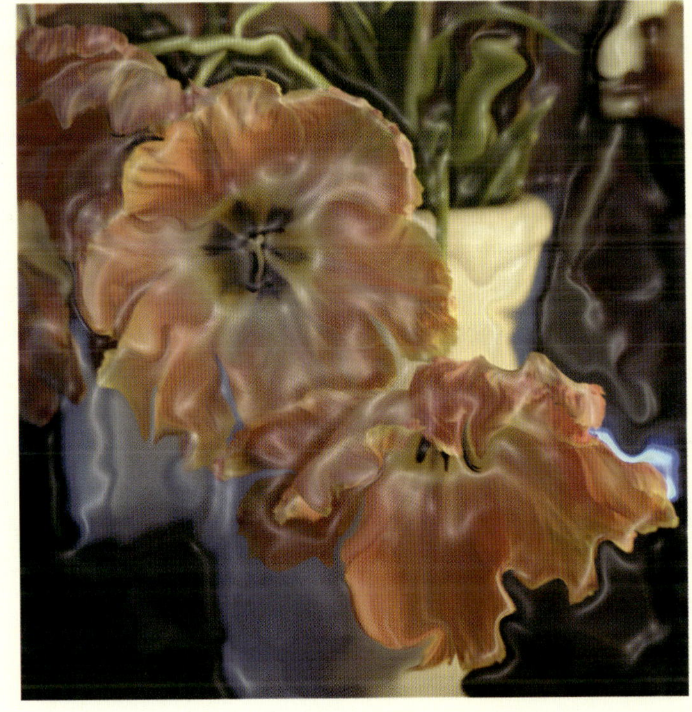

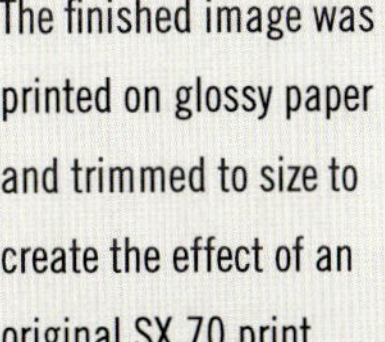

The finished image was printed on glossy paper and trimmed to size to create the effect of an original SX 70 print.

Polaroid transfer effects

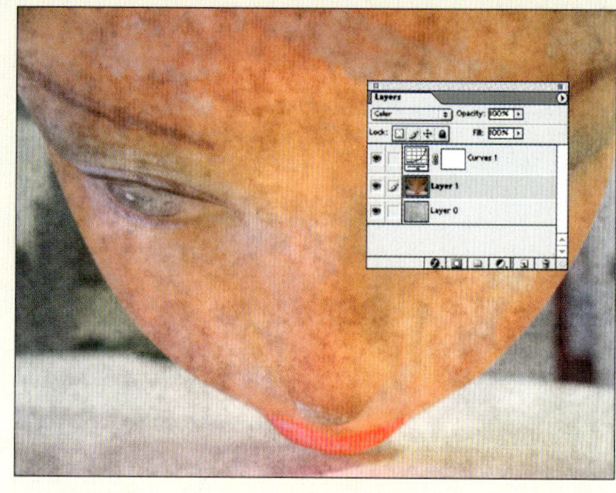

Fig 6

The original image was taken on a Pentax Optio camera. The image is then dragged on to the paper shown in Fig 5 as a second layer, and Color blending mode is selected to brings the underlying texture through. Now the Opacity of the image layer is reduced to about 50–60%, which slightly softens the colours. If the background layer is smaller than the image, the edges of the image effectively stop at the edge of the background painting, adding to the "hand-produced" effect. To make the final product as effective as possible, it is best to print on one of the many fine art papers on the market, such as PermaJet Portrait paper, which is 100% cotton rag. Remember also that this is in effect a contact-printing process, so selecting an image size that relates to normal Polaroid film will add extra authenticity.

Fig 5

Background paper with a layer of watercolour paint.

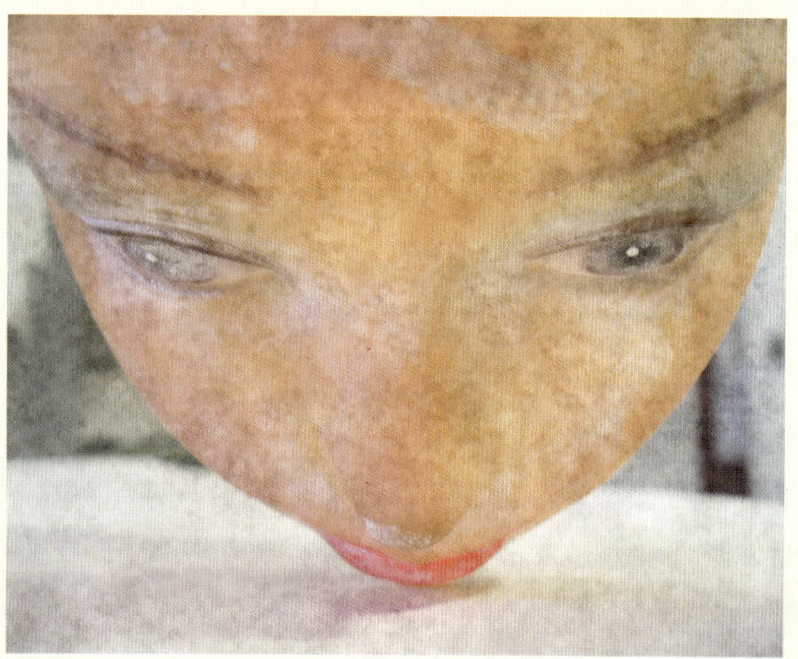

Mask

rollered onto another surface. The image will then continue to migrate to this surface – hence Polaroid transfer. The resulting image is usually softer and more muted in colour than a normal Polaroid, and the surface qualities and texture of the receiving surface become part of the final image.

A similar effect can easily be achieved digitally. The technique involves blending an image with a suitable background. One way is to use a fine art textured paper, which has been coated very thinly with watercolour paint to form the background (see Figs 5 and 6).

Other effects

Whenever a Polaroid transfer is accomplished, the original receptor sheet is usually thrown away. However, some of the image starts to transfer before the initial separation has taken place, resulting in a faint orange/red image. With some subjects this can be interesting in itself (see Figs 8 and 9).

Rather than painting a background layer onto fine art paper, I went back to one of my original image transfers. This was scanned on a flatbed scanner, but the central image was cloned out to produce a blank canvas. Using this technique retains some of the unique edge effects.

This digital image was taken at a fish market in Cornwall.

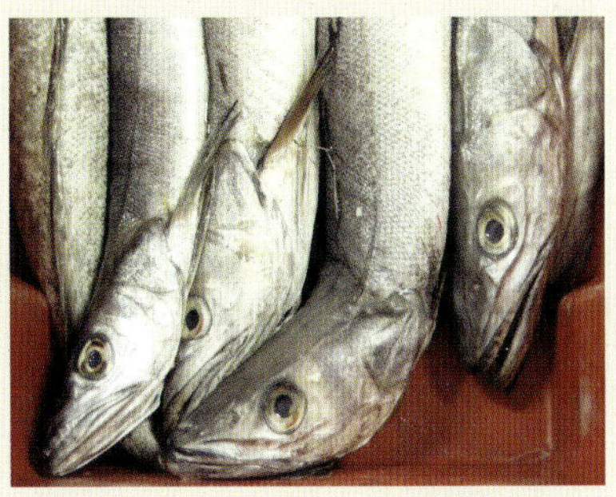

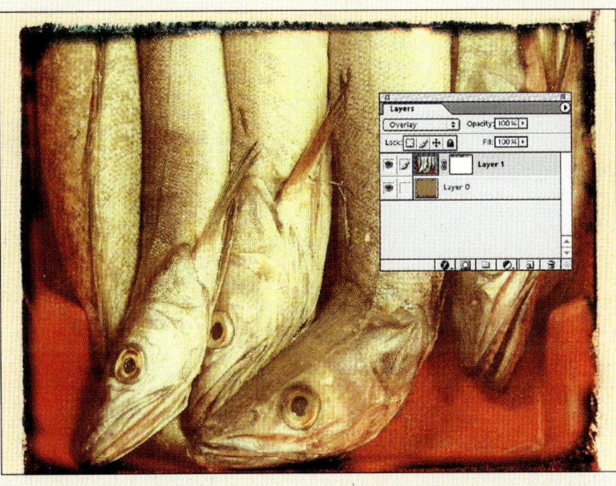

Fig 7

The fish image was blended with the Transfer Mask using Overlay mode. Any areas that did not blend satisfactorily were removed using a Layer Mask.

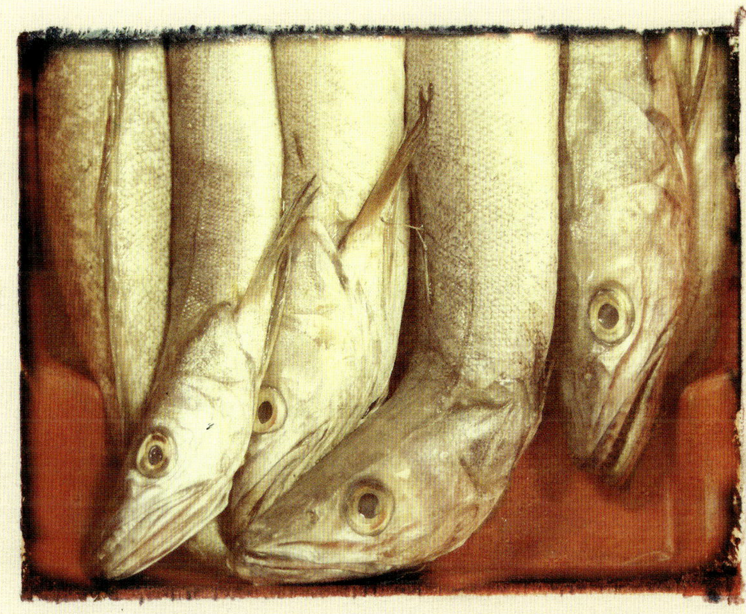

The final image was printed on a fine art paper.

Fig 8

To mimic this result, the image content from a previously discarded Polaroid receptor sheet was cloned out, leaving only the base colour.

Fig 9

A desaturated original image was added to the layer stack in Lighten Blending mode.

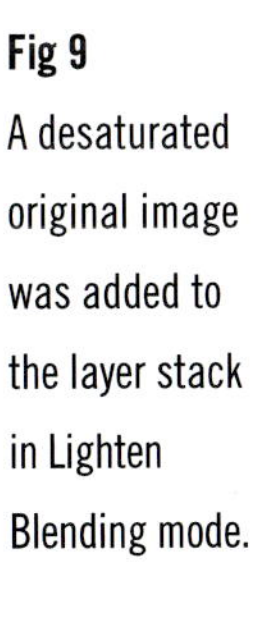

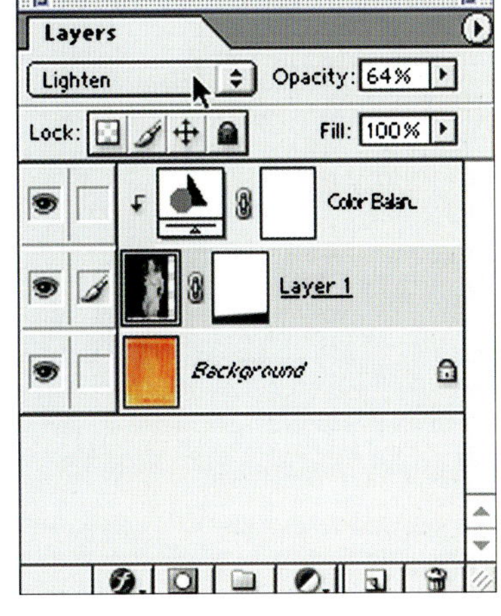

The original image was taken on a Fuji S2 Pro camera. The image was desaturated and slightly masked at the base before being blended with a prepared "receptor sheet".

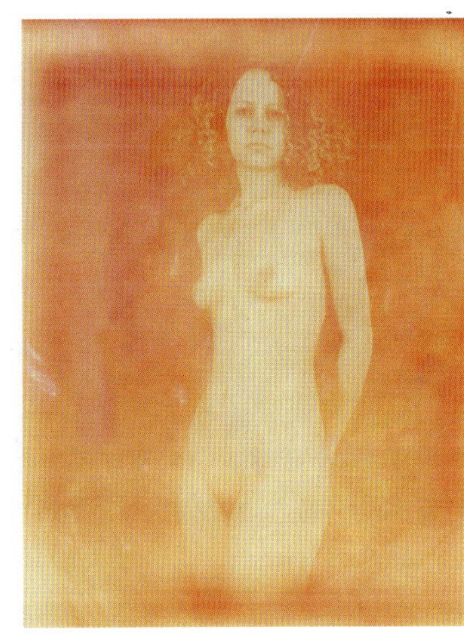

The colour was then slightly modified using a Color Balance Adjustment Layer.

11 Alternative processes

Anyone who has worked with historical printing processes appreciates the satisfaction in creating an image produced from simple raw materials: from the selection of paper, to the mixing and coating of sensitizers, the production of large-format negatives, the nuances of daylight exposures and finally the toning with precious metals.

HOWEVER, THIS TAKES specialist equipment and raw materials, a great deal of time and an acceptance that failure rates may be significantly high. Fortunately, very similar results can be created digitally without any specialist equipment or chemicals, and with an extremely high success rate.

Processes such as Cyanotype, salt, carbon and gum bichromate are unique and have their own special qualities. They should not be

Creating a Cyanotype effect

Fig 1

Many masks can be created to give variety within a body of work. Brush black watercolour paint onto art paper to the rough size of the image. Don't make the paint too dense, and only coat once in one direction, leaving any brushmarks to show. (This can easily be modified later using Edit > Transform > Scale). When the paint is dry, scan with a flatbed scanner and save.

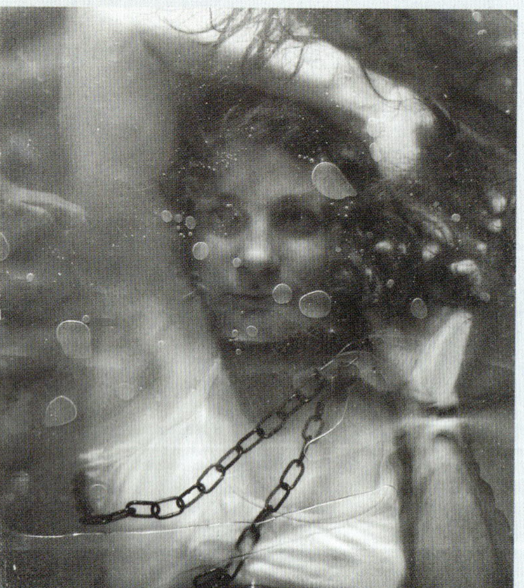

Fig 2

To create a hand-coated look, select an appropriate image and convert to greyscale. Open up the previous scan of the painted paper and drag it onto the image to create a second layer. Initially it will obscure the image, but go to the Blending modes and select Screen or Lighten. Adjust the size of the image as appropriate using Edit > Transform > Scale. Now flatten the image and convert to RGB (Image > Mode > RGB) to allow colour to be added.

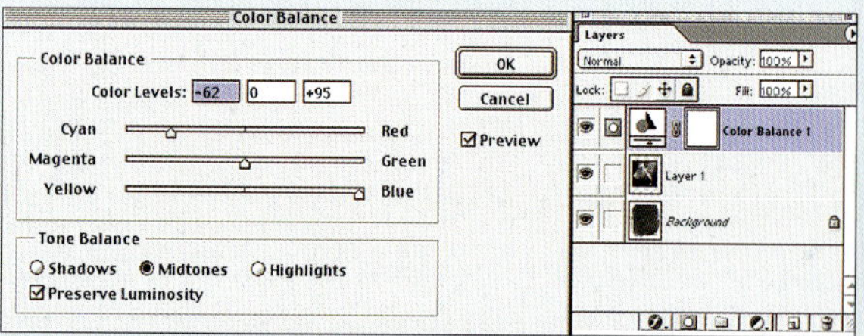

Fig 3

Depending upon your printer/paper/ink combination, applying colour may need a little experimentation. Create a Color Balance Adjustment Layer and set the mid-tones to 62 Cyan and 95 Blue as a starting point.

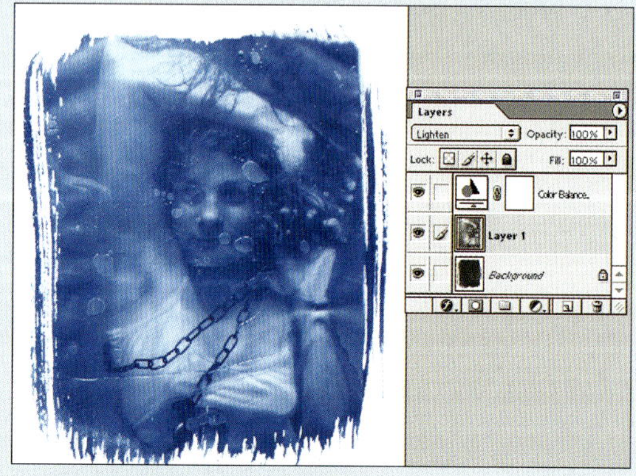

Fig 4

Try a test print and if this is satisfactory, drag the Adjustment Layer onto any other desaturated image to apply the same colouration. The action can be saved as an Action or Droplet for future use.

compared to a black-and-white fibre print any more than a digital print. However, a digital print using carbon pigments on a 100% cotton rag paper comes close to that produced by platinum or carbon printing processes. Many darkroom workers have moved towards digital printing because of the wonderful range of art papers and the physical feel of the printing process, both of which have many similarities to some of the traditional alternative processes.

Cyanotype

The Cyanotype or blue print process was invented by Sir John Herschel and was used by Anna Atkins to produce a series of photograms of plants as early as 1843. It has survived to the present day and is still used by many contemporary artists such as Betty Hahn and Bobbi Carey.

Creating a digital Cyanotype involves a little more than just toning the image blue – a traditional Cyanotype is produced by coating the paper with a mixture of iron salts, using a brush or other applicator. The salts sink in to the fibres of the paper, so the resulting image may show evidence of both uneven coating and the paper surface, and the artefacts thus produced can be aesthetically pleasing.

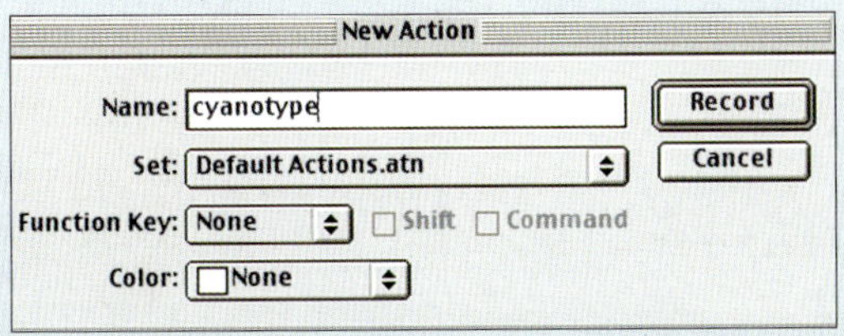

Fig 5

Open the Actions palette (Window > Actions), click on the upper right arrow and select New Action. Name it "Cyanotype" and click on Record. Now go to Color Balance and enter the Cyan and Blue adjustments and click OK. Click on the Stop button at the bottom of the Actions palette. Now any image can have the same adjustment simply by opening it and clicking on the Cyanotype option and pressing the Play button

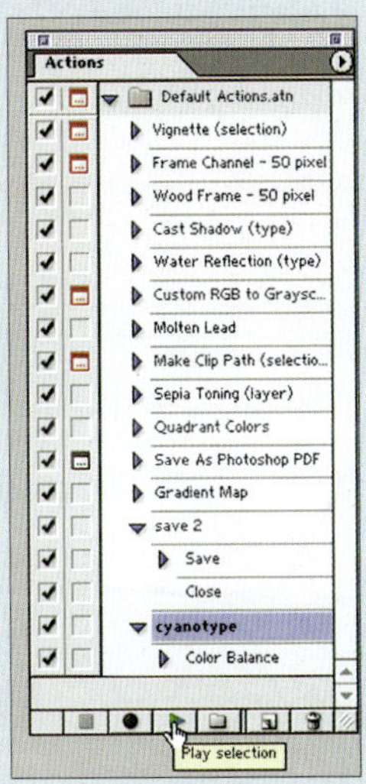

Fig 6: How to save an Action

Once you are satisfied with a colour, you can save the process using the Actions Palette. This is very useful for repeated processes.

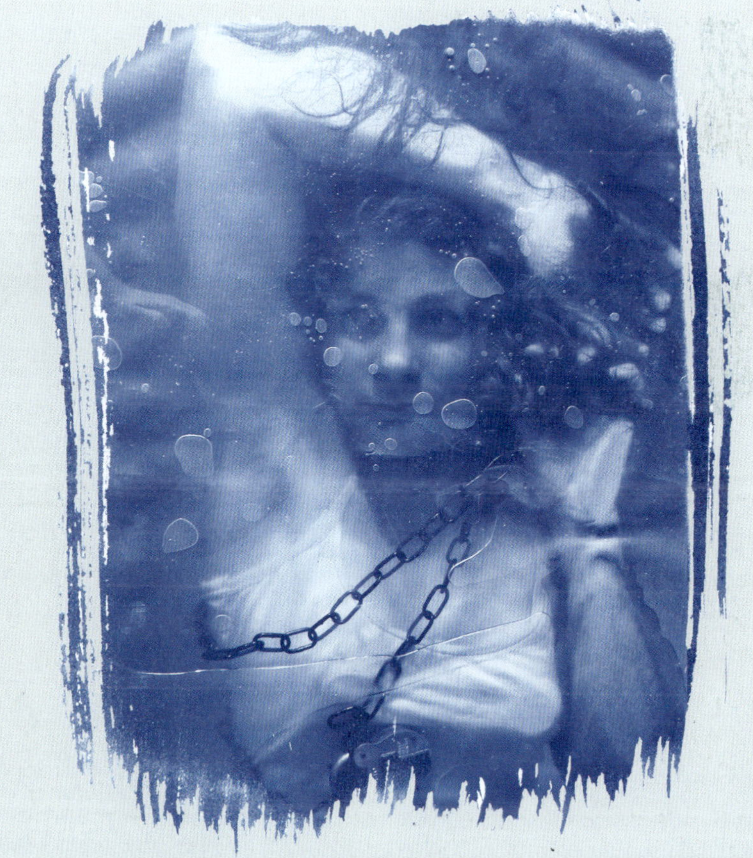

This image was created by photographing the model in a studio with a Fuji S2 Pro camera. She was lying on a thick perspex sheet that had water trapped between two polythene sheets sandwiched under her. This gave the effect of being underwater. The original colour image was then desaturated and given the digital Cyanotype treatment.

Chair

This scene was photographed on conventional black-and white 120 film. I wanted to retain the film feel and produce a rather more graphic result, so I created a blue base layer in the computer and blended the image with it, without introducing edge and brushmark effects.

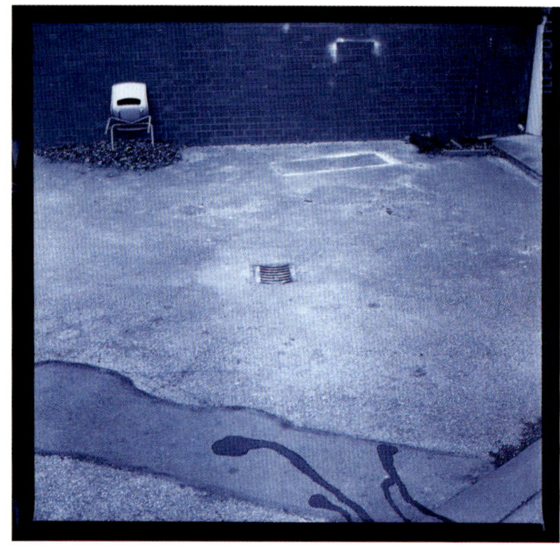

Printing

There are many digital art papers on the market that are ideal for printing convincing-looking Cyanotypes. The advantage of using custom-made digital papers is that the image does not "bleed".

You can experiment with other non-coated papers, but be prepared both for slight bleeding of the inks and a loss in contrast. In the past, Cyanotypes have been created on a variety of surfaces – fabric, stone, wood and so on. Some modern printers can now accept unusual surfaces such as metal and plastics. There are also a number of products that allow digital images to be transferred to fabrics.

Introducing colour

The Cyanotype has not always been used in isolation – Edward Steichen printed Cyanotypes over platinum prints, and contemporary workers such as Betty Hahn use hand-coloured cyanotypes and other mixed-media sources. Once a digital Cyanotype has been produced it can, of course, be worked on with more traditional

How to introduce colour

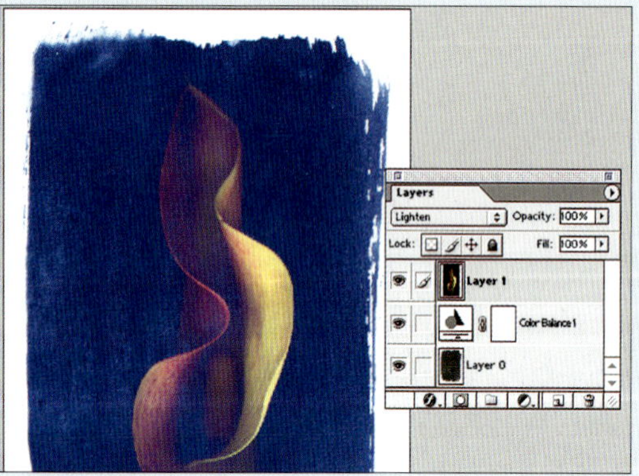

Fig 7

To introduce colour to the digital Cyanotype, the image of the flower was retained in its original colour and included above the Color Balance Adjustment Layer. As the lily was photographed against a black background, the Lighten Blending mode was used to merge the image.

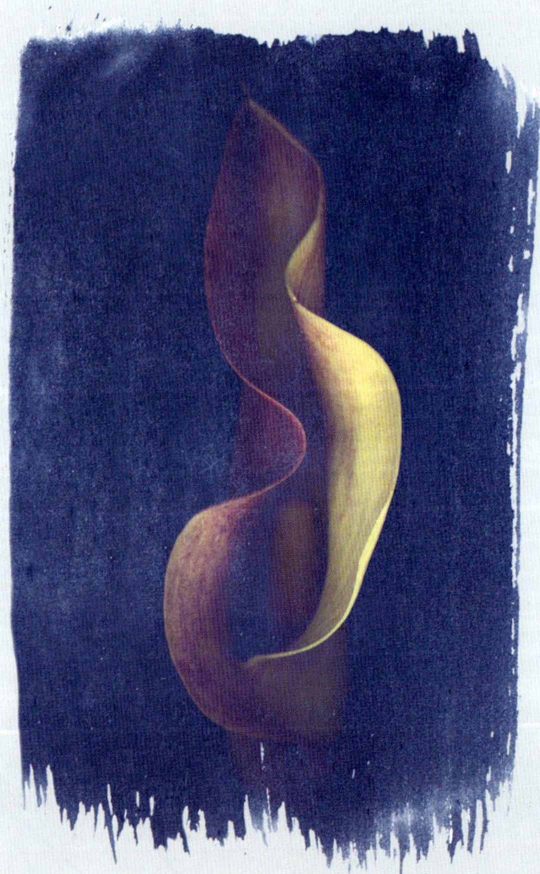

The lily was scanned on a flatbed at 300dpi with the lid left up. This created a black background, which was made to disappear in the final image by using the Lighten Blending mode.

media, or alternatively colour can be introduced by digital paint techniques (see Fig 7).

Tea-stained Cyanotype

A popular method of "toning" Cyanotypes is to soak them in strong tea. The tannins stain the lighter areas brown, giving a subtle, bronzed look to the prints. Much trial and error is required as to strength of tea, temperature and time left to soak, and a digital version can dispense with the uncertainty factor (see Fig 8).

Salt prints

Silver salts have formed the basis of photographic emulsions from the early experiments of Wedgwood right through to the present day. The images of Henry Fox Talbot and his contemporaries were mainly printed on "salted paper". Common salt and silver nitrate were combined to form light-sensitive silver chloride. This was painted onto paper and contact-printed with a negative to produce a photographic print. Depending upon the type of paper, time of exposure, after-toning and fixing processes, the end result was anything from a neutral black to a warm brown colour. As the sensitizer sank into the paper fibres, the image lacked biting clarity, and the texture of the paper surface was easily visible. Without optical brighteners, the highlights took on the colour of the paper base (see Fig 10).

Gum prints

Much loved by pictorialists and art photographers of the early 19th century, gum prints are a crossover between photography and painting, where an image is built up using a number of layers of coloured pigment. Gum

Toning digital Cyanotypes

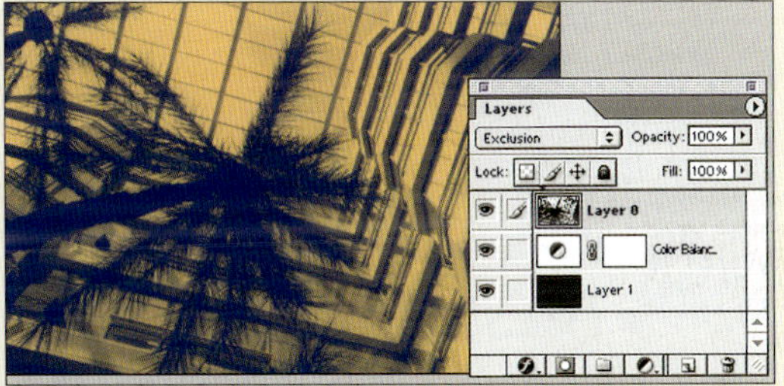

Fig 8

Using the Desaturated Image layer as the top layer of the stack, and Exclusion as the Blending mode can create a very convincing digital version of a tea-stained Cyanotype.

This graphic image of a modern building interior was taken with a Pentax Optio camera pointed to the skylight to produce a relatively contrasty image that contained a reasonable amount of light tone. Used in the Exclusion Blending mode, this combined with the lower blue layer to produce the effect of tea staining.

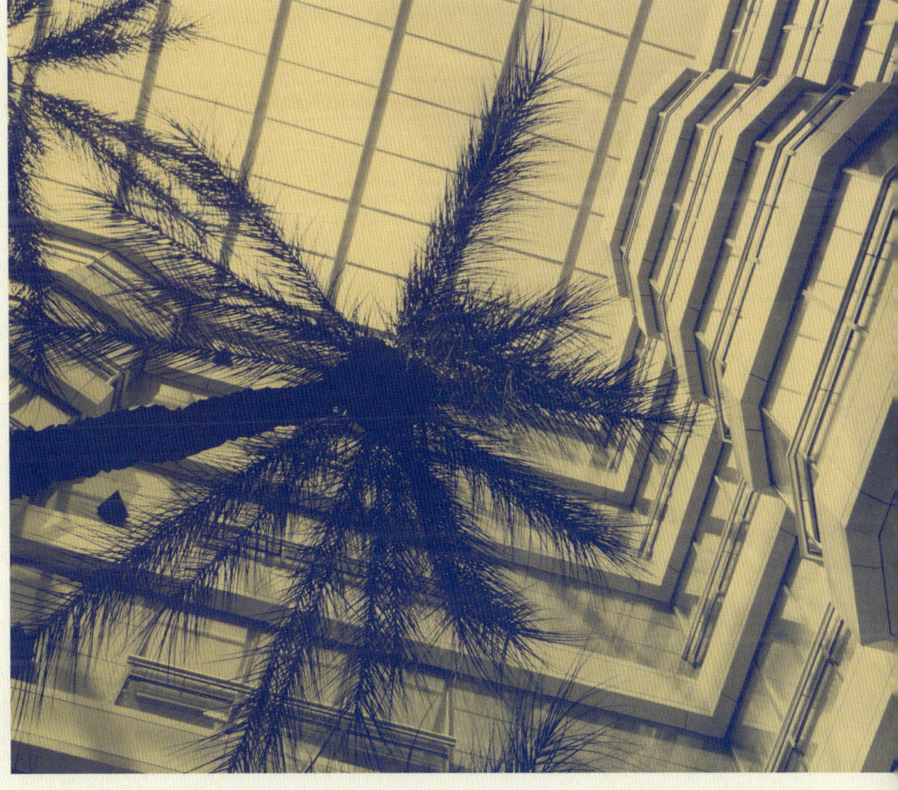

Making a salt print

Fig 9

The first stage of creating a digital salt print is similar to producing a digital Cyanotype. The "hand-

produced" effect of brushing silver nitrate over a previously salted paper, to cover the negative area, can easily be replicated by painting a weak dilution of watercolour paint on a piece of fine art paper, wich is then scanned in RGB and used as the first layer.

Fig 10

Next, import, desaturate and drag an image to form a new layer. Resize the image if necessary using Edit > Transform > Scale, and change the Blending mode to Screen or Overlay, depending upon the effect required; adjusting the opacity of the top layer will allow more or less of the

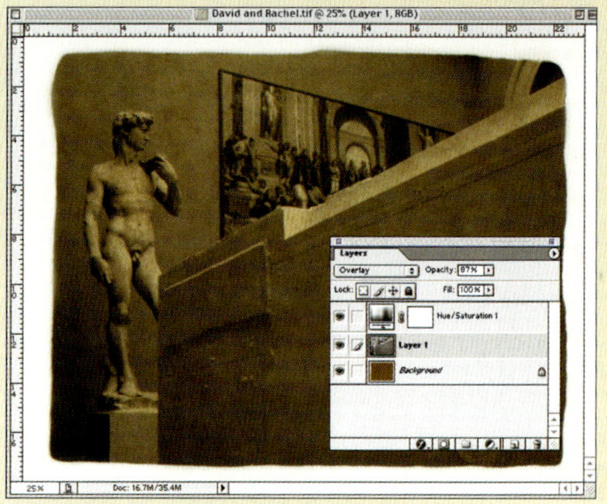

textured paper to show through. Finally, fine-tune the colour using Image > Adjustment > Hue/Saturation. Make sure the Colorize box is checked, and start with a setting of Hue 29, Saturation 18.

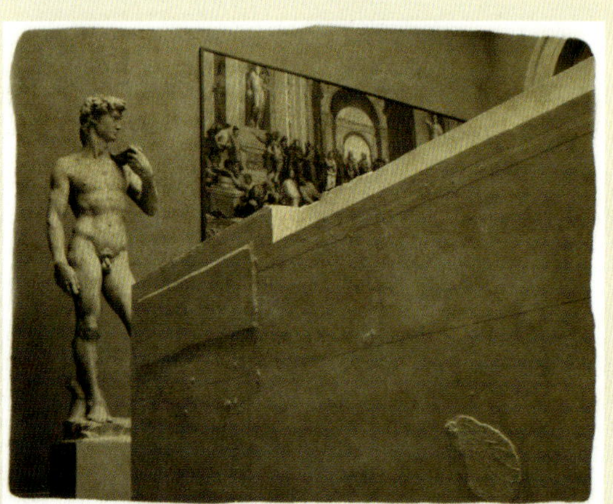

The Cast Room in London's Victoria and Albert Museum juxtaposes Michelangelo's *David* with Rachel Whiteread's cast of Room 101, in which George Orwell worked. The image was taken on a Pentax Optio camera, and the only manipulation was to remove a label from the base of the cast of David. The rough-edged effect was deliberately left in, and the image colour was toned down slightly using a Hue/Saturation Adjustment Layer.

arabic is used as the binding agent and light-sensitive medium, and the process involves the multiple coating, exposure, washing and drying of papers before the final effect is achieved. Negatives need to be accurately registered between each exposure, and the paper must not shrink between washing and drying. Each colour that is laid down affects the underlying layer. Washing or the use of brushes can manipulate the image. It is one of the most complex, time-consuming and frustrating of all the historical processes, but those who persevere can produce beautiful "painterly" effects. One of the features of the gum print is the evidence of handiwork, in particular brushmarks that are used to selectively remove pigment. Study early masters such as Edward Steichen or Robert Demachy to appreciate this technique at its best.

Liquid emulsion effect

One of the easiest alternative printing processes to emulate is the liquid emulsion effect. It has become quite fashionable over recent years to paint liquid emulsion directly onto watercolour paper, which then reveals the tell-tale brushmarks when processed. This

Gum prints

Venetian facade

Taken from a black-and-white negative, scanned in RGB mode.

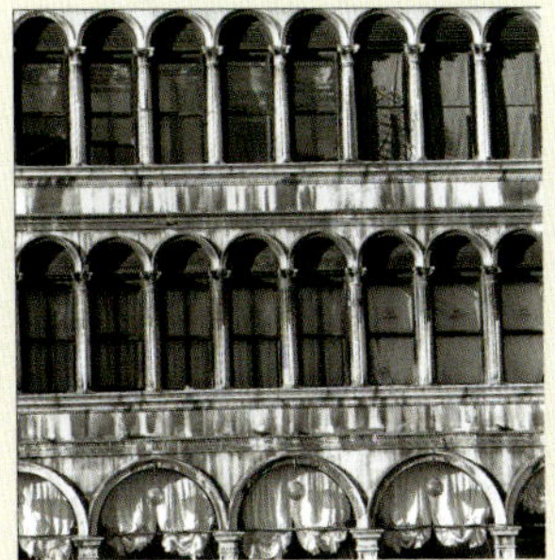

The brushstroke image was scanned and made into the background layer, then the façade was selected and imported over the background to create the second layer. The two layers were merged and coloured using Color Balance.

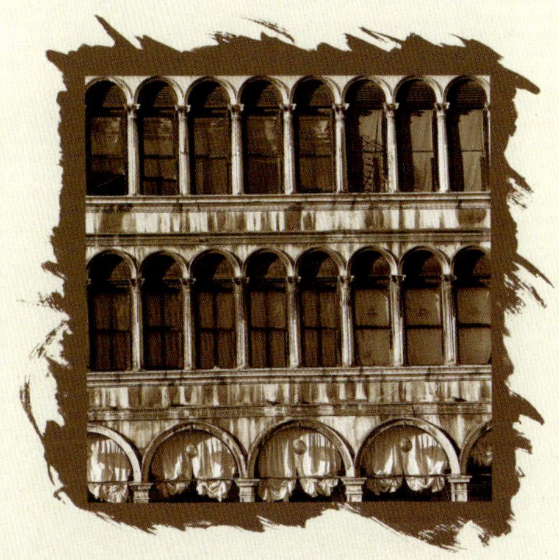

When aiming to mimic any process, it is important to understand it and then to apply a digital process that closely replicates it. A gum bichromate is produced by applying a successive sequence of colours onto the same piece of watercolour paper, resulting in the telltale brushmarks on the edges. To achieve this digitally, I created two separate layers comprising the façade image and a separate brushstroke image. Each was coloured separately using Color Balance. These two layers were then stacked, and by using the Opacity control I was able to carefully move one layer over the other in order to achieve perfect registration. In this way I was also able to secure the best balance between the two coloured layers. The final image was then printed onto a heavy-duty art paper.

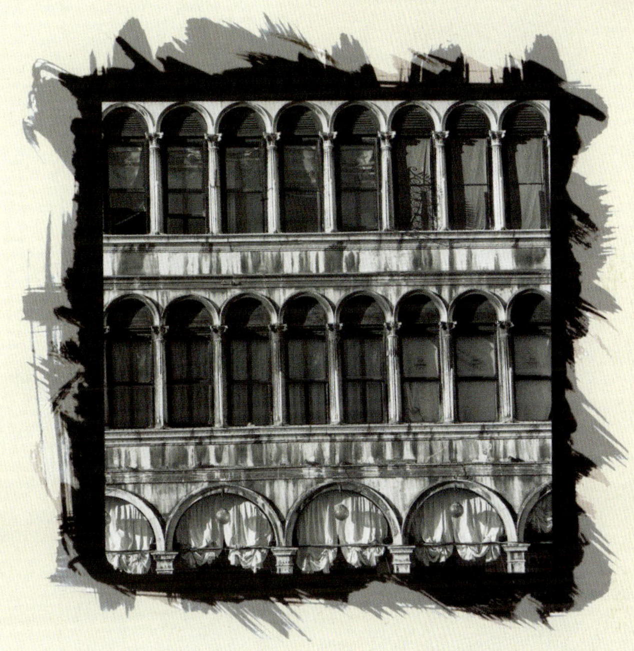

effect can easily be mimicked digitally, particularly if the results are printed on an art paper such as Perma Jet Museum Classic.

Digital negatives for alternative processes

Alternative printing processes such as platinum/palladium, salt, Cyanotype and Kallitype, are contact-printing processes that require a negative the same size as the required print. In addition, each process requires a slightly different negative in terms of contrast and tonality to produce the optimum results. The traditional way to achieve this is to use a large-format camera and to process each sheet of film specifically for the method being used – however, this allows very little manipulation of the original image.

With digital technology, a contact negative can be created in a variety of ways, and can lead on to experimentation with combined images and the contrast and tonality of the negative. It also means that any size of negative or digital file can be used. The main problem is reproducing a negative, which acts in the same way as a silver-based sheet of film. One solution – to print on transparency film material using black ink only – has posed

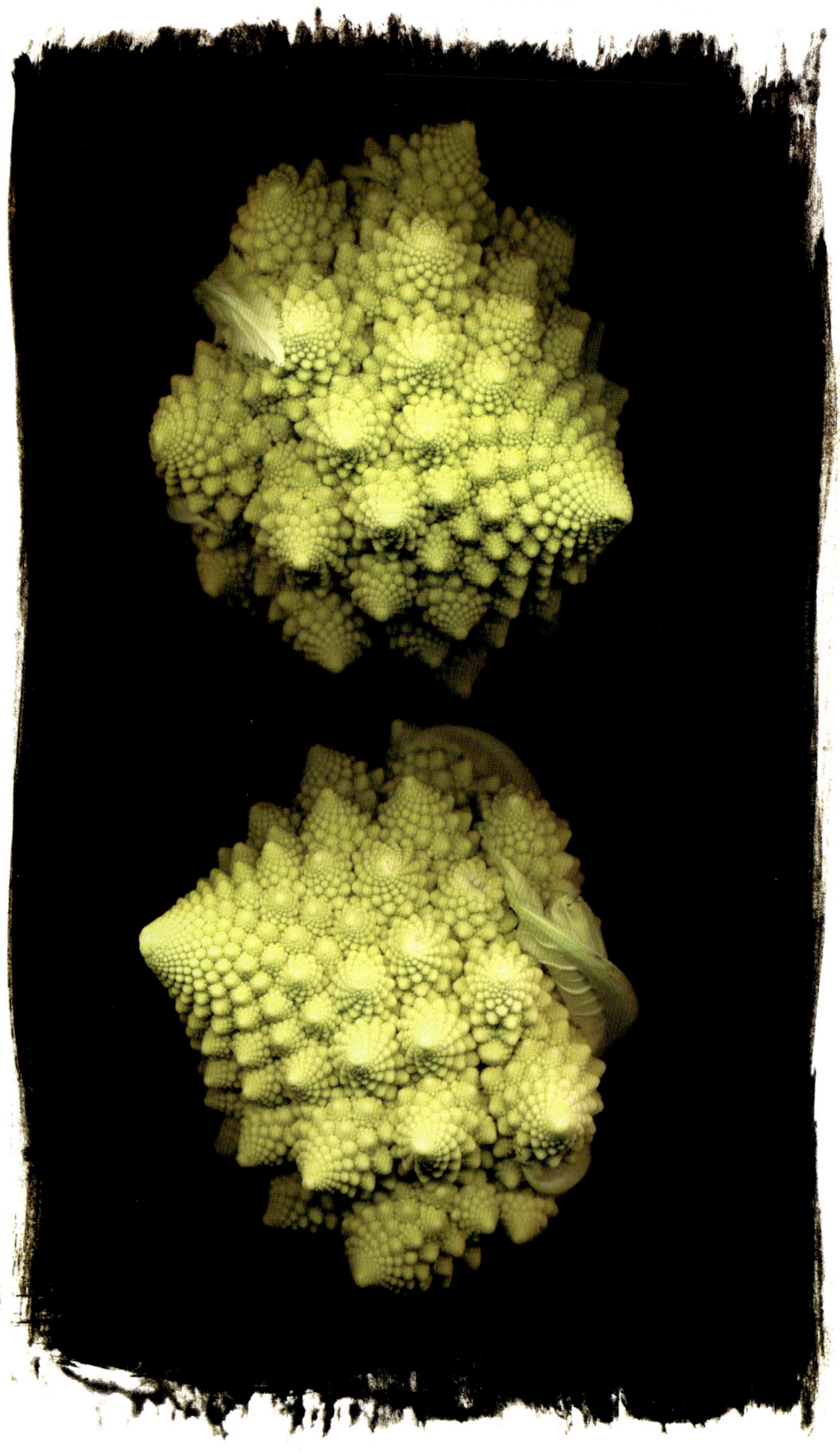

However, materials have improved greatly over the past few years, and Pictorico OHP digital negative film produces excellent results from most inkjet printers. Available in 215 x 280mm (8$\frac{1}{2}$ x 11in), 280 x 430mm (11 x 17in) and 330 x 485mm (13 x 19in) sizes, it needs to be printed using colour dyes, with the printer set at Photo Glossy Film. One side has a receiving layer, the other does not, so it is important to load the film correctly in the printer. To help, there is a notch in the top right corner. To create the file for the negative, the image should be desaturated or reduced to greyscale and inverted (Control 1) It should also be laterally reversed so that it will print the correct way on contact. One alternative approach is to use "chromagenic negatives" (see Figs 11–14).

certain problems in the past, mainly due to the fact that the density of inks is not the same as that of silver particles – in order to achieve a sufficient density, the acetate has to be over-inked, which leads to loss of fine detail.

Digital negatives

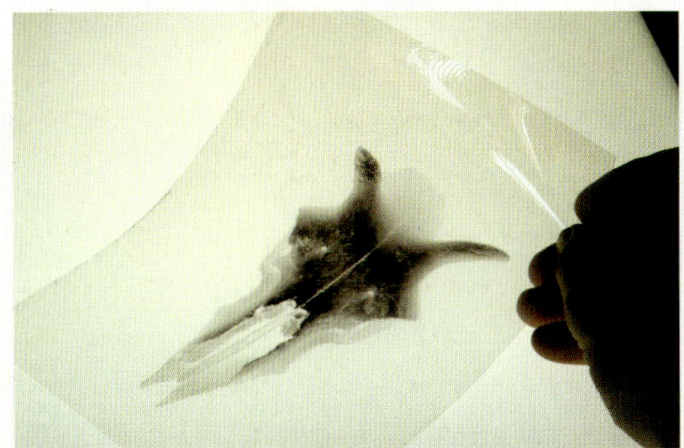

Fig 11

"Chromagenic" negatives work on the basis that light can be absorbed by colour dyes, rather than just using density. This means that there is less tendency to over-ink the negative to reach the required density. Generally speaking, the red end of the colour spectrum absorbs most of the image-forming light, therefore negatives created with a preponderance of red will be effective at cutting out light and UV. This works well with images printed on the cheapest Epson photo paper, especially if the paper is then gently oiled with sunflower oil on the reverse side, to produce greater transparency. (For a detailed explanation, refer to Dan Burkholder's book *Digital Negatives for Alternative Processes*.)

As a starting point, the scanned image should be in negative form. The appropriate controls should then be used to produce detail and tone as required. Be careful of trying to make shadow areas too dense. Curves are available for different processes, but a good place to start is to colourize the negative (see Figs 12–14).

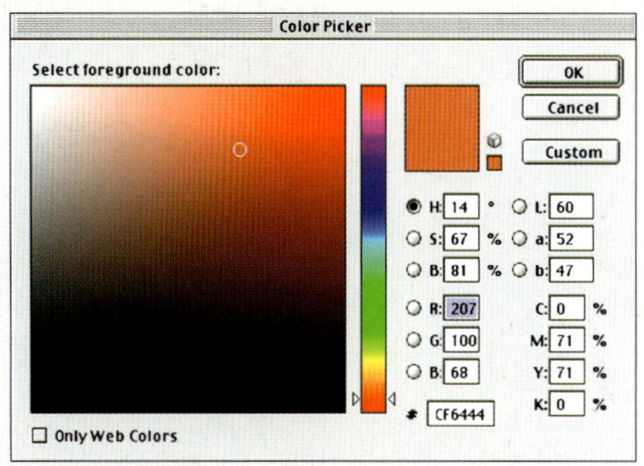

Fig 12

Select the foreground colour by using the Color Picker. Choose Cyan 0, Magenta 71, Yellow 71 and Black 0.

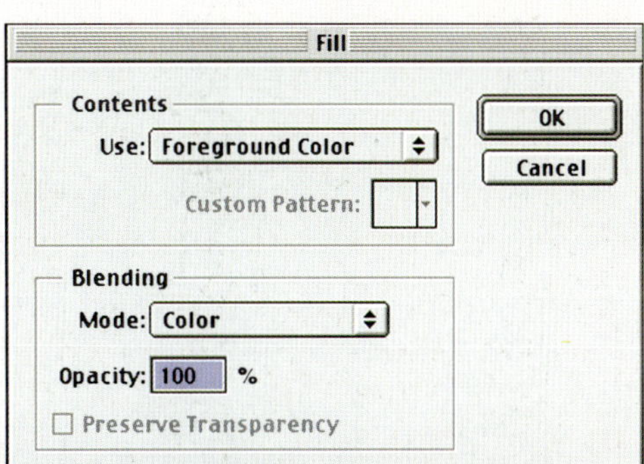

Fig 13

Go to Edit > Fill and choose Use: Foreground Color and Blending Mode Color, Opacity 100%.

Fig 14

The image will turn a reddish colour and can now be printed as an RGB image.

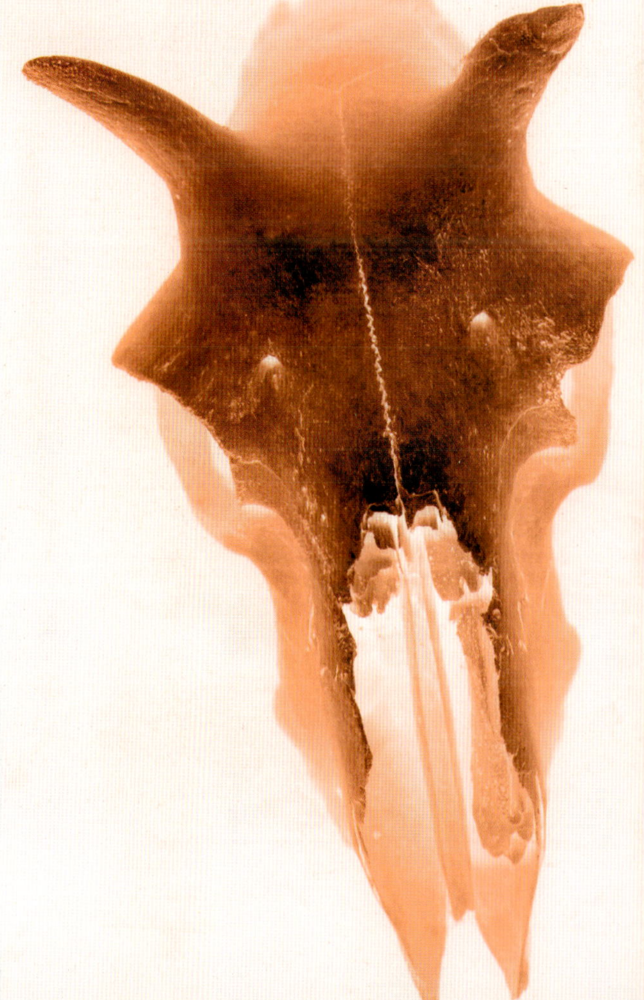

12   Creating a pinhole effect

As film and cameras have become increasingly more sophisticated, there has been an awakened interest in alternative means of capturing images; consequently, some photographers are now beginning to explore very simple technologies, such as pinhole cameras, as a means of exploring the visual world. This might be regarded as a backward step, but as modern photographic hardware becomes more advanced, there is a genuine desire to celebrate the quirky and ephemeral qualities of these old processes.

A PINHOLE CAMERA CAN capture haunting and wistful images that cannot be achieved with modern cameras. The pinhole camera process is fraught with difficulties, not least in estimating the correct exposure – luckily, very similar results can be achieved digitally.

It is also worth considering the aesthetic issues. Photography currently occupies the role that painting occupied several centuries ago, but since the middle of the 19th century, painters have been able to explore new and more interesting ways of reflecting the visual world – increasingly they make only casual reference to reality, and as a consequence their

Pier 1

A charming, but otherwise quite uninteresting seascape.

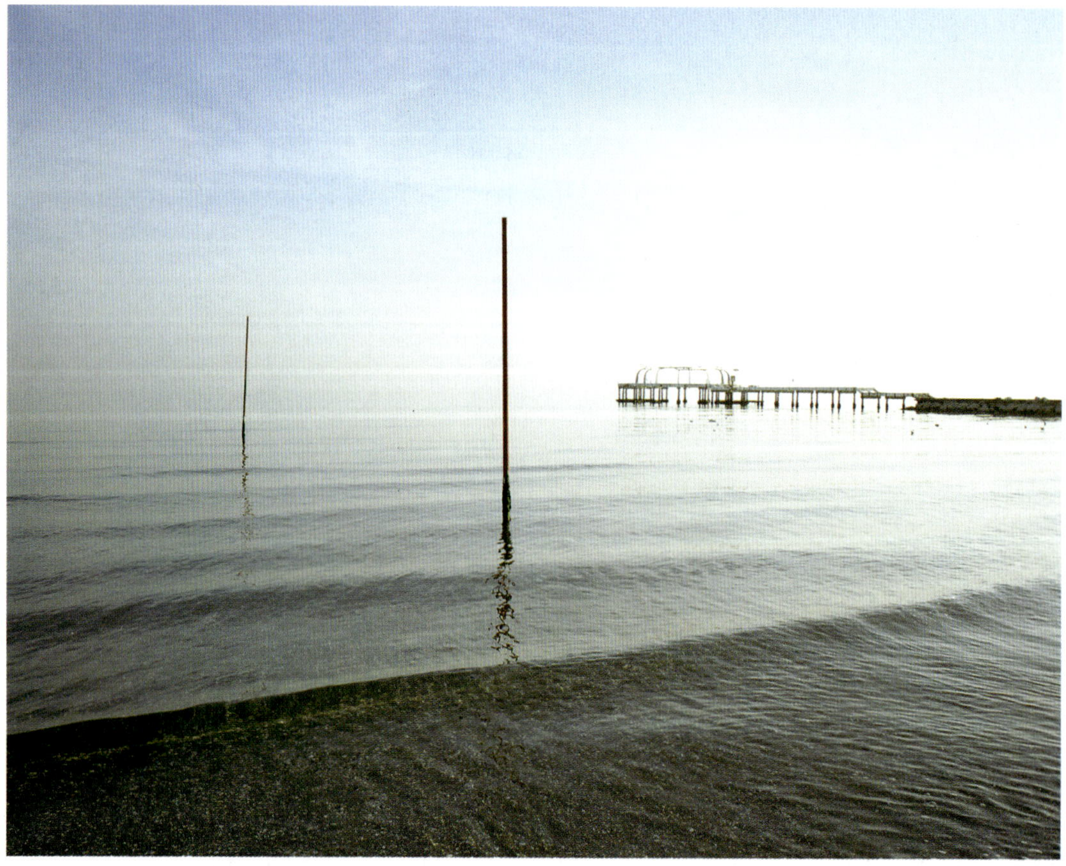

images are more personal and engaging. The technical aberrations that are the hallmark of pinhole photography can now be created in other ways, and surely the argument should be not about how these aberrations are created, but that we are prepared to accept them in the first place.

What are the distinguishing characteristics of pinhole cameras?

1 They are normally characterized by very slow exposures, which even in good lighting conditions can take up to 30 seconds, although some take up to several hours, depending on the size of the aperture and the available light.

2 As there are no lenses to correct the aberrations, the images are slightly soft in appearance.

3 Vignetting is likely to occur, especially with home-made pinhole cameras.

4 Light can often be seen bleeding in from the edges, if home-made pinhole cameras are used.

5 The image will appear as a negative if using a paper negative. A positive is achieved by contact-printing, but occasionally the image is more interesting left as a negative.

How are these effects created digitally?

The ideal way to create the blurred effect due to a long exposure is to use an image that has been exposed for a prolonged period. There are several filters in Photoshop that can also create a sense of movement, and possibly the best is Motion Blur: Filter > Blur > Motion Blur. Remember, these filters can be used selectively so that the sense of movement can be restricted to a specific area.

Pier 2

By using the Omni filter, a sense of mystery has been created. Sometimes a photographic image can appear too perfect, and deliberately reducing its quality can introduce a heightened sense of intrigue. The sense of movement in the water has been created by selectively applying Motion Blur.

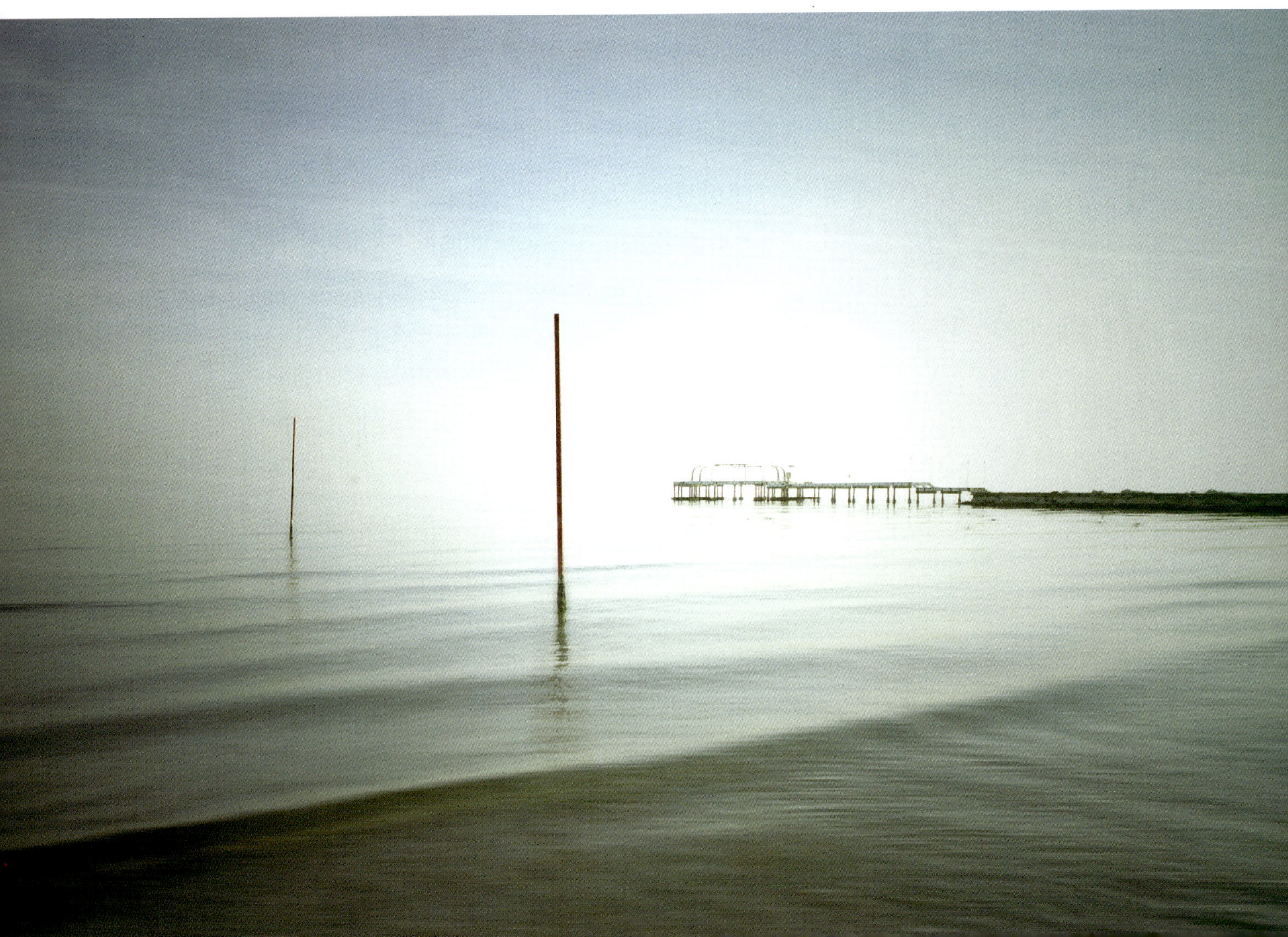

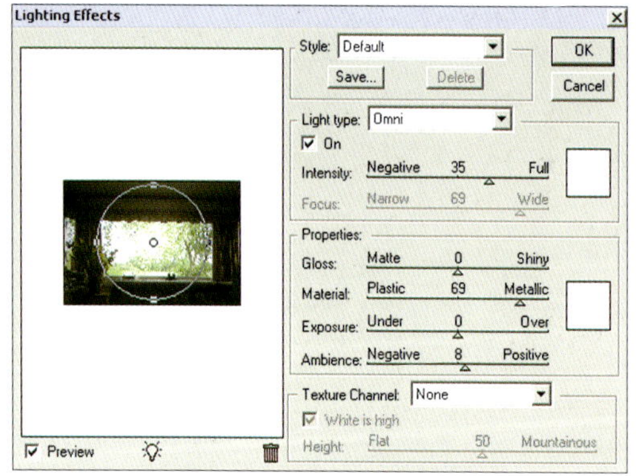

Another characteristic of a pinhole image is the level of sharpness fall-off at the edges; this can easily be simulated using Gaussian Blur: Filter > Blur > Gaussian Blur. Select the area you feel ought to remain sharp, but feather your selection and then inverse. Use the Radius slider to establish the extent of the blur; usually 3 pixels should be sufficient (see Fig 1, page 102).

Vignettes

The effect of vignetting can be obtained by simply selectively darkening the corners, although a more dramatic way of achieving this is to use the Omni filter: Filter > Render > Lighting Effects > Light Type. The Omni creates the suggestion that there is a strong area of illumination within the centre of the image, with dramatic fall-off towards the edges. When using a pinhole camera, the centre of illumination is governed by where the pinhole is in relation to the film or paper; working digitally, it is merely a matter of placing the small white circle where you want it to be. It can be best to place it on a darker area somewhere within the centre of the picture, otherwise areas can look bleached out. Surrounding the small white circle is a circular line with grey anchors which can be moved to modify the intensity of the illumination. Similar effects can also be achieved by using Spotlight. The extent of the lighting is controlled by the Intensity slider.

Light

One of the idiosyncratic qualities of pinhole camera images, particularly if the camera is home-made, is the unpredictable bleeding of light that sometimes occurs at the edges. The effect is identical to the bleeding that so often happens with roll film when the paper backing is not as tight as it ought to be. Using one of these, scan it with its imperfections, and make it the first layer; then scan the pinhole image. Making sure that the size and resolution of both layers match, use the Layers option to blend the two images.

Negatives

Be prepared to accept some of your images as a negative. When using paper negatives, the exposed paper appears as a negative; normally this is resolved by treating the image as a paper negative and making a contact print to create a positive. Occasionally the negative form is more interesting than the positive. To achieve this digitally, merely invert by going to Image > Adjust > Invert.

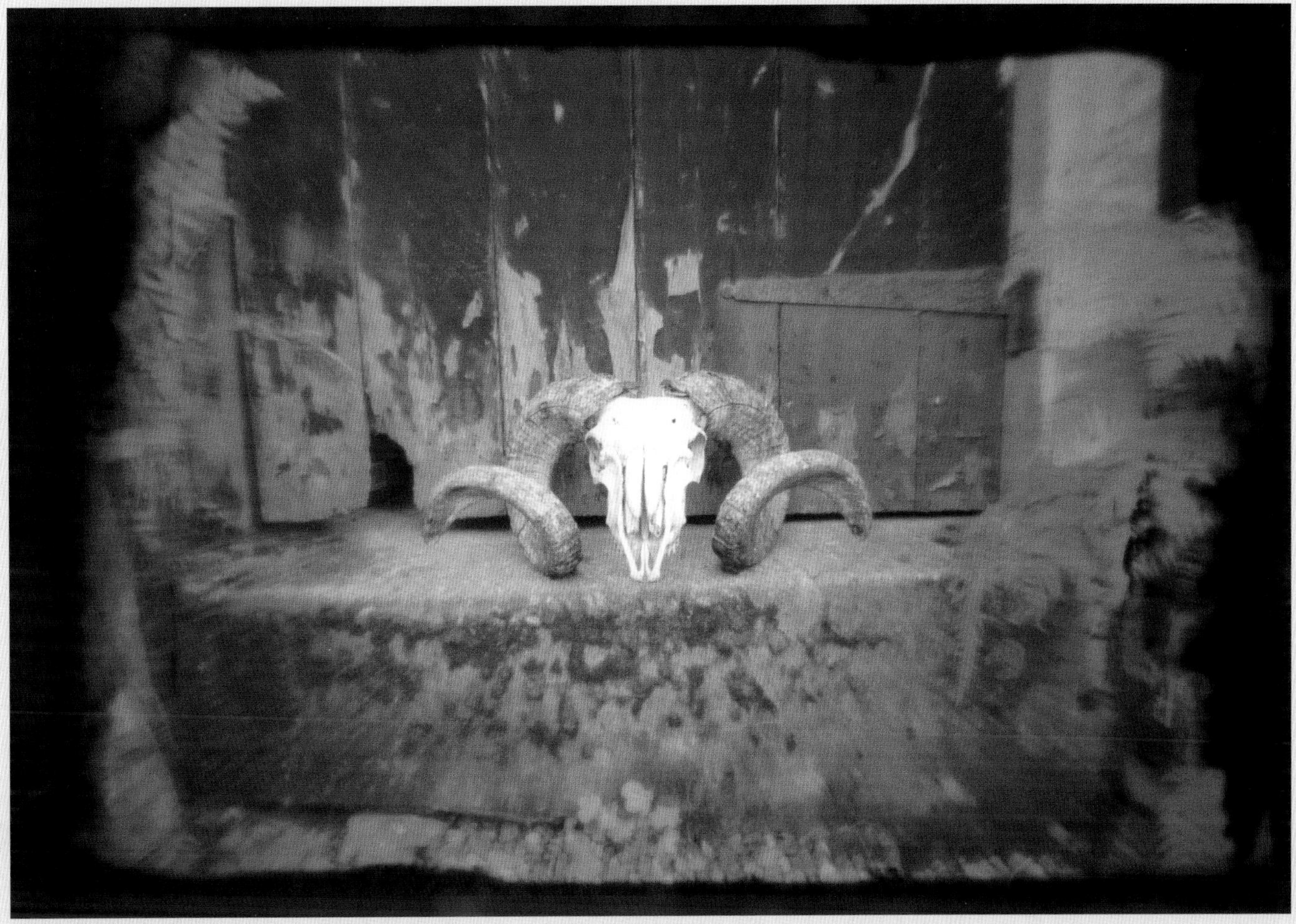

Still life, Inversnaid

Originally taken on a Pentax Optio camera at fairly low quality,
this image was first desaturated and then a rough selection
was made in an oval shape around the ram's skull. This was
heavily feathered and then slightly blurred using Gaussian
Blur. The selection was then inverted, and a larger Gaussian
Blur and a small amount of Radial Blur were applied to the
outer edges of the image. Finally, scanning an original
pinhole image and incorporating only its edge into the final
composition produced the uneven edge effect.

Using the character of pinhole images

Resplendent interior 1

As advancing technology offers us increasingly sharp film and optically improved lenses, it is easy to become over-obsessed with image sharpness. However, more and more photographers are beginning to appreciate that the limitations and imperfections which characterize pinhole photography can sometimes more effectively communicate mood and interest. It is almost as if having marched endlessly in the direction of super high-fidelity imaging, some of us now wish to take a step backwards. This image was scanned from a black-and-white negative in RGB mode, but was not desaturated, and consequently retains the arbitrary colours that scanned black-and-white images often assume.

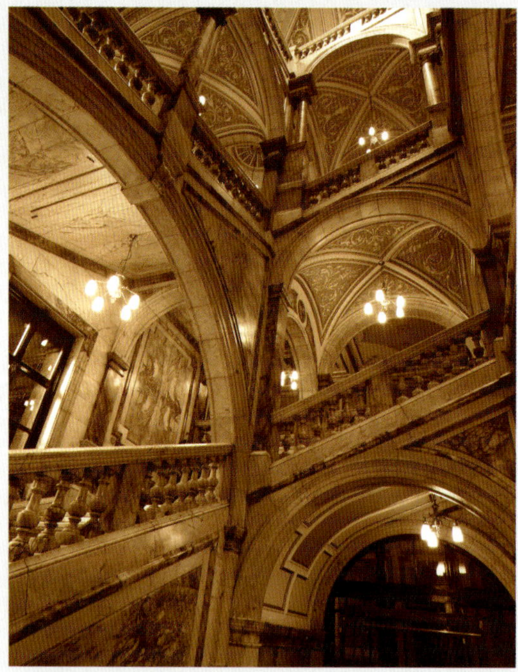

Resplendent interior 2

An altogether more interesting image is created by using Filter > Render > Lighting Effects, which focuses the illumination in the centre of the image, while giving the impression of vignetting in the corners. These characteristics are typical of an image taken using a simple, single-aperture pinhole camera.

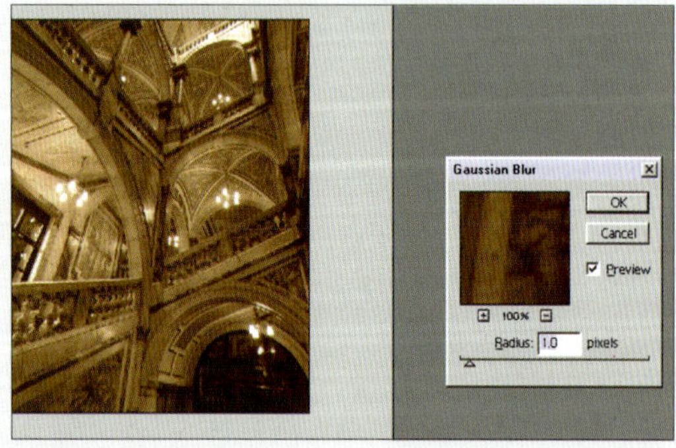

Fig 1

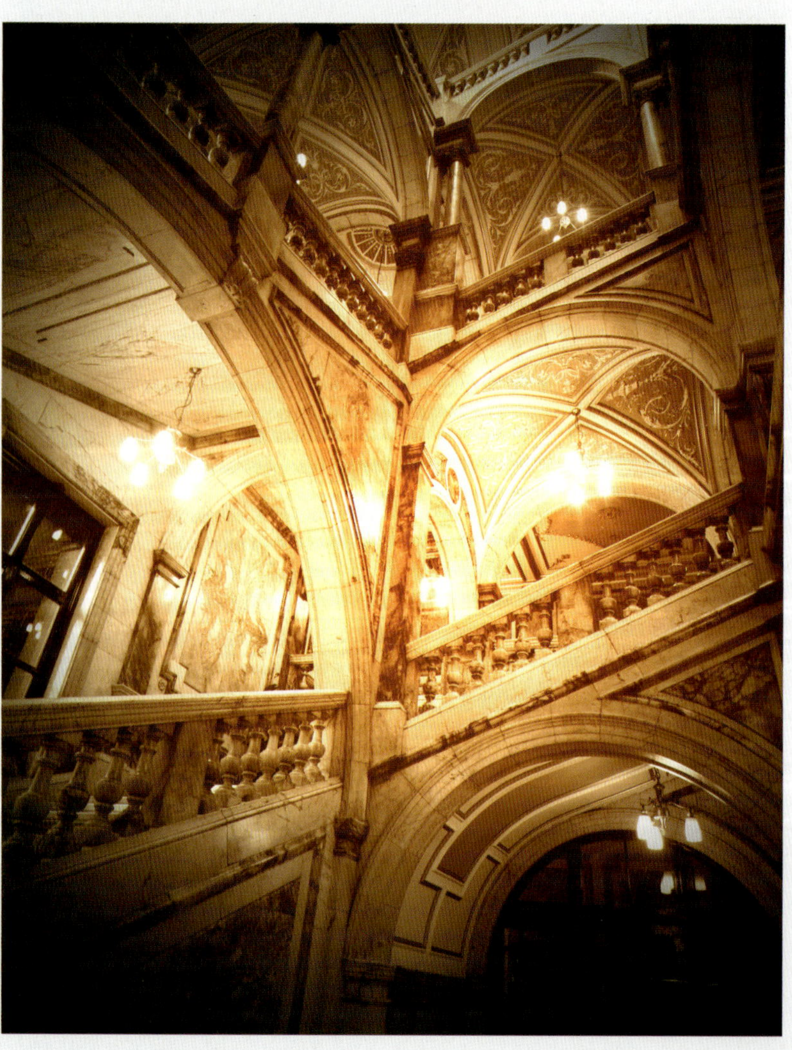

Resplendent interior 3

Unusual objects, such as biscuit tins, books, shoes and even the human body, can be used to make pinhole cameras, providing they are made to be lightproof. This, of course, is the big imponderable, as often these constructed cameras require exposures of between 30 seconds and several hours. Inevitably there will be some light leakage, but this is a defining characteristic of this kind of photography. In order to simulate this effect digitally, a second layer was created using a discarded piece of roll film, which had been subject to light leakage (see Fig 2), and then the two layers were merged using the Layers option.

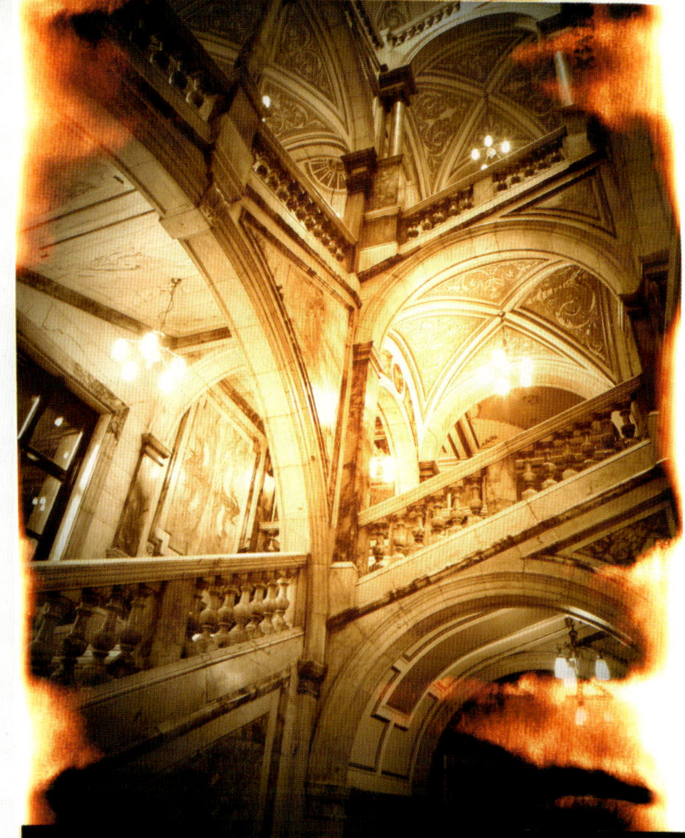

Fig 2
A discarded piece of roll film was used for the second layer.

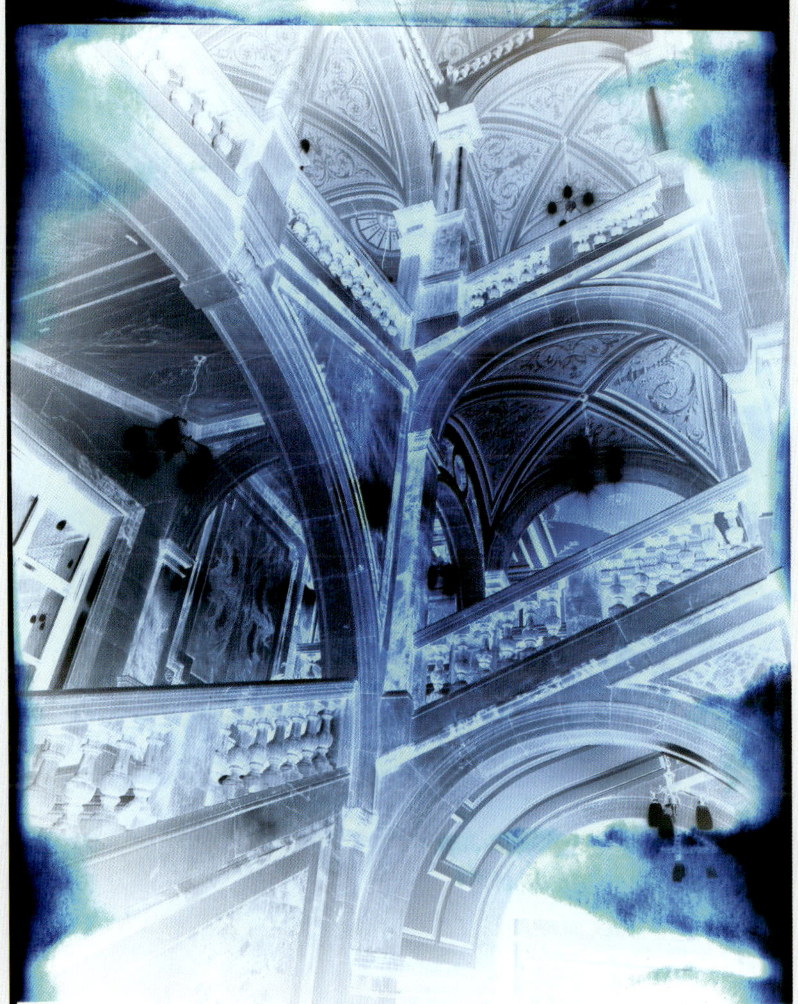

Resplendent interior 4

Depending on the design of the pinhole, either film or printing paper can be used; if you select the latter, the image will appear as a negative. You can then opt to use this image as a paper negative in order to achieve a positive, although occasionally choosing to retain the image in its negative form offers a more challenging alternative.

13 Working in sequences

There are numerous occasions when we take a sequence of shots; usually we do this because we are uncertain about the final outcome or when the lighting situation appears unpredictable. Whether you capture images digitally or on film – in the long run – taking those extra shots usually turns out to be cost-effective.

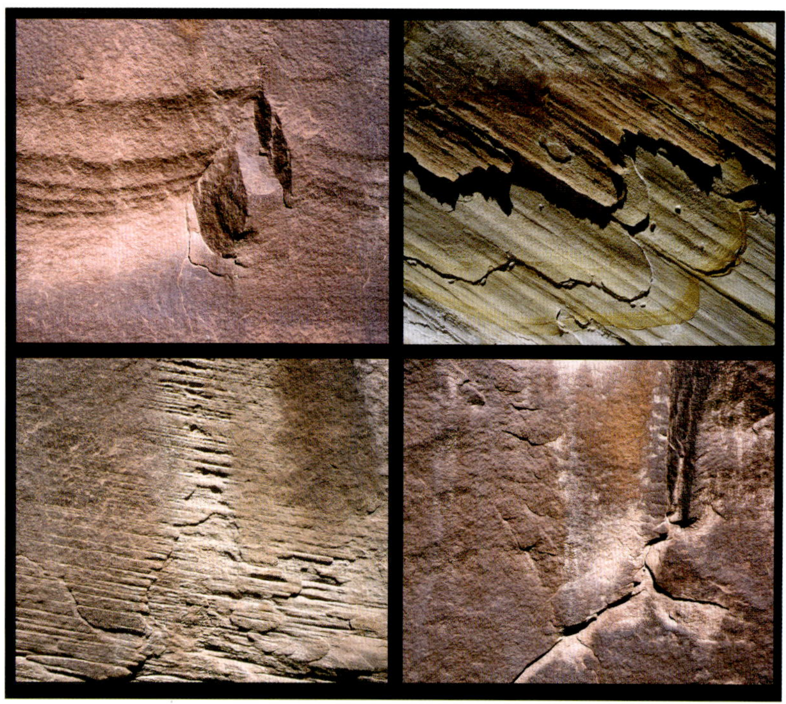

Red sandstone
When grouping related images together, a white background is traditionally used, but occasionally a black or even a coloured background can prove to be more effective. When working digitally, it is easy to experiment and try out the different options.

HAVING TAKEN a sequence of related images, we are conditioned to select just one that, in our opinion, most perfectly encapsulates the qualities of all the others. This view is reinforced because as photographers we learn to produce contact prints and then to carefully review each single image, so that we can make this decisive and critical choice. This is not to suggest that careful editing should not remain an important process within photography, it is just that sometimes a single image does not adequately express the richness of our visual experiences. There are occasions when, compared to the contact sheet, the final image can prove to be a disappointment.

From single shot to sequence
This is not to argue that the single image does not have value. On the one extreme, photography is about capturing the critical moment, and the shots just before and after that moment appears inconsequential; this is a tradition that is best exemplified by photographers such as Henri Cartier-Bresson and the highly objective Robert Frank. But objectivity can be expressed in many ways: the German photographers Bernhard and Hilla Becher have methodically documented domestic and industrial structures, which on the surface look very similar but, when closely examined, reveal individual characteristics. Their studies of blast furnaces, water towers and half-timbered buildings illustrate that while these structures reveal a certain uniformity, they are uniquely different. In order to make their point, the photographers present their work in carefully constructed sequences, and invite the viewer to cross-reference each image in order that they may make their own judgements.

A subjective approach to this tradition has been eloquently expressed by the fictional photographer, Duane Michals, who has constructed highly cinematic sequences that

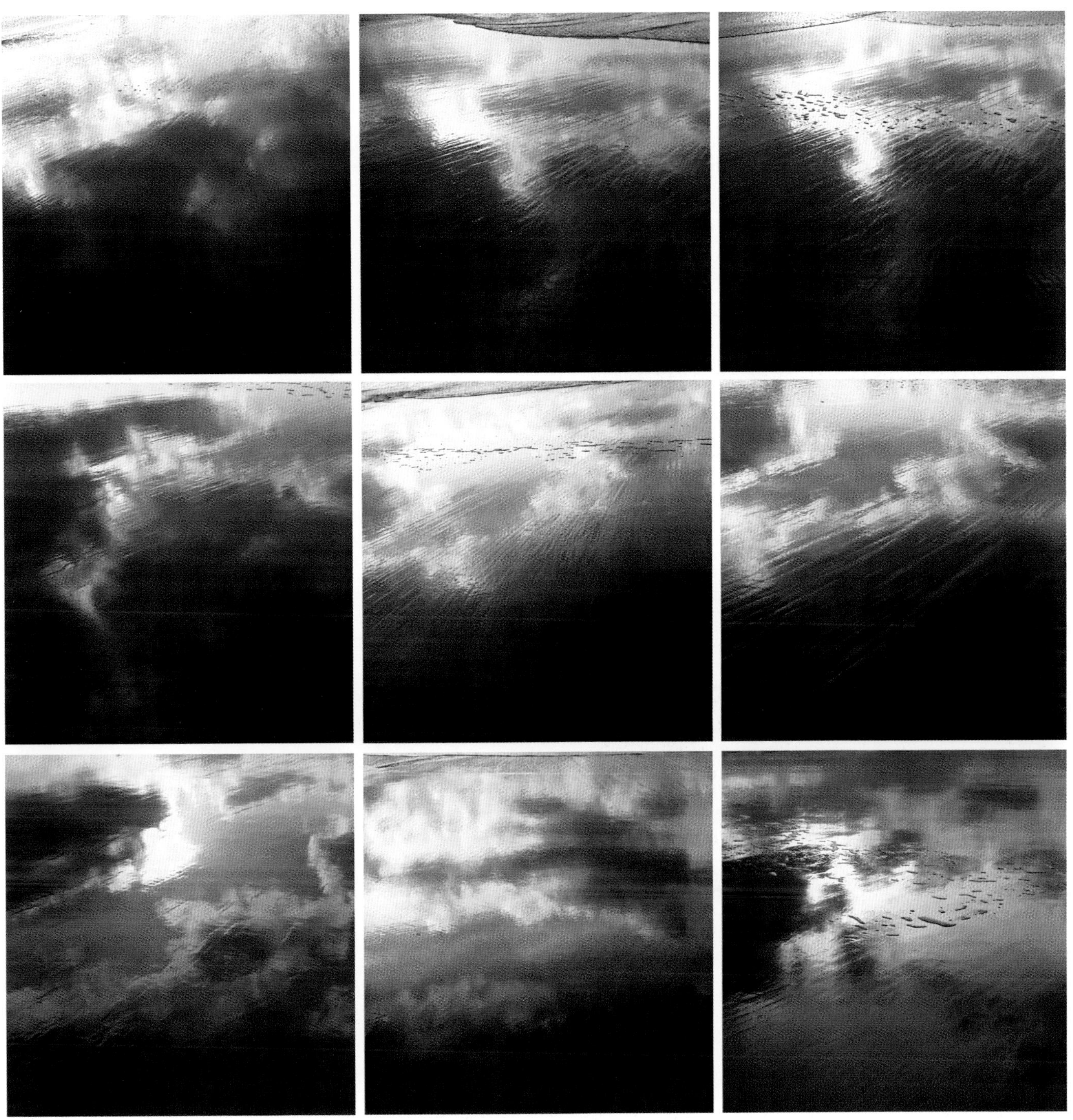

seek to tell a story. In fact, Michals plans his work with care and sketches out his ideas beforehand. Each shot is carefully thought out so that every image within the sequence makes a a constructive contribution. He has learned how to reduce his narrative to the smallest

Reflected sun

Photographically, one of the great advantages of producing sequences is that it is an incentive to try to capture images that appear inconsequential when presented singly. In this example, I was fascinated by the reflection, in wet sand, of the sun appearing and then disappearing behind a cloud. Often sequences such as these are a wonderful way of expressing the notion of time.

Fig 1

Even when using the same film size, there is often a need for some cropping, which needs to be done with great accuracy, as any unevenness will show up once the images are placed within the

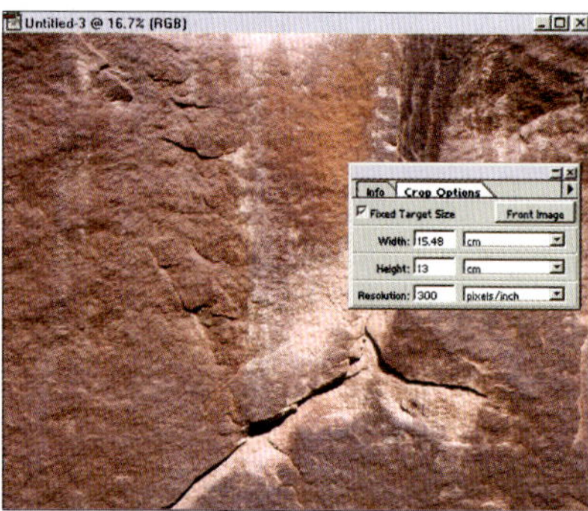

sequence. First, crop one of the images to the dimensions that best represent the final required outcome, but take note of its width, height and resolution (which for printing purposes, should be set to 300ppi). When cropping the remaining images, use the Crop option, tick Fixed Target Size, and type in the dimensions and resolution of the previously cropped image in the empty boxes. This will ensure that all further crops match the first. When determining the crop size, some thought should also be given to the number of images to be used, the overall size of the print and the intended gaps: in effect, will it fit?

Fig 2

In order to create a sequence, a new file needs to be opened, which will serve as a canvas for the sequence. Go to File > New. The New File dialog box will appear; type in the required height and width,

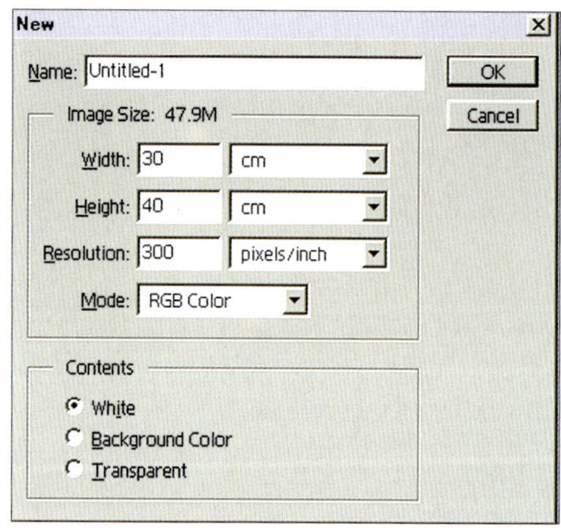

which of course should match the final print size. Assuming that you wish to print this, set the resolution to 300ppi. Another option offered is the background colour; while the new file will default to white, any colour can be chosen, although this requires setting the background colour first. You can also choose transparent, which means that it is possible to layer the sequence over another image.

Sand dunes, Death Valley

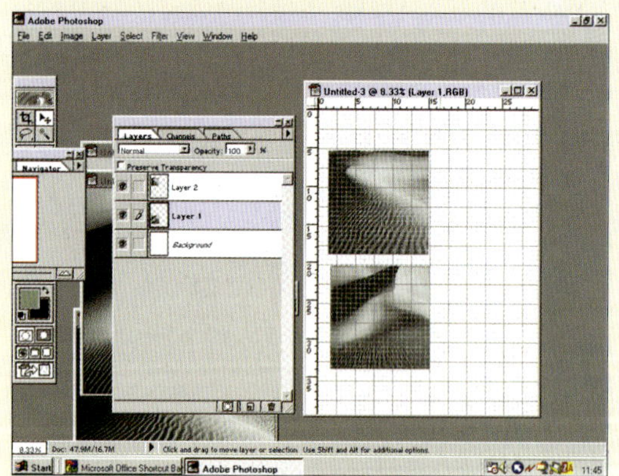

Fig 3

Select the first image you wish to move into the new file and drag it by using the Move tool to where it should appear in the final sequence. In order to make this task a little easier, use the grid and ruler. Go to View > Show Grid, then go to View again and > Show Ruler.

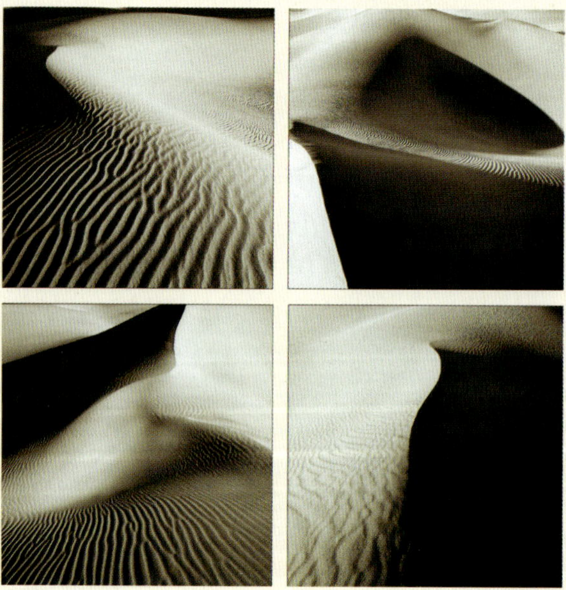

Sand dunes, Death Valley

Photographing in this wonderful Californian location, I was fascinated by the simple light and dark shapes created by the early morning light. Once I had processed the film, it was difficult to identify one single frame which was markedly better than the others; in effect, the taking of all the images was the photographic experience. By grouping the shots in this way, a more accurate record of the totality of the experience is illustrated.

All the images were taken on black-and-white film, scanned and coloured using Duotone.

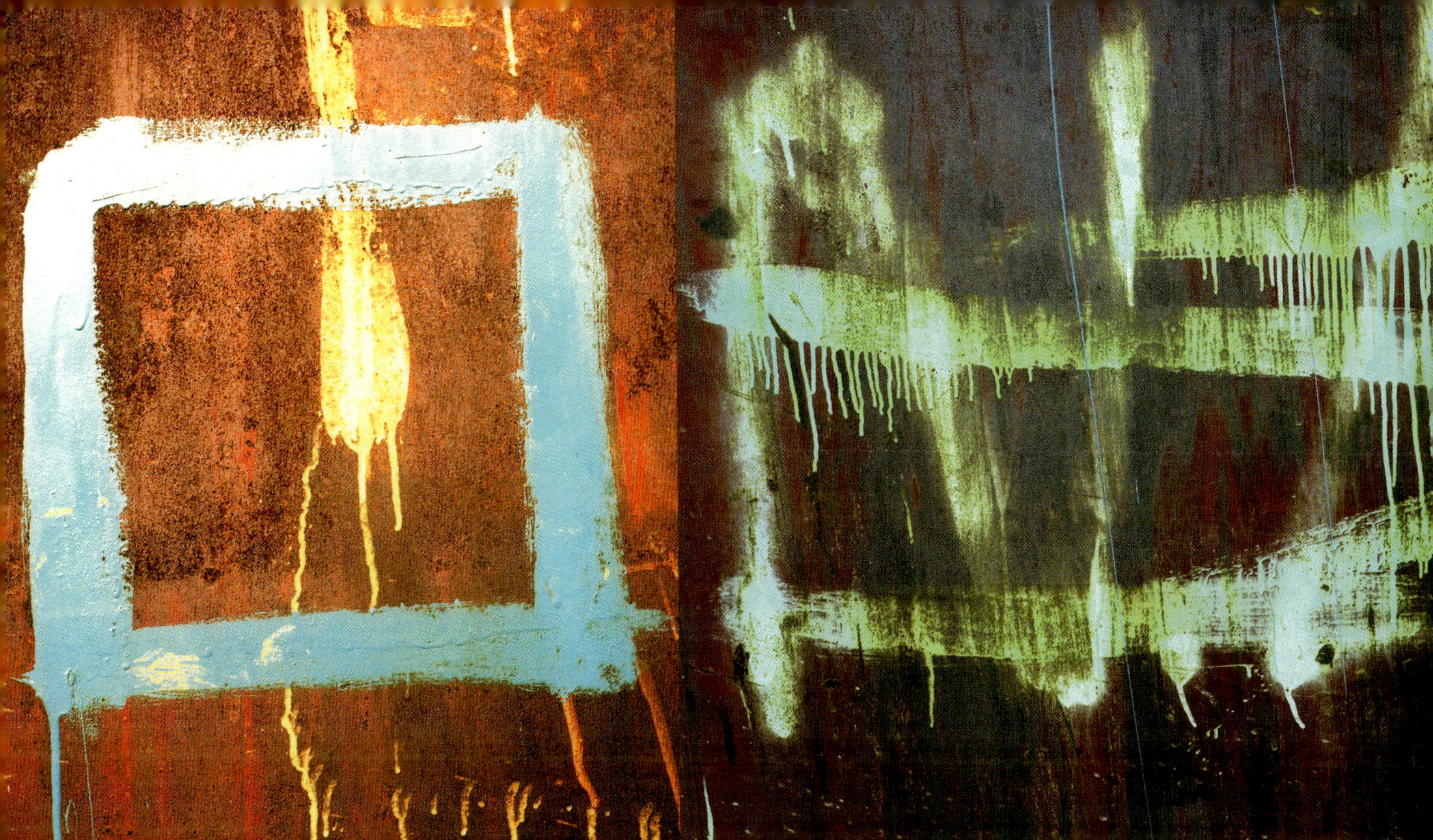

number of shots, and by skilfully directing the pose, body language and gestures of his models, he is able to ensure that each image counts. These quirky stories are recollections from his imagination, and he uses photography to explore fantasy, much in the same way as a film director might do.

The tradition of presenting sequences of photographs is steadily growing, although the process can pose technical difficulties, particularly when working traditionally in the darkroom. Printing numerous images on a single sheet of paper demands exceptional organization, and of course the more images you wish to include, the more likely it is that a mishap will occur. But when working digitally, this becomes an altogether much simpler task.

Organizing images

By their very nature, sequences need to be planned; therefore it is useful to store all the required images in the same folder. Obviously it depends on the desired outcome,

but it is often desirable that they are all of the same size. This is easily achieved at the cropping stage.

Accurately positioning images

Where each image is placed, and the space allowed around each one, are clearly important issues when planning out sequences. In general terms, the order in which each image is placed will already have been sorted out before any of the images are imported into the new file (see Fig 2), although once placements have been made, some alterations may be required. It is important to appreciate that the new file represents a single layer, and that each of the imported files creates another separate layer; so if six images are imported into a new file, seven layers will be created.

Making a greetings card

Producing any kind of greetings card is quite an easy task, but one that clearly involves a

Venetian lido

Fig 4

Remember that neither the grid nor the ruler will appear in the final print. Obviously it depends on the overall shape of the sequence, but often it helps to place the middle components first and then work outwards. Once one of the "keystones" has been established, import the next image, but this needs to be placed with great accuracy, as even the slightest misalignment will show up in the final print. Use the Navigator to focus in on the corners; once these are accurately aligned, the other elements can be positioned.

When all the images are in place, an overall assessment can be made,

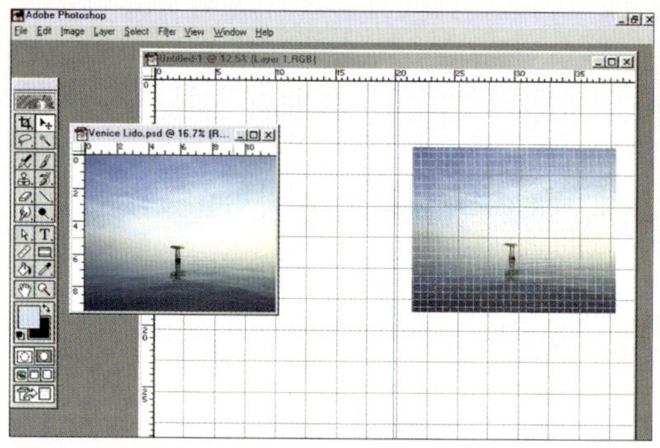

and if you feel that a particular image needs to be changed in some way, select the layer within the Layers dialog box, and only that layer will then become active. It is possible to alter the tonality or the position, or make any other required changes at this stage.

Once the final sequence has been satisfactorily completed, flatten the image to reduce file size.

Fig 5

To make a greetings card, select the image you wish to import into the new file and carefully position it on the right side of the new file (see Fig 6), assuming of course that that you wish to see the image on the front of the card.

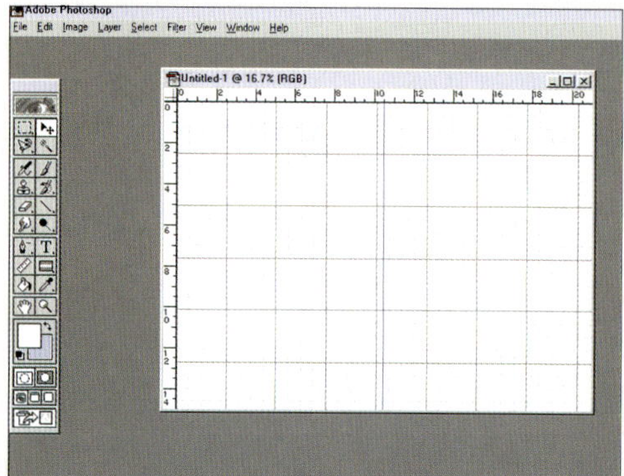

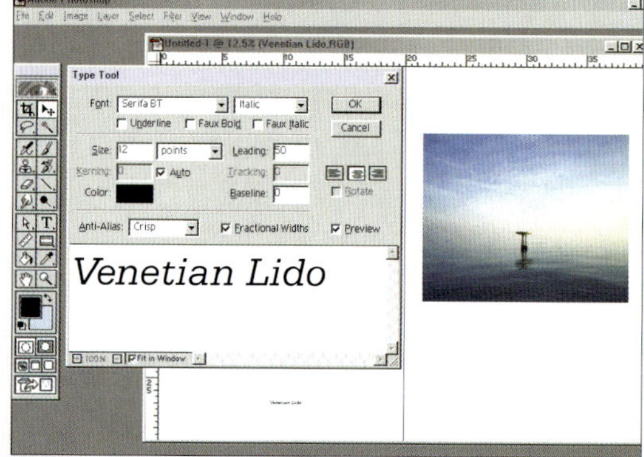

Fig 6

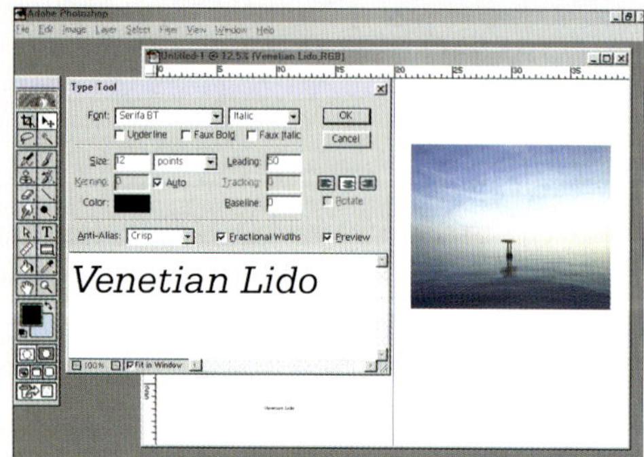

Fig 7

Once the desired text has been completed, click OK and it will appear with the established settings. If you need to reposition the text, place the Move cursor directly on the text and move it to where you want. It is important to place the cursor accurately over the text, otherwise you risk moving the background instead.

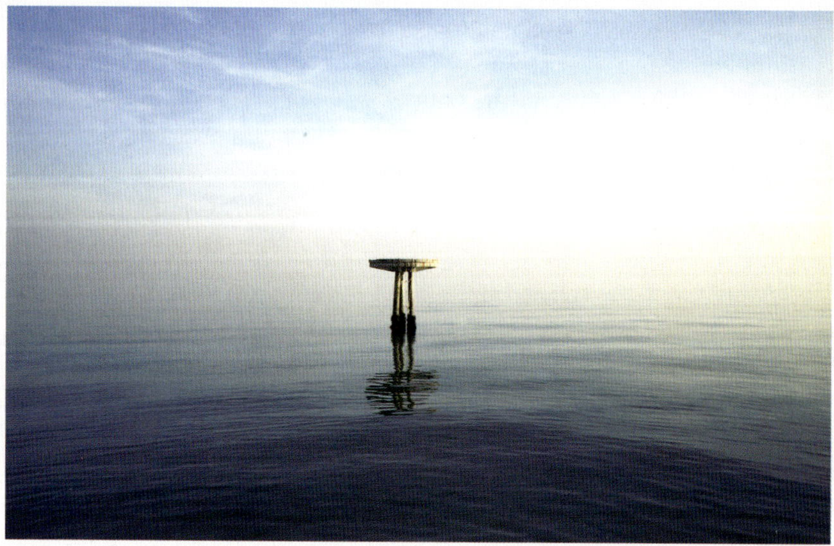

Venetian lido

Simple, clear-cut images are ideal for greetings cards.

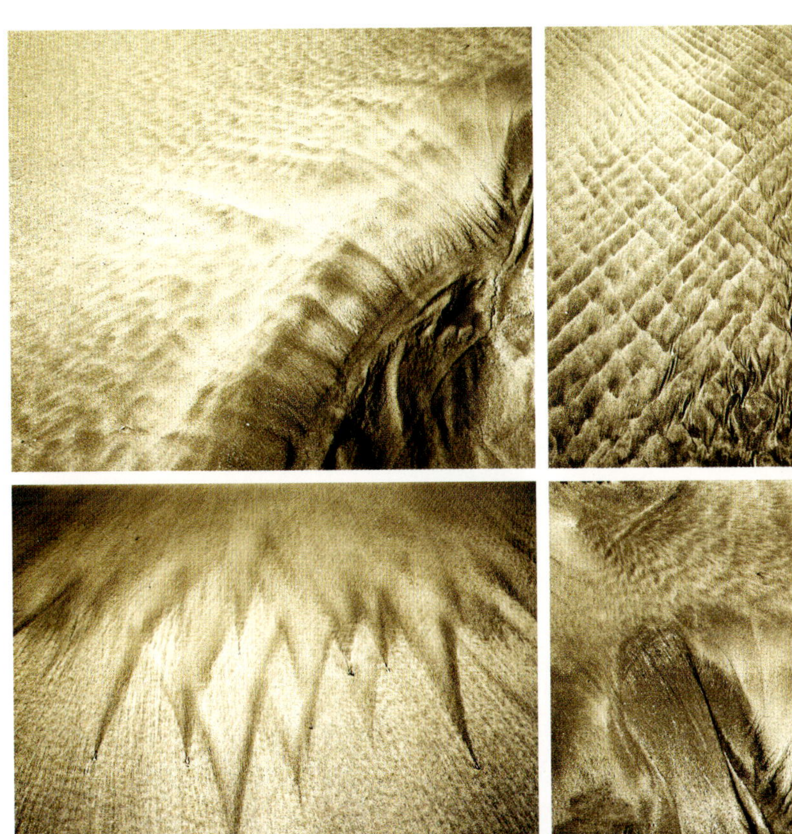

One of the advantages of working in sequences is that it encourages us to photograph minimalist subject matter we might otherwise ignore. Grouped together, the inherent rhythm in each of the individual images becomes far more apparent.

little bit of planning. In essence, what is required is a mixture of imaging and text, so it is important to start with a new file. This is usually white but can be any colour you choose, although it is important to consider the text in relation to the intended background colour. It is possible to buy purpose-made folded blank cards, which are capable of being printed on both sides. When designing work, decide what is required on the outside of the card, and this will become New File 1. Create the file to the same dimensions as the opened-up card and then apply the grid. Accurately establish the halfway mark, which represents the intended fold in the card (see Fig 5).

Introducing simple text

Text is introduced by selecting the Type tool. When using type, it creates its own layer, so it is easy to make adjustments without altering the other layers, and you can afford to place the Type cursor approximately and make a more considered adjustment later on. Either the Type tool or the Vertical Type tool can be used. Place the cursor inside the image, click, and the Type tool dialog box will appear (see Fig 7). Select the font, style and size of the text and then specify the required colour – not all text need necessarily be black. Think carefully about the text alignment you require; often the preferred mode is centred, but occasionally aligning text to the left or right can appear stronger.

Shadow

Whilst staying at an
apartment in the south
of Spain, I noticed that
the shadow cast over
our balcony wall by an
adjacent building changed
rapidly as the sun rose.
Traditional photography
 is all about capturing
the single moment, but
when presented in timed
sequences, other interesting
visual relationships can
also be explored.

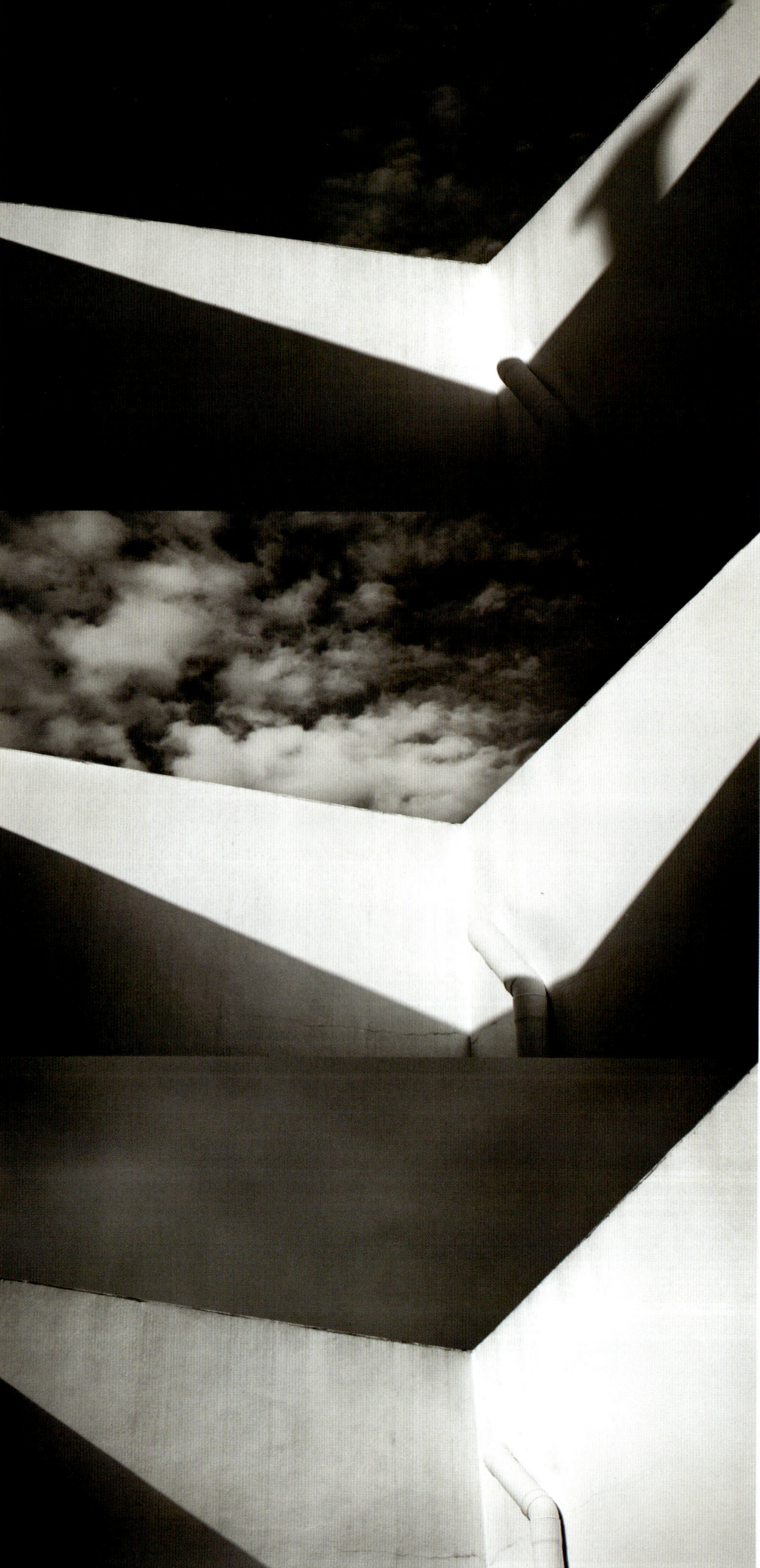

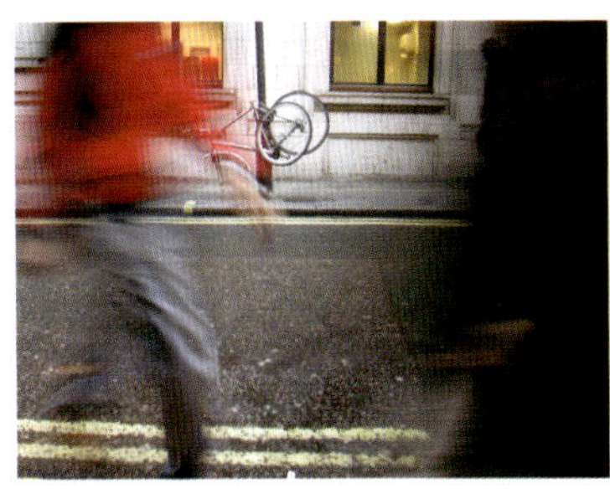 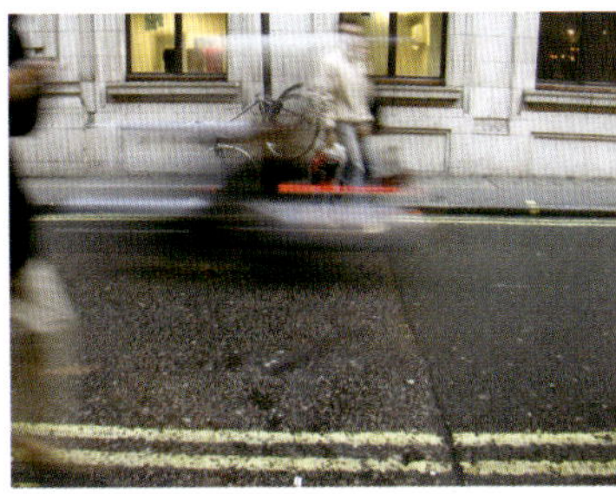 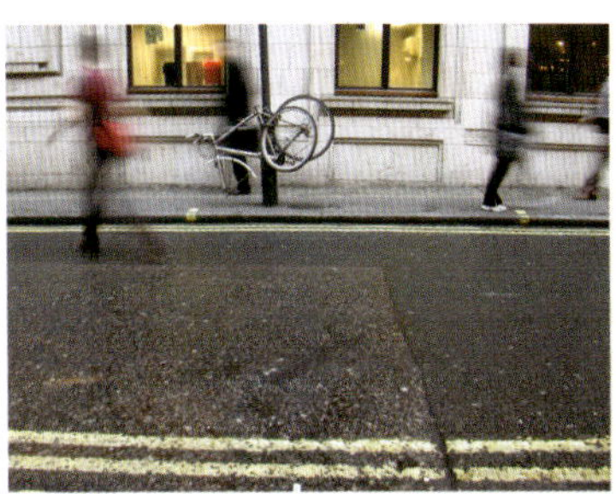 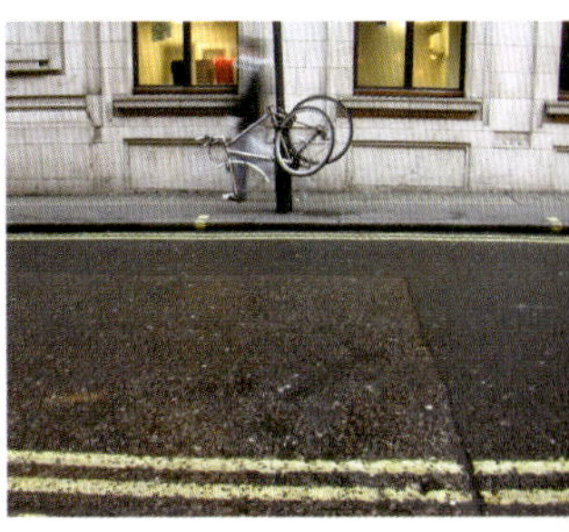

Passing time

This was exactly what I was doing. During a residential visit to London with about 100 students, I escaped to a local pub. The barstool by the window allowed me to observe the passers-by hurrying home from work. As always, I was carrying my Pentax digital camera in my pocket and was able to produce a series of sequences by photographing through the window. Using the playback screen I could determine the best shutter speed to use to produce the motion blur. After that it was just a matter of letting things happen.

Model with drape

A permutation of a theme is a common approach in art; however, photographers are a little less comfortable with this notion, which can provide some interesting images. In this example, a single black-and-white negative was scanned in RGB mode and then digitally manipulated in various ways to produce this sequence.

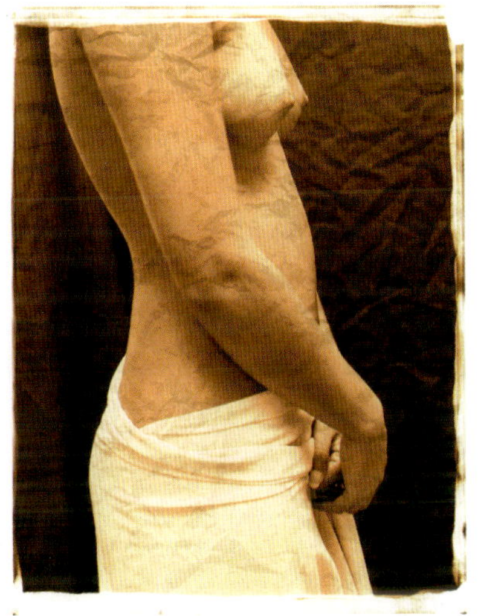 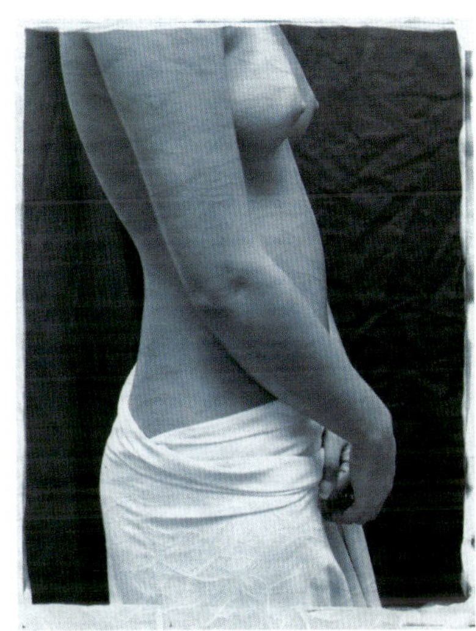

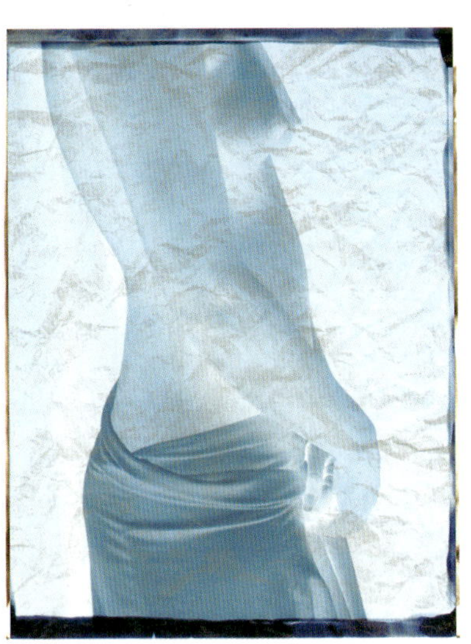 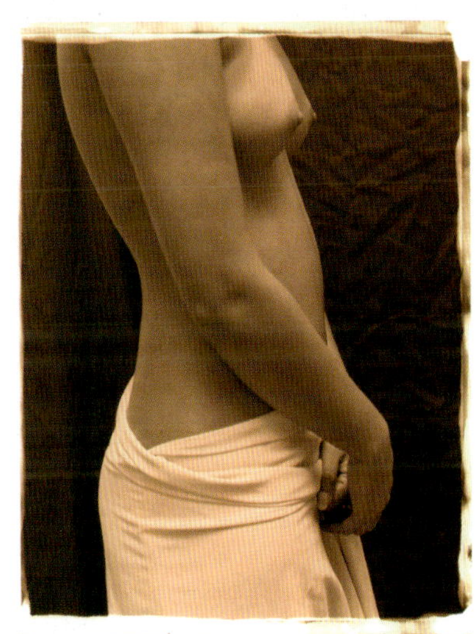

14   Joiners and Panoramas

Panoramic images are not new, but they are seeing a resurgence at the moment. Some of the most famous panoramic images were taken by Eadweard Muybridge of San Francisco. Well known for his sequence images of human and animal locomotion, Muybridge was also an accomplished landscape photographer and created panoramas by combining a number of negatives to create a single image.

WHEN MUYBRIDGE CLIMBED to the top of the Hopkins Tower in San Francisco in 1877, he wanted to produce a unique image of the city. A single exposure with the cameras of the day could not capture the wide, sweeping vista that lay below him. His solution was to use an 8 x 10in plate camera to photograph 11 separate plates, which were then printed and combined to form a panorama that was 2.12m (7ft) long. Flushed with the artistic and commercial success of this venture, he later returned with a 18 x 22in plate camera and repeated the shots, producing a 5.18m (17ft) panorama composed of 13 images. The "joining" of separate images to form the panorama was obviously necessitated by the existing technology. Nearly 130 years later, NASA has two mobile craft on Mars equipped with so-called "Pancams" that provide fantastic digital panoramic images from another planet.

Nowadays, with specialist panoramic cameras, even 360° shots can be taken with a single exposure. However, it is not necessary to purchase a specialized camera dedicated to panoramas. Now any type of camera can be used for everything from slightly wide formats to full 360° shots. The key factor is the stitching together of adjacent images to produce a convincing panorama. There are a variety of software programmes that automate the process, including one of the features in Photoshop Elements and Photoshop CS. However, it is not a difficult process and more control is available for the manual worker.

Classic seamless panoramas

Everyone has experienced the problem of trying to represent the grandeur of a magnificent landscape vista in a single image: too much foreground and sky, with the main interest forming a thin line in the middle of the image. Using a lens with a longer focal length and concentrating on a section of the landscape will produce a far better image, but may not give any idea of space.

A classic panorama is usually a combination of adjacent images taken with a slightly telephoto lens. Each image should overlap by at least 20%, and it is imperative to work on manual exposure to ensure consistency between images – if exposure is changed between images, it is far harder to match up colours and tonality. To keep horizons level, a tripod with a three-way head is recommended, although with practice, holding the camera at the eye and swinging from left to right can be very effective. The main thing to watch is the position of the horizon. Keep this consistent: many cameras have screen grids, which can help, but a simple spirit level is just as good.

Once the images have been scanned or downloaded to the computer, they must be "stitched" together.

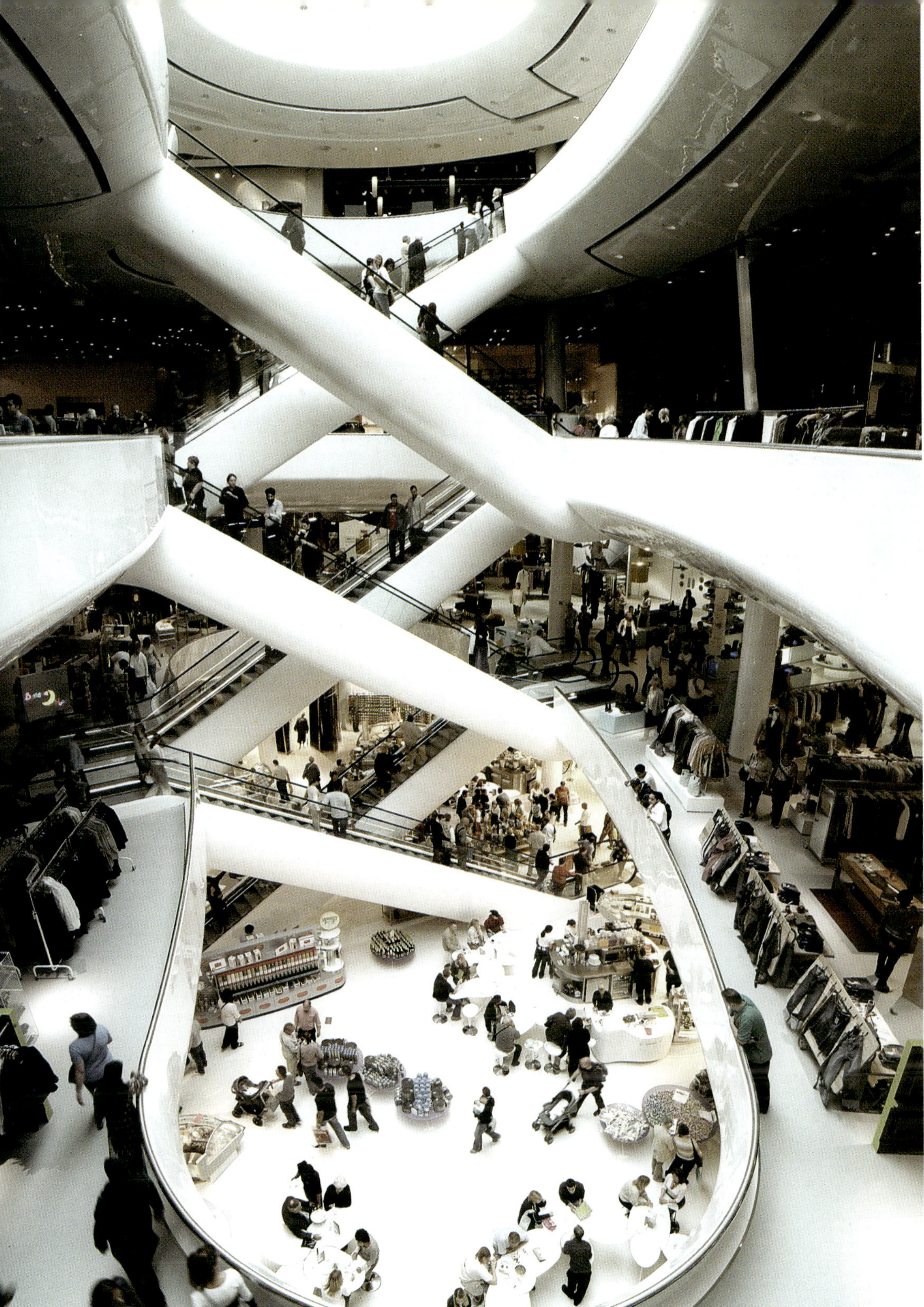

Stitching shots together

Both Photoshop Elements and Photoshop CS have automated functions for stitching a panorama from appropriate single images. If you have followed the above advice, they will do an excellent job. However, you may on occasions need to make some adjustments, particularly at the joins, and it is worth considering the manual process so that you have complete control.

1 Create a blank canvas about 10% larger than the final image. This will give some space for minor errors which may have occurred at the taking stage.

2 Open up all the images and resize them as appropriate, ensuring the resolution is the same as the canvas, usually 240–300dpi for printing; (see Fig 2).

3 Using the Move tool, drag each individual image onto the canvas, where it will automatically become a separate layer. If there are a lot of layers at this stage, it is worth naming each one appropriately (see Fig 1).

4 Starting with the first image on the left of the panorama, drag the second image over the top so it is roughly in position. Reduce the opacity of image 2 to about 50%, using the Opacity slider in the Layers palette. Zoom in on the join and use the keyboard arrows to register the two images. The opacity of layer 2 can now be returned to 100% (see Fig 3).

5 Drag image 3 over image 2 and repeat step 4. Continue this process until the panorama is complete.

6 Select the Crop tool to remove excess canvas or to produce a neat edge to the panorama, and flatten the image.

This process works if everything is perfect at the taking stage. This is not always the case – the join may be harsh due to exposure differences and a distinct line will show, as in Fig 3. Use Levels to ensure exposure is consistent between images. To prevent any harsh line, some blending between images is advisable – this is why each image needed to overlap.

Use of the Eraser

One simple way to achieve a blend is to use the Eraser tool set to a relatively large, soft-edged Brush. By gently moving along the edge of the join, the edge of the image can be effectively "feathered". This can be done gradually by using the Eraser set at lower opacities, for instance about 15–20%. The only problem with this method is that it permanently deletes part of your image.

Use of Layer Masks

A more controllable and non-destructive method is to use a Layer Mask. By painting onto the mask, parts of the image can be selectively concealed or revealed.

1 Set the foreground and background colours to their default black and white.

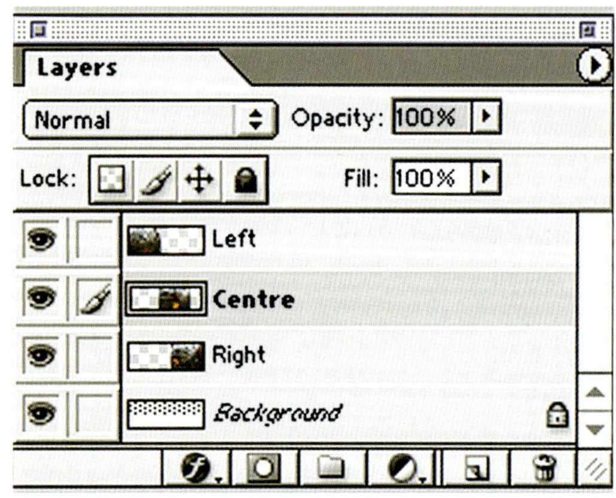

Fig 1

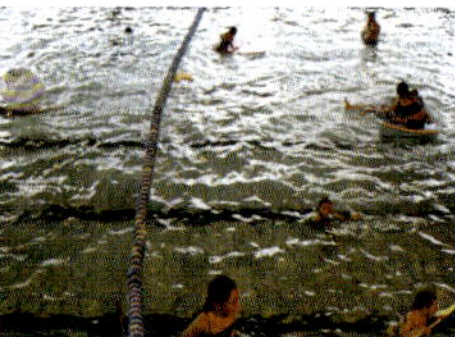
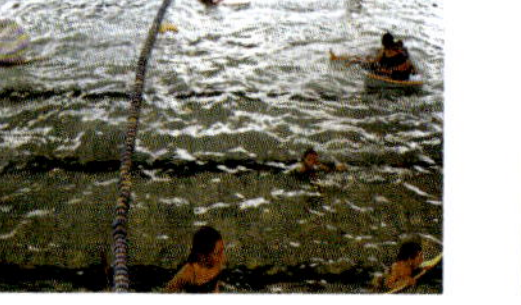
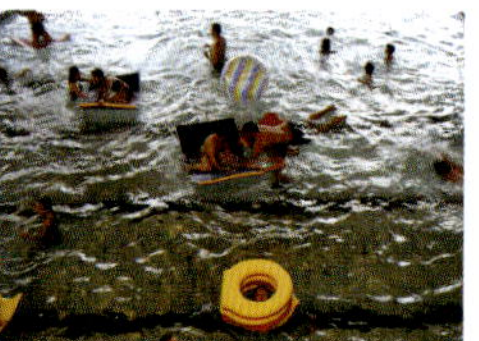
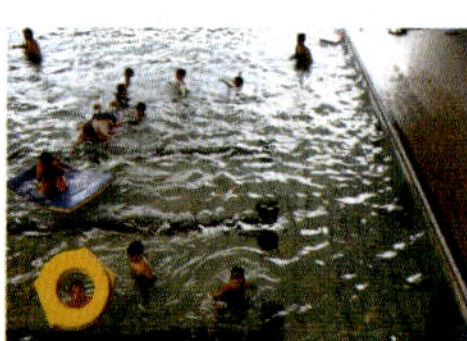

Fig 2

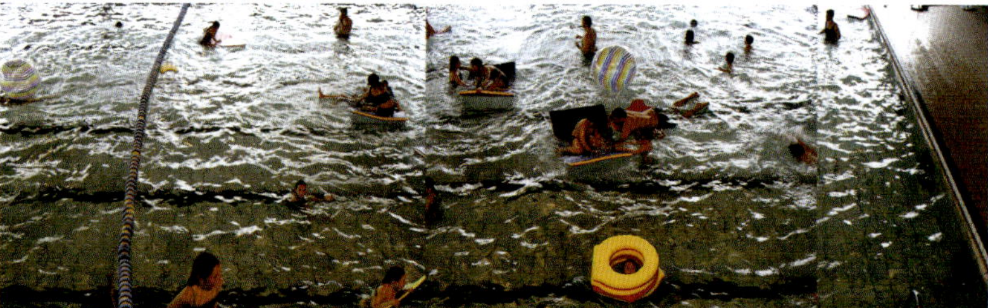

Fig 3

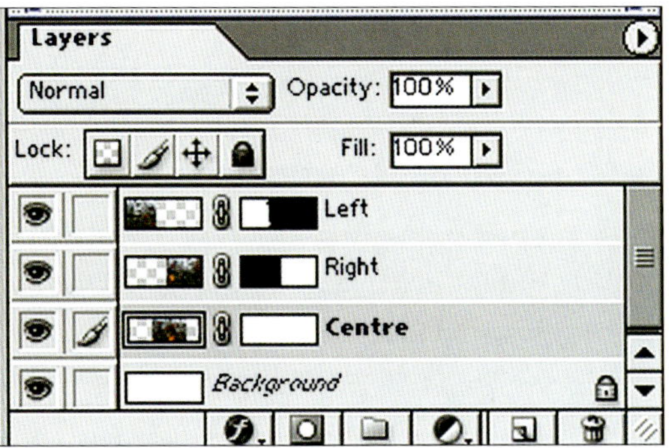

Fig 4

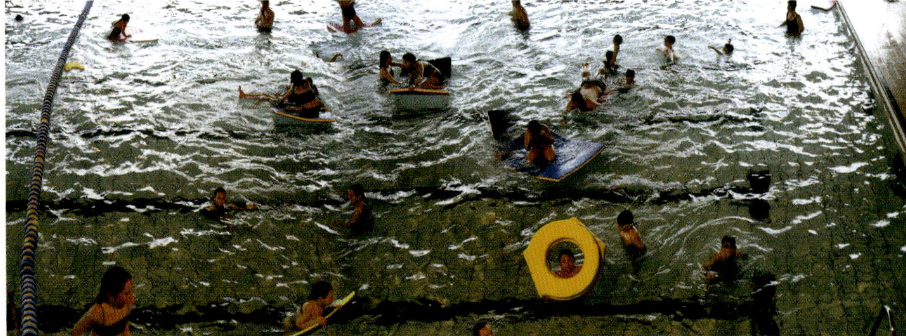

Fig 5

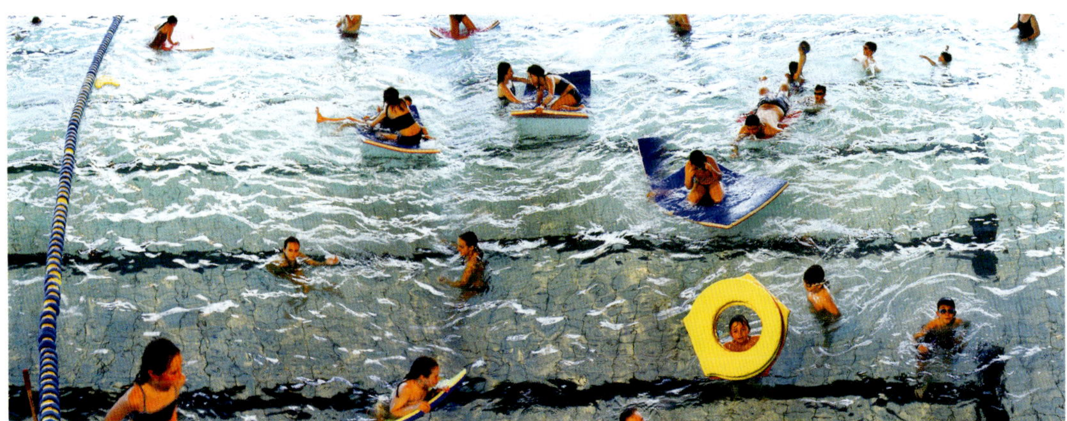

2 Select the image that you wish to work on by clicking on its layer. Use the Auto Select Layer option in the Tools palette to help determine the correct layer.

3 Create a Layer Mask by clicking on the Add Layer Mask icon at the bottom of the Layers palette.

4 Select the Linear Gradient tool, ensuring that the Foreground to Transparent option has been selected. Click and drag horizontally across the dividing edge of the image. A gradient mask will be applied, which will produce a gradual fade on the edge of the image. This is usually sufficient to create a seamless blend (see Fig 4).

5 On some occasions – for instance if subjects have moved between frames – there may be a need to edit the join. This can still be achieved on the same Layer Mask using an appropriate-

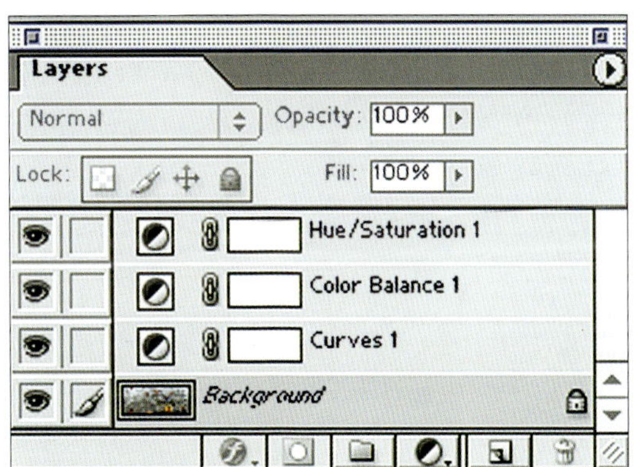

Fig 6

This image resulted from combining three images taken with a Pentax Optio camera; permission was obtained from the leisure centre to photograph. By using Layer Masks as described, the joins were made. As the initial exposures were produced using manual settings, there was a reasonable consistency between each image, which only required minor changes. The raw images from the camera did look a little dull, however, and adjustment layers were used to increase contrast and colour saturation.

sized Brush. Painting with black adds to the mask; white subtracts.

Distortion

Sometimes adjacent images do not quite match and may need to be distorted slightly. Select the correct layer and use the Transform function: Edit > Transform > Distort. By moving the corner handles slightly, any discrepancies in initial viewpoint can be matched up.

Finally, check each image for matching tonality, contrast and colour balance. The image can now be flattened and printed.

If further treatment, such as changing to monochrome, toning, colour balance and so on is to be attempted, it is best to do this after flattening.

Creating panoramas using Photoshop Elements
Adobe Photoshop Elements is the cheapest and most basic form of Photoshop, but it has a facility many of the more expensive versions (except the new CS) don't have – namely Photomerge. (In fact, Elements is often included free as part of the package when buying certain scanners or printers, but is often left ignored as users opt to use the more sophisticated and expensive options.)

To access Photomerge, go to File > Photomerge. An empty Photomerge dialog box will appear into which the source files should be imported. Simply click on Add and select the folder with the images that require stitching. Once all the source files have been added, click OK.

A new screen will appear, with the source images appearing as thumbnails at the top of the screen; use the Select Image tool to move each one into the work area in the order you wish them to be stitched. Each image will appear much larger, so use the Navigator to reduce size so that all the images appear within the work area.

As it is important to establish just one vanishing point, make sure that both the Snap to Image and Use Perspective boxes are ticked. Drag the Vanishing Point tool over the entire panorama and then select one of the images in order to establish the vanishing point for all the others. Any of the images can be used, although using one of the middle ones helps to reduce distortion; when this is done, a blue box will appear around the selected image. If the composition does not line up as anticipated, use the Select Image and the Rotate tools to make further slight adjustments.

In order to balance out the varying exposure differences, tick Advanced Blending, similarly, if the composite appears "bow-tied", tick the Cylindrical Mapping option. By selecting Preview, you can then have an overview of how the final panorama

Photomerge can deliver very successful panoramas, although whenever a single perspective point is applied, some small measure of distortion is inevitable.

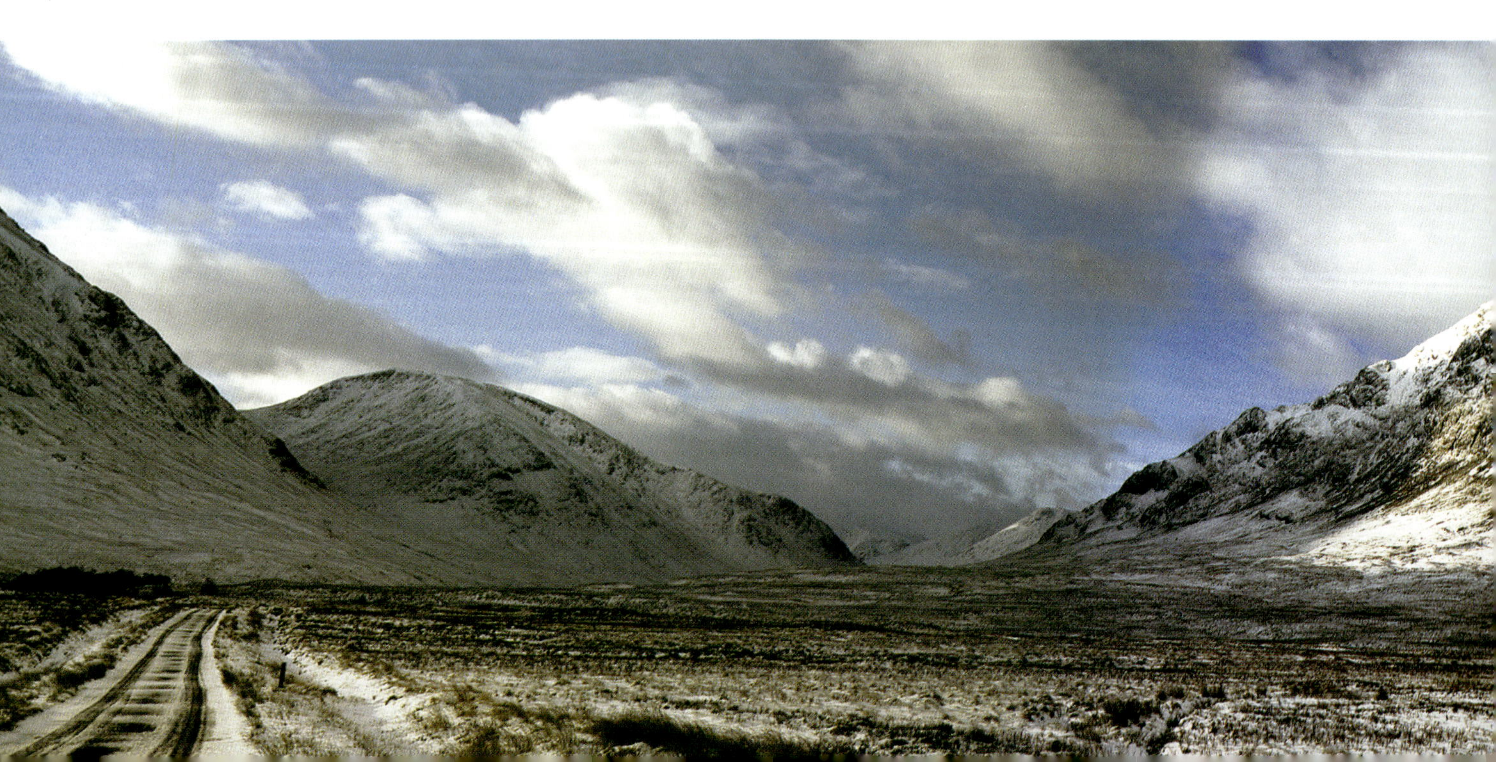

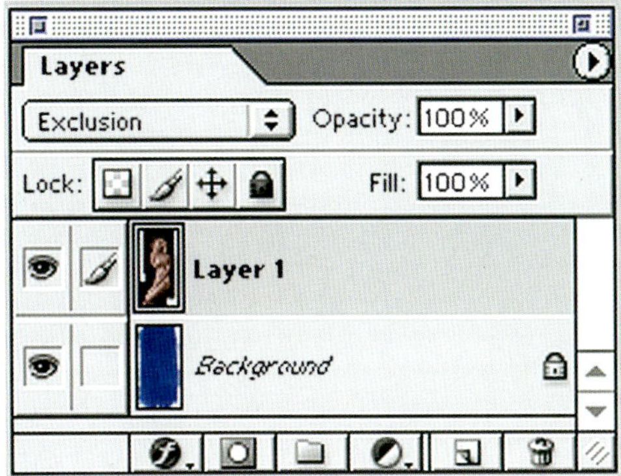

Fig 7

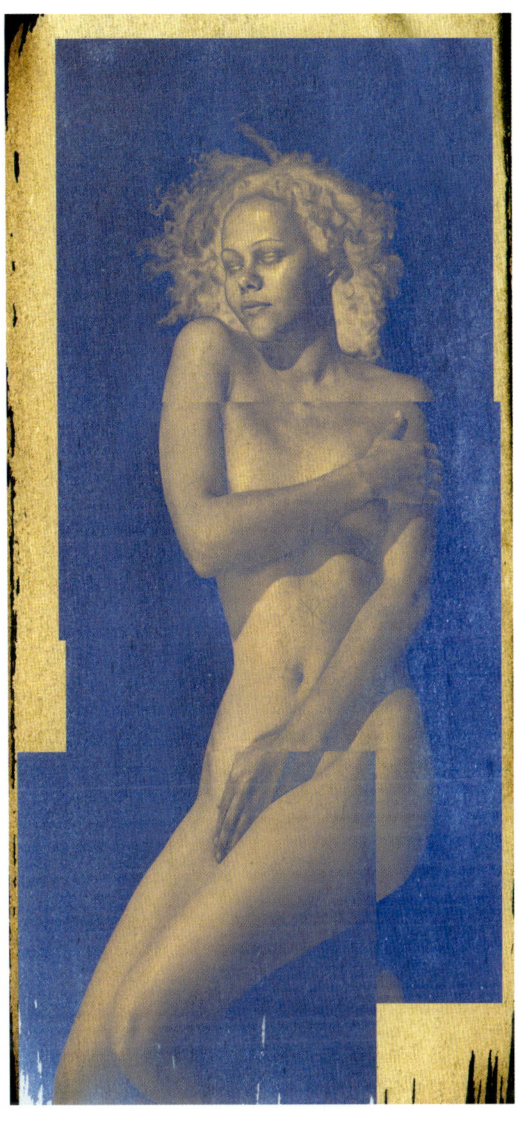

A very simple joiner image created by overlapping three images taken on a Nikon digital Coolpix camera. The gold colour was created by using a lower blue background layer and blending the figure using Exclusion mode.

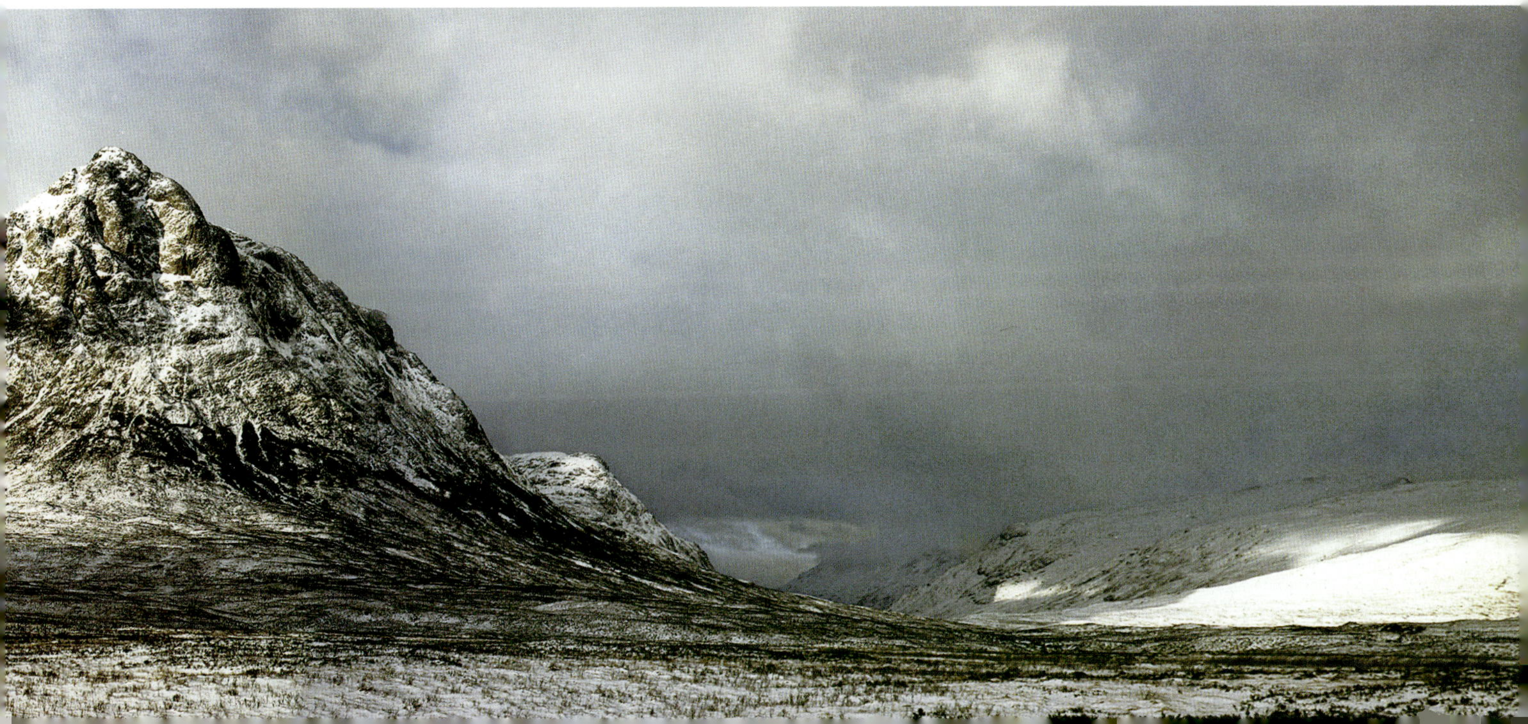

will appear. If you are satisfied with the final result, click OK in the Photomerge dialog box.

Once the panorama has been created, any irregular edges can be cropped and the entire image can then be tonally adjusted. If you are unhappy with the limitations posed by Elements, the image can be saved, imported and subsequently manipulated manually.

Ignoring conventions

Though traditional panoramas are very effective, it can be interesting to extend the normal boundaries of vision. An obvious first step is to consider panoramas in the vertical plane. Usually, a longer focal length lens

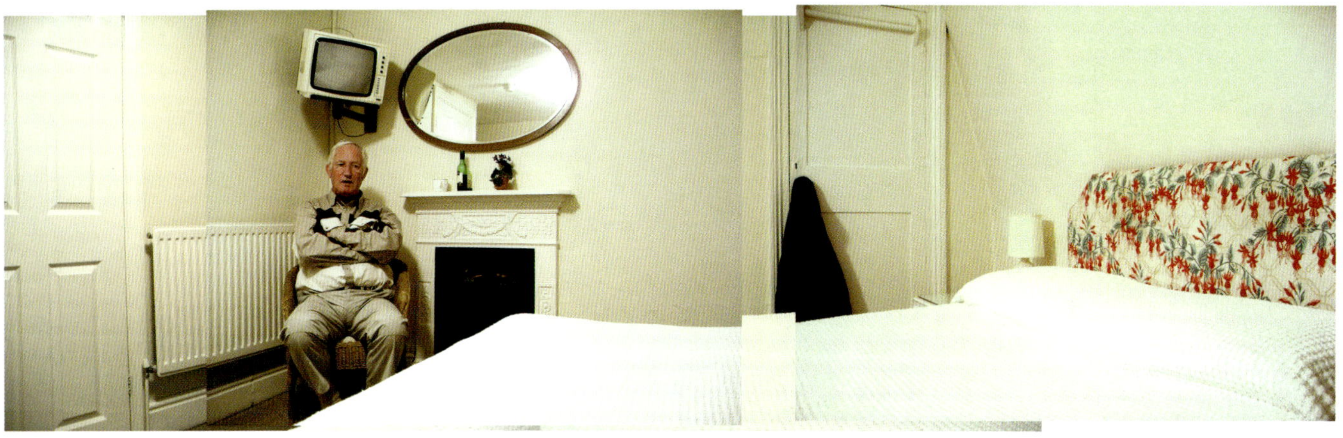

would be used to produce optical accuracy, but changing to a wide-angle provides much more dynamic images.

Joiners

The tradition for producing joiners is a relatively recent one, and the artist David Hockney was possibly the first to truly exploit its potential. It involves taking numerous related photographs of a particular scene and pasting them together to create a much larger tableau. Hockney was captivated by the idiosyncratic qualities of photographs, particularly the way perspective is affected and the way the element of time can be incorporated. It is a process that celebrates the distortions and irregularities one encounters when capturing images through the lens, and the imperfections that are created by matching one picture alongside another.

Photoshop truly is an awesome program, capable of achieving tasks that seem unimaginable in the darkroom, but that is not to say that we need to use all its facilities. It is so tempting to use it to iron out these visual aberrations, but occasionally they are best left unaltered. When working traditionally, the joiner needs to be glued to a background, which leaves little room for error; however, when working digitally it is far easier to change and edit your work in a more thoughtful and considered fashion.

Using filters

Probably the most abused of all camera accessories, lens filters proliferate in inverse proportions to their usefulness. Many photographers have dozens of expensive filters gathering dust, because after that first impulse buy they are rarely used. Due to the specific limitations of photographic

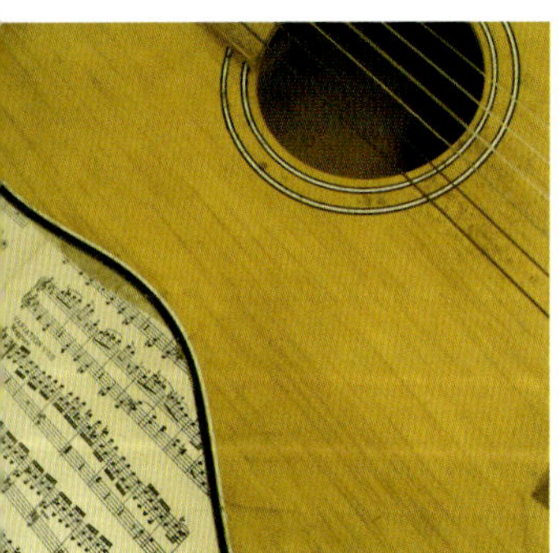

A simple digital image of a guitar and music.

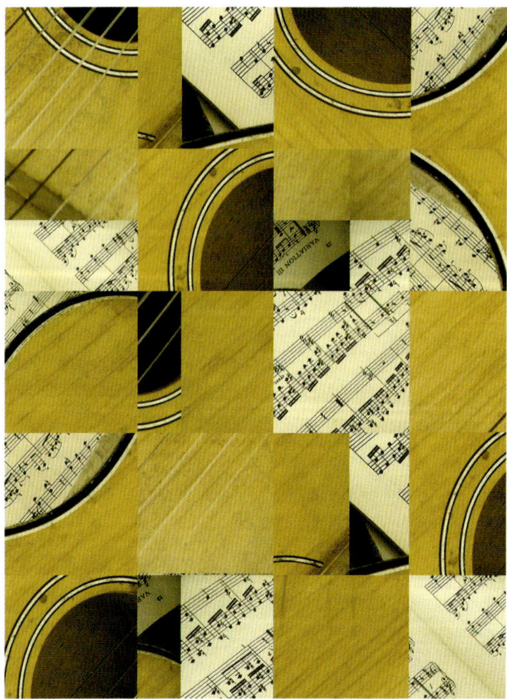

The Square Wave filter produced an effect similar to that of a Cubist painting.

emulsions, some filters are indispensable – colour correction in artificial light, red and green for monochrome, infrared, and neutral density in bright light are a basic set. The starburst, multifacet, tobacco graduate, motion and other filters may have made Mr Cokin a great deal of money, but add very little to creative output – the problem is that they are unnatural and quickly become a recognizable cliché.

Digital cameras can make use of the same filters, and many have built-in filters. The great thing about digital imaging, however, is the ability to apply filter effects at the manipulation stage rather than the time of taking – at least you can conserve your original unadulterated image if things go horribly wrong.

Photoshop has an enormous range of filter effects, which can be added to by using third party plug-ins. At the touch of a button, an image can be completely transformed. The excitement of this process can easily addle the brain, leading to total loss of taste and aesthetic appreciation. This phenomenon has spread like a pandemic quickly engulfing the known photographic world, producing technical clones with little or no sense of artistry. A little harsh? No! You have to be cruel to be kind.

The great advantage of Photoshop filters is that they can be applied very subtly if necessary, and to specific areas of an image. In many of the best cases of filter use, the filter effect is not noticeable. However, subtley is not always advisable, and if confidently applied in the right situation, dramatic results can be achieved. The golden rule is that the addition of a filter effect should enhance an image, rather than detract from its true purpose. Forethought is a key element and filters should not be used in an attempt to disguise poor photography.

Joiner effects can be created with the Wave filter found by going into the menu Filter > Distort > Wave. Select the Square Wave option and set the Number of Generators at 1. Then experiment with Wavelength, Amplitude and Scale.

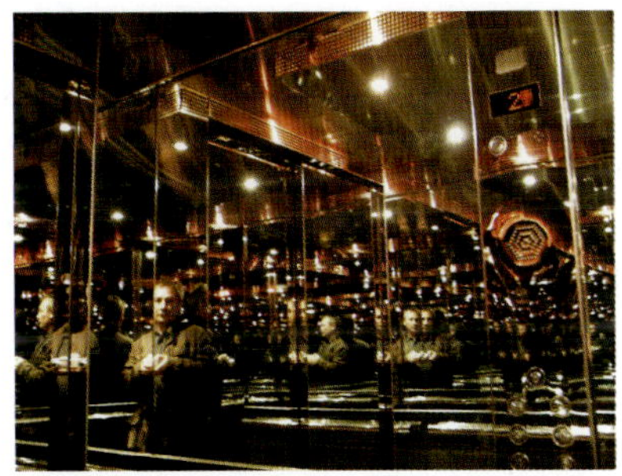

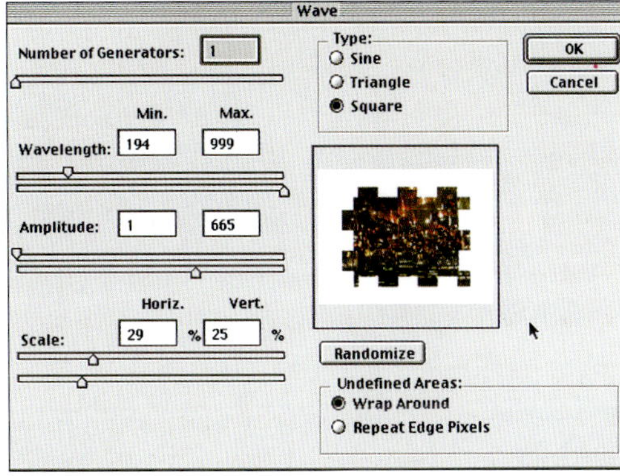

Fig 8

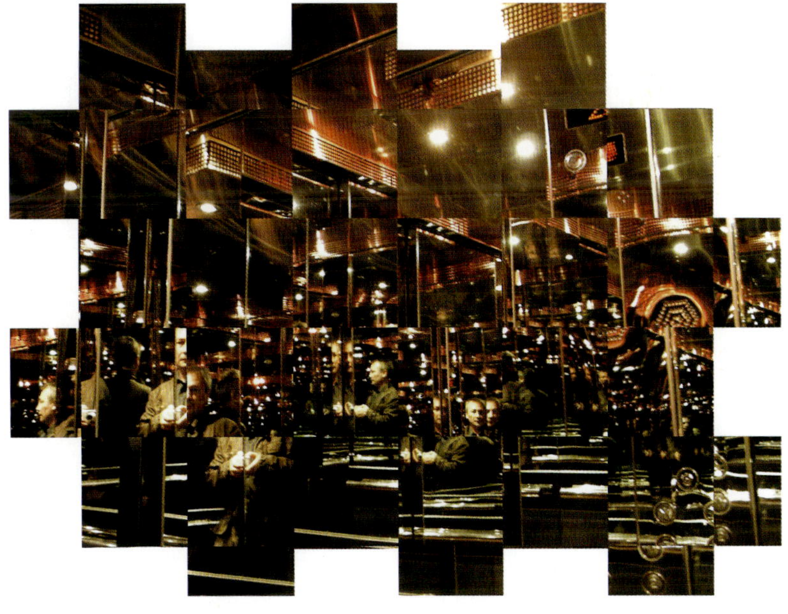

Starting with an image, that already has a multifaceted structure makes sense. This was taken in an elevator in the famous Midland Hotel, Bradford, which had repeating mirrors all around.

15 Printing on unconventional materials

Many contemporary photographers cast an envious eye towards artists who are able to exploit a much greater range of media and materials and are, as a consequence, able to explore visual issues in far greater depth. The standard view of a photograph is something that has been printed on paper, approximately A3 or A4 in size, although with the advent of digital imaging, much of this is changing.

AS PHOTOGRAPHERS ARE gaining increased access to professional printers capable of printing rolls of 1.52m (5ft) or more in width, it is becoming far easier to produce large and imposing images. To pretend that size does not matter is clearly to miss the point; there are countless images that gain impact, merely by being presented at a large size. Another alternative is to print on specially adapted rolls of canvas. These are marketed by Perma Jet and Fotospeed, who offer widths of 915–1125mm (3ft–3ft 8in) and lengths of 10 or 12m (33 or 39ft). Bearing in mind the robustness of canvas, compared to printing paper, this might prove to be an attractive alternative.

Stretching canvas

Canvas, of course, needs to be supported, and the most convenient way is to stretch it onto a frame. This could be made, although frames can also be bought quite cheaply from most good art stores. Generally these pre-made stretchers come as kits and are very easily assembled.

While there are some similarities between artist's canvas and the material produced for digital printing, there are also certain key differences. The most important one is that photo canvas has a substantial white coating, which makes it less flexible and therefore more difficult to stretch; which is not to say that it cannot be done (see Fig 1). Furthermore, the stretching needs to be done after the image has been completed, so some thought needs to be given to ensure that the print precisely fits the stretcher. As you need to wrap the canvas around the stretcher, it is

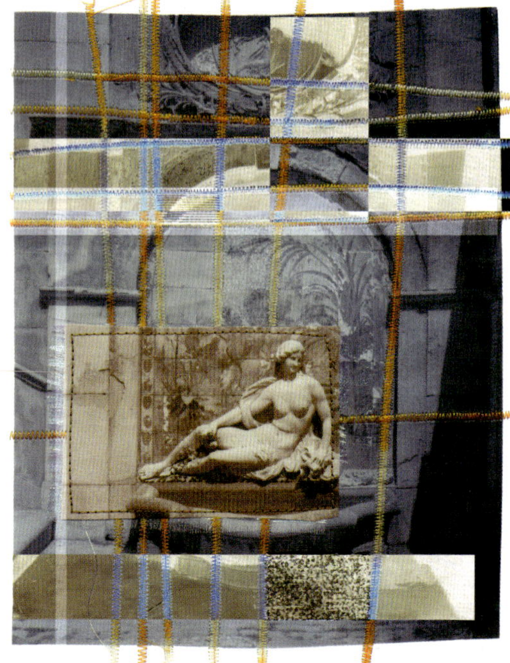

Portuguese façade

Appliqué is an interesting art form, which uses scraps of material to create an image. By working digitally, it is possible to marry photography with appliqué. In this case, two separately coloured examples of the same image were printed on T-shirt transfer paper and then ironed onto fine cotton. Part of one was then cut and stitched over the other. Appliqué can be made more interesting by adding further layers of other translucent materials, such as silk or rice paper.

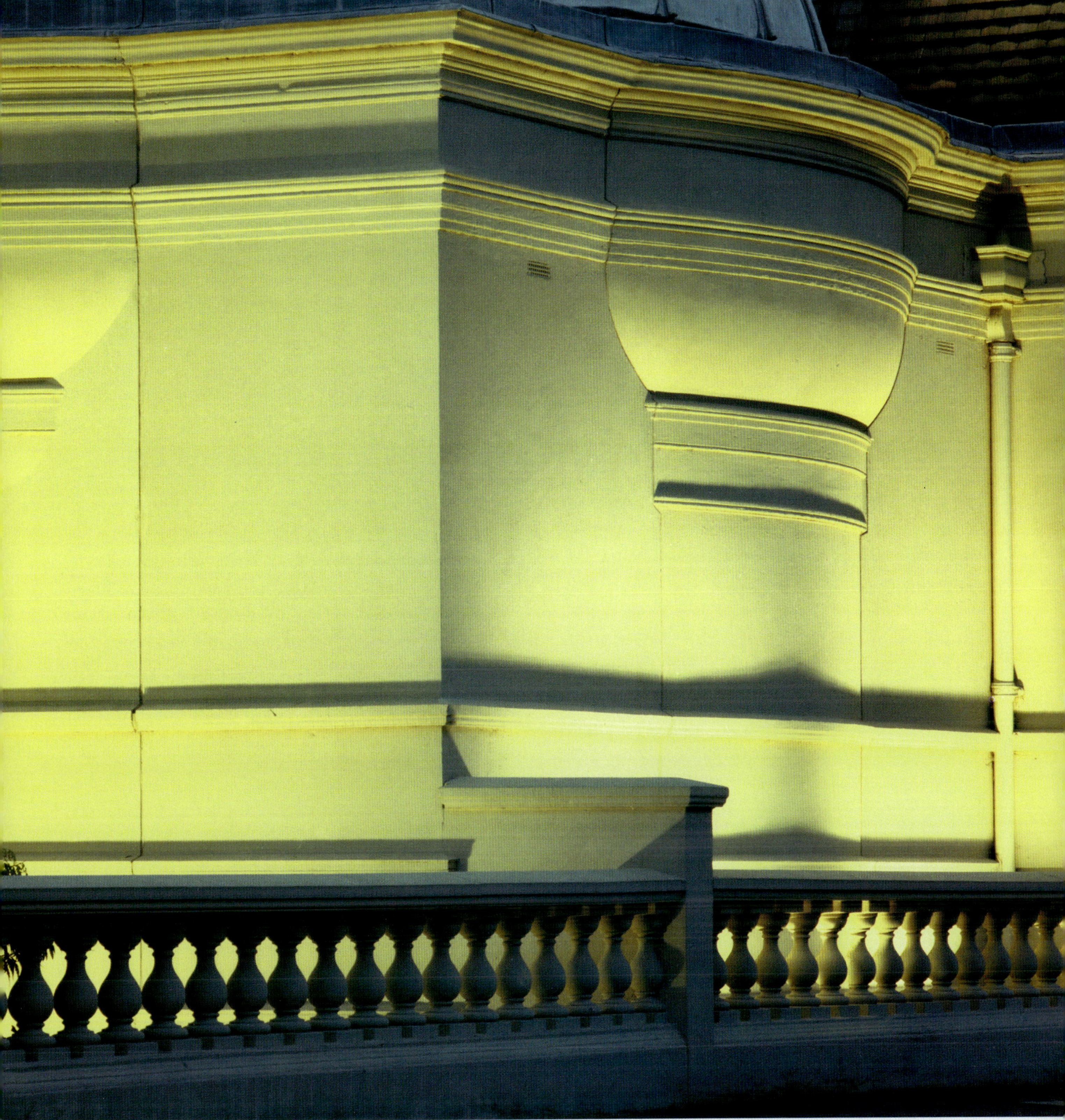

Façade: the Russell Coates Museum

While there has never been a restriction on the size photographers print in the darkroom, in reality very few have been prepared to produce images much larger than 405 x 510mm (20 x 16in), simply because processing dishes rarely come much larger than that. By printing onto photo canvas and then stretching the image, it is now possible to produce large and imposing photographs; such images should be protected with Giclée varnish.

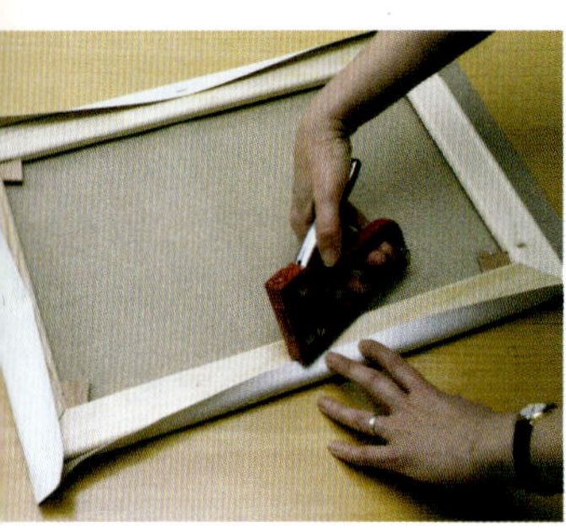

Fig 1

Photo canvas is best attached to the stretcher using a staple gun. Starting from the centre of one side of the frame, stretch the canvas so that it becomes taut and then secure another staple directly opposite the first. Repeat this process on the two sides of the adjacent frames. Once the centres are secured, methodically staple the remainder, working from the centre towards the corners.

important to leave a border of approximately 50mm (2in), otherwise part of the image will disappear behind the frame. Because the stretchers are constructed of wood, it is quite easy to attach a decorative frame.

It helps to seal the surface of the print to protect it from UV light and other pollutants; use Perma Fix (made by Perma Jet) or Frog Juice (marketed by Fotospeed), both of which come as aerosols, or alternatively use Giclée Varnish (available from DCP Systems, Thorncliffe Park Road, Chapeltown, Sheffield S35 2PH), which is painted directly onto the surface of the image. All three products should only be applied once the image has been attached to the stretcher.

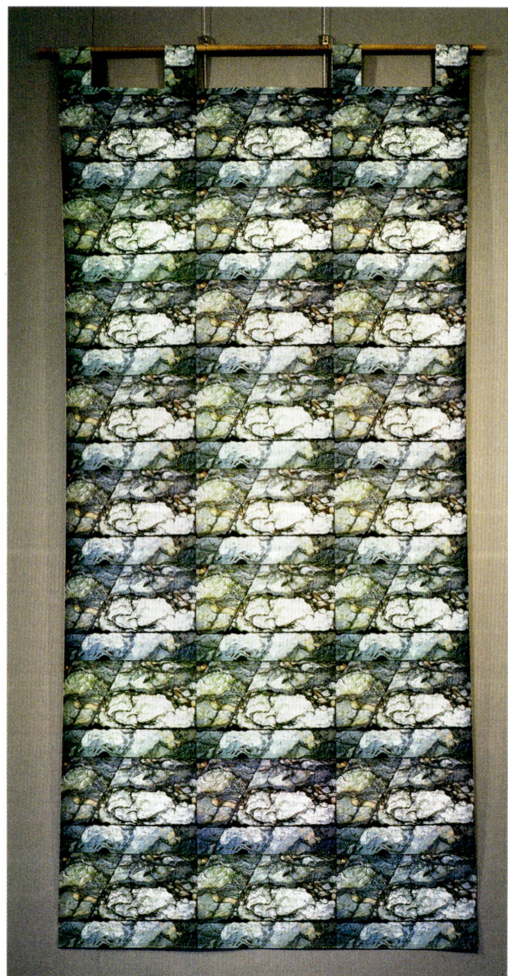

Using T-shirt transfer paper

The material used for photo canvas may well prove to be too heavy for some purposes, and a much finer fabric may be required. One way round this is to print onto T-shirt transfer paper, and then to iron this directly onto a more suitable material (although it needs to be one which can cope with a hot iron – a fine cotton material works best).

Before printing, it is important to flip the image horizontally, otherwise it will appear reversed once ironed. Print as normal using high quality or high resolution, but increase the brightness by about 10%. Allow the print to dry for at least 30 minutes. Place the printed inkjet sheet face down on the material, which should have been pre-ironed to ensure that there are no wrinkles. Place the hot iron on the backing paper and slowly and methodically iron the entire surface. Do not use the steam facility. Once the paper has cooled down, carefully peel it off the material.

Further materials

Manufacturers are increasingly producing imaginative new materials to print on. In addition to the wonderful art papers currently available, it is now possible to print on linen, canvas, acetate, clingfilm and highly translucent or reflective surfaces. It is even possible to explore body art, as Folex Imaging has introduced a film that allows the user to produce personalized tattoos. Don't be blinded

Wall hanging

This impressive wall hanging, produced by the artist Alan Hayward, illustrates just how imaginative photographs can become once one is prepared to step outside what is considered conventional. The multiple image, which uses a small detail of rock as its source, has been printed on coated polyester banner material, and attached to a bamboo support. It measures 2 x 1m (6ft 6in x 3ft 3in).